(Continued)

Making Friends in School:
Promoting Peer Relationships
in Early Childhood
PATRICIA G. RAMSEY

Play and the Social
Context of Development in
Early Care and Education
BARBARA SCALES, MILLIE ALMY,
AGELIKI NICOLOPOULOU, &
SUSAN ERVIN-TRIPP, Eds.

The Whole Language Kindergarten
SHIRLEY RAINES & ROBERT CANADY

Good Day/Bad Day:
The Child's Experience of Child Care
LYDA BEARDSLEY

Children's Play and Learning:
Perspectives and Policy Implications
EDGAR KLUGMAN & SARA SMILANSKY

Serious Players in the Primary Classroom:
Empowering Children Through Active
Learning Experiences
SELMA WASSERMANN

Child Advocacy for
Early Childhood Educators
BEATRICE S. FENNIMORE

Managing Quality Child Care Centers:
A Comprehensive Manual for
Administrators
PAMELA BYRNE SCHILLER
PATRICIA M. DYKE

Multiple World of Child Writers:
Friends Learning to Write
ANNE HAAS DYSON

Young Children Continue to Reinvent
Arithmetic—2nd Grade: Implications
of Piaget's Theory
CONSTANCE KAMII

Literacy Learning in the Early Years:
Through Children's Eyes
LINDA GIBSON

The Good Preschool Teacher:
Six Teachers Reflect on Their Lives
WILLIAM AYERS

A Child's Play Life:
An Ethnographic Study
DIANA KELLY-BYRNE

Professionalism and the Early Childhood
Practitioner
BERNARD SPODEK, OLIVIA N. SARACHO,
& DONALD L. PETERS, Eds.

Looking at Children's Play:
The Bridge from Theory to Practice
PATRICIA A. MONIGHAN-NOUROT,
BARBARA SCALES, JUDITH L. VAN HOORN,
& MILLIE ALMY

The War Play Dilemma:
Balancing Needs and Values in
the Early Childhood Classroom
NANCY CARLSSON-PAIGE
DIANE E. LEVIN

The Piaget Handbook for Teachers and
Parents: Children in the Age of Discovery,
Preschool–3rd Grade
ROSEMARY PETERSON
VICTORIA FELTON-COLLINS

Teaching and Learning in a Diverse World:
Multicultural Education for Young Children
PATRICIA G. RAMSEY

Promoting Social and Moral
Development in Young Children
CAROLYN POPE EDWARDS

Today's Kindergarten
BERNARD SPODEK, Ed.

Supervision in Early Childhood Education
JOSEPH J. CARUSO & M. TEMPLE FAWCETT

Visions of Childhood:
Influential Models from Locke to Spock
JOHN CLEVERLEY & D. C. PHILLIPS

Starting School:
From Separation to Independence
NANCY BALABAN

Young Children Reinvent Arithmetic:
Implications of Piaget's Theory
CONSTANCE KAMII

Ideas Influencing Early Childhood
Education: A Theoretical Analysis
EVELYN WEBER

Diversity in the Classroom:
A Multicultural Approach
FRANCES E. KENDALL

The Joy of Movement in Early Childhood
SANDRA R. CURTIS

Quality in Family Child Care and Relative Care

Susan Kontos

Carollee Howes

Marybeth Shinn

Ellen Galinsky

Teachers College, Columbia University
New York and London

Published by Teachers College Press, 1234 Amsterdam Avenue, New York, N.Y. 10027

Library of Congress Cataloging-in-Publication Data

Quality in family child care and relative care / Susan Kontos ... [et al.].
    p.   cm. — (early childhood education series)
  Includes bibliographical references (p.   ) and index.
  ISBN 0-8077-3409-8 (cloth : acid-free paper)
  1. Family day care—United States.   2. Family day care—United States—Statistics.   3. Family life surveys—United States.
  I. Kontos, Susan, 1949– . II. Series.
  HQ778.63.Q35   1994
  362.7'12'0973—dc20.   94-37696

ISBN: 0-8077-3409-8

Printed on acid-free paper
Manufactured in the United States of America
02 01 00 99 98 97 96 95 8 7 6 5 4 3 2 1

Contents

Acknowledgments

This study was made possible by funding from the following organizations:

The Annenberg Foundation
The Carnegie Corporation of New York
Dayton-Hudson Foundation
The Harris Foundation
The A.L. Mailman Family Foundation
Mervyn's
The David and Lucile Packard Foundation
Smith Richardson Foundation
The Spunk Fund, Inc.
Target Stores

Appreciation is expressed to Dr. Susan McBride, Iowa State University, for providing factor loadings for items on the Maternal Separation Anxiety Scale, and to Kathy Modigliani, Wheelock College, for providing salary data from the Economics of Family Child Care Study. Barbara Norcia and Nik Elevitch, Families and Work Institute, provided valuable staff support. We also appreciate Susan Liddicoat's patient, careful editing of the manuscript. Finally, we would like to acknowledge the assistance of the family child care providers and mothers who participated in the study and without whom it would have been impossible.

The following staff participated in the study:

Site Coordinators
California: Deborah Norris
North Carolina: Patricia Busch
Texas: Grace Wei
Texas Site Supervisor: Dr. Charles Mindel, University of Texas at Arlington
Mathematica Policy Research, Inc.: Dr. Anne Ciminecki, Project Director

Research Assistants/Interviewers

New York University and Families and Work Institute: Djuana Stoakley

California: Leslie Phillipsen, Kristen Droege, Ellen W. Smith, Margo Alfaro, Amanda Phan, Theresita Bermudez

North Carolina: Linda Johnson

Texas: Pam Greenwood, Kathleen Johnson, Clare Kosmicki, Marie Mitz

1

Introduction

The last decade has seen the emergence of family child care as a newly dynamic segment of the child care profession. A major part of this new dynamism are the numerous initiatives at the national and state level to improve the quality of family child care (Dombro, 1994). It is particularly good timing, therefore, to release the results of a new study on quality in family child care and relative care. The results of an observational study reported in this volume, combined with findings from a recent large-scale telephone survey of a nationally representative sample of family child care providers (Hofferth & Kisker, 1992), provides researchers and policymakers with information of unprecedented depth and breadth.

The Study of Family Child Care and Relative Care (as it was originally called) was conducted between September 1991 and December 1992 in Charlotte, North Carolina, Dallas/Fort Worth, Texas, and San Fernando/Los Angeles, California. These sites were selected because a companion study we were conducting examined the impact of family child care training programs in these communities.

The terms *family child care* and *relative care* are defined in particular ways. The term *family child care* is used to refer to the care of unrelated children in the home of the provider, and the care of related children (other than the provider's own children) is termed *relative care* in the relative's home (e.g., Hofferth, Brayfield, Deitch, & Holcomb, 1991). Grouped together, these two forms of care constitute the most frequently used child care arrangements in the United States among employed mothers with children under 5 years of age. As shown in Table 1.1, 32.6% of children are cared for in this way as compared to 28.3% cared for in centers and 27.7% cared for by their parents. The use of these two forms of care by mothers who are employed *full-time* is even greater

TABLE 1.1. PRIMARY CHILD CARE ARRANGEMENTS FOR YOUNGEST CHILD UNDER 5

Primary Child Care Arrangement, without school	Percentage of Employed Mothers (n = 1,180)
Center	28.3
Parent	27.7
Relative—child's home	6.5
Family child care and relative care	32.6
Relative—own home	12.7
Nonrelative—own home	19.9
Sitter	2.8
Self care	0.1
Lesson (music, athletics, etc.)	0.4
Other	1.6
Total	100.0

Source: From *National Child Care Survey, 1990,* (p. 46) by S.L. Hofferth, A. Brayfield, S. Deitch, and P. Holcomb, 1991, Washington, DC: The Urban Institute. Reprinted by permission.

(see Figure 1.1). Comparing center usage (35%) with the use of care by nonrelatives and relatives in the provider's home (38%), it becomes even more evident that a plurality of children under 5 years of age in America whose mothers are employed full-time are cared for in the homes of a neighbor, friend, family child care provider, or relative.

When one examines child care arrangements by age of child (see Table 1.2), one can see that family child care and relative care is used most frequently by families with children 2 years of age and under; a dramatic shift into center care occurs when children reach 3 years of age (Hofferth et al., 1991). This pattern of child care usage does not necessarily result in family child care providers caring primarily for infants and toddlers. This is because there are fewer infants and toddlers than preschool-aged children in any type of out-of-home care (Hofferth et al., 1991) and because many states limit the number of infants and toddlers cared for by regulated providers (Children's Foundation, 1993). In any case, the pattern of family child care and relative care usage reveals its dominance as a child care arrangement for working mothers of young children and reinforces the need for current information about it.

The study had several purposes. One was to fill the vacuum created by a nearly 15-year hiatus in the publication of a large, multisite observational study of family child care. Given the prevalence of this form of care, the resulting absence of timely information on the context of family child care for families, providers, and children created a noticeable gap in the family child care literature. Another reason for conducting the study was concern about the typical level of quality in family child care and relative care. Several small studies of family child care

TABLE 1.2. Primary Child Care Arrangements for Youngest Child, by Age, Employed Mother

Primary Child Care Arrangement, Without School	Percentage of Employed Mothers—by Age of Child						
	Total	<1	1–2	3–4	5	6–9	10–12
Center	20.5	13.6	22.7	42.8	31.9	15.0	3.2
Parent	30.5	37.7	28.6	20.7	23.5	35.4	33.1
Father	18.0	22.5	18.4	12.1	13.5	20.2	18.6
Mother	12.5	15.2	10.2	8.6	10.0	15.1	14.1
Relative—child's home	9.7	9.0	6.7	4.9	7.5	11.1	17.4
Family child care and relative care	24.3	33.4	36.4	27.9	28.4	18.0	10.4
Relative—own home	11.5	13.0	13.8	11.4	14.5	11.2	7.3
Non-relative—own home	12.8	20.4	22.6	16.5	13.9	6.8	3.1
In-home provider	3.1	3.4	3.0	2.4	1.7	4.5	1.6
Self-care	2.1	0.0	0.2	0.0	0.0	1.3	10.1
Lesson	8.4	0.5	0.3	0.6	6.5	13.6	22.4
Other	1.4	2.4	2.0	0.7	0.5	1.1	1.8
Total	100.0	100.0	100.1	100.0	100.0	100.0	100.0
Population estimate (in thousands)	15,997	1,529	3,152	2,754	1,148	4,835	2,579
Sample size	2,539	243	500	437	182	768	409

Note: Percentages do not add to 100 in some cases because of rounding error.
Source: From National Child Care Survey, 1990 (p. 50) by S.L. Hofferth, A. Brayfield, S. Deitch, and P. Holcomb, 1991, Washington, DC: The Urban Institute. Reprinted by permission.

3

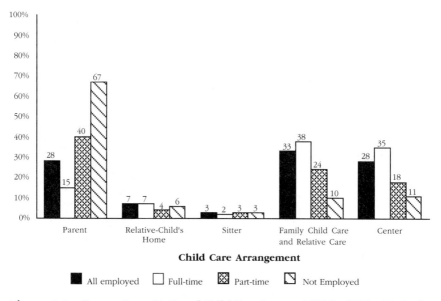

Child Care Arrangement

■ All employed □ Full-time ▨ Part-time ◩ Not Employed

Figure 1.1. *Source:* From *National Child Care Survey, 1990* (p. 50) by S.L. Hof-ferth, A. Brayfield, S. Deitch, and P. Holcomb, 1991, Washington, DC: The Urban Institute. Reprinted by permission.

have been conducted that suggest quality may be minimally adequate and widely ranging (Kontos, 1992). These studies are small, single-site studies, however, and include primarily regulated providers. Little infor-mation is available on nonregulated providers and even less is avail-able on relative providers. Thus, there was a need to document the range and typical level of quality of family child care and relative care.

Although we were concerned about the level of quality of family child care and relative care in general, we were especially concerned about the quality of care received by children from low-income families and by minority children. The National Child Care Staffing Study (Whitebook, Howes, & Phillips, 1989) found that children from low-income and upper-income families enjoyed higher quality, center-based care because of access to subsidized care for low-income families and the ability of upper-income families to pay for quality. Middle-income families were caught in-between because of their inability to qualify for subsidized care or to pay for quality care. Other, smaller studies have also observed this pattern (e.g., Kontos, 1991). Thus, one pur-pose of the study was to determine the relationship between family income and quality of family child care or relative care. Because minor-ity children are more likely than their nonminority counterparts to be low income, we believed it was important to also examine the relation-ship between minority status and quality.

The importance of including relative care in the study was brought about by the passage of three federal child care subsidy programs—Child Care and Development Block Grant, Title IV-A At-Risk Child Care Program, and the Family Support Act—which allow parents to purchase family child care services from relatives (Blank, 1994). As a result of these programs, what had previously been regarded as an entirely private matter beyond public scrutiny has now become an object of public concern.

The study was designed with these overall purposes in mind and in light of what we already know about family child care and relative care. In spite of our concern about the lack of a recent, large, multisite, observational study of these two forms of care, we felt it was crucial to ground our study in the existing knowledge base. It is to this subject that we now turn in the following section.

RESEARCH ON FAMILY CHILD CARE AND RELATIVE CARE

Several recently published comprehensive reviews of research on family child care are available (cf. Kontos, 1992; Pollard & Fischer, 1992), obviating the need for repetition here. It is important, however, to put the present study in the context of the research that has come before it.

Virtually every survey of parental preference for out-of-home care has found that families prefer more informal, home-like arrangements for their infants and toddlers (Hayes, Palmer, & Zaslow, 1990; Kisker, Maynard, Gordon, & Strain, 1989; Mason & Kuhlthau, 1989). However, existing research on child care and its effects on children tells us little about the quality of these arrangements. Some research shows that those families who are least well educated, have less income from the mothers' jobs, and have higher levels of stress tend to have poorer quality care for their children (Goelman & Pence, 1987; Howes & Stewart, 1987). Recent studies of supply and demand have further shown that the supply of child care is most sparse in low-income areas (Culkin, Morris, & Helburn, 1991; Hill-Scott, 1989). This trend has led the National Academy of Sciences in the book, *Who Cares for America's Children?* (Hayes et al., 1990) to conclude:

> Children from families enduring greater psychological and economic stress are more likely to be found in lower quality care settings. Thus, there are very young children in the United States, especially those from low-income families, in double jeopardy from stress both at home and in their care environments. (p. 77)

Compared to center-based child care, family child care has been underresearched. A recently published monograph that comprehensively reviewed the research literature on family child care (Kontos,

1992) found, however, that there was a surprising amount of information essentially (though not exclusively) beginning with the National Day Care Home Study (NDCHS) (Divine-Hawkins, 1981; Fosburg, 1982). Although these data were gathered nearly 15 years ago, they remain the keystone for the body of family child care research. The NDCHS was the first attempt to comprehensively study family child care in urban settings in order to provide a framework for sound day care policies and programs. It was distinguished by being a multisite, observational study. We learned, for instance, that training makes a difference to the quality of provider–child interactions and that there is a negative relationship between number of children and frequency of interactions between providers and individual children (except for interactions focusing on adult control, which was positively related to number of children). Even more important, we learned that family child care environments were generally safe, home-like settings that were positive for children. In the wake of the NDCHS, the quantity and quality of research on family child care has increased.

The need for additional, comprehensive information about the child care settings serving young children in this country emerged in essence because of the passage of time and the changing family demographics in this country during the decade that followed the NDCHS (Hofferth & Kisker, 1992). In response to this need, the National Child Care Survey (NCCS) mentioned earlier {Hofferth et al., 1991) and A Profile of Child Care Settings (PCS) (Kisker, et al., 1991) were conducted. These studies were unique in that a nationally representative sample was solicited in order to describe the types of care and education (outside of formal school) used by parents to supplement their own care (NCCS) and to describe the characteristics of these arrangements (PCS). A supplement to the NCCS examined a representative sample of regulated and nonregulated family child care homes. Together, these two studies inform us about the needs and resources of American parents with respect to early education and care.

The NCCS and PCS were telephone surveys that contacted either formal early education and care programs or households with children under age 13. The PCS was the first study to reveal that the large majority of family child care homes (regulated and nonregulated) meet their state regulations regarding maximum group sizes and adult–child ratios. It also showed that nearly two thirds of regulated providers, and just over one third of nonregulated providers, have some sort of specialized training in child care or early education. These data help us to characterize the quality of family child care available to families in the 1990s based on aspects of care that are regulated. It is one of the first attempts to obtain data on a *representative* sample of nonregulated providers.

A small but growing body of research is available examining the experiences of children, families, and providers in family child care, including research on the quality of care provided. Most of these studies utilize observational methods to gather their data, but it is rare for studies to involve a focus on multiple ecological levels of family child care or on more than one geographic location, and equally rare for studies to involve nonregulated providers (Kontos, 1992). It is important to consider multiple locations because the regulatory climate, as well as child care supply and demand, vary from state to state. It is also important to understand the intersection of the family's, child's, and provider's worlds in order to fully comprehend processes of influence. Because estimates of the ratio of regulated to nonregulated providers indicate that the latter group is the larger one, research on regulated family child care providers is not representative of the population of providers.

The Quality of Family Child Care

One issue that has driven a number of relatively recent studies is characterizing the quality of family child care. These studies have focused primarily, but not exclusively, on regulated providers and have used observations as the primary data source. Quality of care has been examined using a variety of approaches, including regulated characteristics such as ratio and group size, as well as more process-oriented approaches that examine such things as provider behavior, type of children's experiences provided, and organization of the physical environment.

According to Kontos (1992), six studies conducted in the United States and Canada have measured quality in family child care (excluding relative care) with the Family Day Care Rating Scale (FDCRS) (Harms & Clifford, 1989). Although other rigorous studies of family child care quality have been conducted, because each of these six studies used the FDCRS, it is possible to examine the quality of family child care across samples using a common metric (Fischer, 1989; Goelman & Pence, 1987; Goelman, Shapiro, & Pence, 1990; Howes, Keeling, & Sale, 1988; Howes & Stewart, 1987; Kontos, 1994). The FDCRS is a 33-item scale used to rate six areas of caregiving practices: space and furnishings, basic needs, language and reasoning, learning activities, social development, and adult needs. Each item is rated on a 1-to-7 scale, with a score of 1 indicating inadequate practices and a score of 7 indicating excellent practices (3 = adequate; 5 = good). Scores on the FDCRS are associated with measures of home stimulation (Goelman et al., 1990), provider involvement with the children, and children's competence (Howes & Stewart, 1987).

The average FDCRS item scores across studies ranged from 2.9 to 4.33. The range of quality reported in these six studies indicated that family child care quality varied from inadequate (potentially harmful to children) to good (developmentally enhancing), rarely reaching excellence. The typical quality of these family child care homes was between "just below adequate" and "not quite good" (Fischer, 1989; Goelman et al., 1990; Goelman & Pence, 1987; Howes et al., 1988; Howes & Stewart, 1987; Kontos, 1994). Adequate care is considered custodial, neither developmentally enhancing nor harmful to children (Clifford, Harms, & Cryer, 1991).

Two of the studies included both regulated and nonregulated family child care providers (Fischer, 1989; Goelman & Pence, 1987). In each of these studies, the nonregulated family child care providers were rated lower on the FDCRS than the regulated family child care providers. Researchers have attempted to determine the characteristics associated with quality other than regulatory status. The factors that emerge are stimulation in the home, years of experience of providers, hours per week care is provided and the amount of television viewing (Goelman et al., 1990), affiliation with support networks, training, years of experience (Fischer, 1989), and the number of the provider's own children (Kontos, 1994). So far, the only caregiving characteristic associated with quality (as measured by the FDCRS) in more than one study is regulatory status.

Given the importance of regulation, it is important to underscore the limitations of regulation requirements for family child care in the United States. A review by the Children's Defense Fund (Adams, 1990) notes that although experts recommend that one adult care for no more than three or four infants, 13 states allow a single family child care provider to care for five or more infants and toddlers. Furthermore, 22 states exempt family child care providers serving five or fewer unrelated children from regulations, and 36 states exempt providers serving three or fewer children. The Children's Defense Fund further estimates that "nearly three fourths of all children cared for in family child care homes are in programs that are not regulated or registered and, therefore, are not required to comply even with the basic health and safety standards" (Adams, 1990, p. vi). This fact makes the need for research on regulated and nonregulated care even more urgent. We also need to know how differing regulatory requirements affect quality.

The Quality of Relative Care

Although there is a growing body of literature about non-relative family child care, little is known about relative care, despite its prevalence. The NDCHS (Fosburg, 1982) provided a glimpse into this segment of potential child care arrangements utilized by parents. Relative providers were found to exhibit a pattern of behavior that suggested less inter-action (teaching, playing, helping) with the relative's child than providers caring for unrelated children. On the other hand, relative providers engaged in more directing of children's behavior and more household work. Relative care was characterized as less structured, less formal, and less focused on the children.

A study of young mothers' use of relative care found that grand-mother care was the most common form of relative care and that, unex-pectedly, about one third of the grandmothers providing care to their grandchildren had other employment (Presser, 1989). The result was a significant amount of schedule-juggling on the part of both grand-mothers and mothers. About one third of grandmothers received cash payment for their child care services, sometimes supplemented by in-kind payments. Presser interpreted these results as evidence that, con-trary to many parents' beliefs that grandmothers are the ideal child care arrangement (Mason & Kuhlthau, 1989), use of grandmother care may entail certain costs that counterbalance the benefits (Presser, 1989).

A recent study (Jendrek, 1993) investigated the extent to which car-ing for grandchildren was disruptive to the lives of grandparents in a sample of grandparents providing daily care to their grandchildren. Par-ticipating grandparents responded to advertisements and referrals to the study. Their socioeconomic status was not indicated, but their aver-age educational level was one year of college and the entire sample was white. The results of the study revealed that, for grandparents provid-ing child care, as opposed to foster care, for their sons or daughters, disruptions were surprisingly minimal. Of course, these grandparents organized their day around the children, but neither their friendship and family networks nor their marriages were substantially affected. Some of the grandparents were quite pleased to provide care for their grandchild, and others were resentful of the intrusion. This study pro-vides important background information for understanding the context of relative care but did not examine the caregiving arrangement itself or focus on the child's perspective, as our study was designed to do.

The Effect of Quality on Children

Although considerably more research on the impact of quality child care on children has been conducted with center-based rather than with family-based arrangements, there is a growing number of stud-ies delineating the effect of quality on children in both types of care. These efforts have focused on what Phillips (1988) has dubbed the "iron triangle"—group size, adult–child ratio, and provider educa-tion/training—and on links to positive developmental outcomes in children in family child care. Larger groups (and thus poorer adult–child ratios) have been linked to poor social interaction and cognitive development (Clarke-Stewart & Gruber, 1984; Fosburg, 1982; Howes, 1983; Howes & Rubenstein, 1985). Other studies have found the reverse to be true (Kontos, Hsu, & Dunn, 1994) or have found no associations (Dunn, 1993). Additional research is needed to determine how regulable characteristics of family child care relate to quality and to children's development.

The NDCHS (Fosburg, 1982) found that providers with training were most likely to engage in more positive teaching and supportive interactions with children than were providers without training. Rosenthal (1990) reported similar results with an Israeli sample. Unfortunately, only one quarter of states require preservice training for family child care providers (Hayes et al., 1990).

Other ingredients of quality that affect children include the stability of the provider (either provider turnover or number of caregiving arrangements experienced by the child), the physical design of the home, supervision, care for own children, and, as previously noted, the regulatory status. One study found that children experiencing more turnover in staff as infants and toddlers do less well in their preschool years (Howes & Stewart, 1987). In family child care, whether the home space is child- or adult-centered can make a difference. Howes (1983) found the child-centered space to be linked to a more positive emotional climate and social relationships. Rosenthal (1991) documented a relationship between provider supervision by the sponsoring agency and the quality of interactions with children. In a midwestern sample of providers, those whose own children were at home were more warmly involved with the unrelated target children (Kontos, in press). Finally, the regulatory status of the home—whether or not the provider belongs to a family child care and relative care association—and the age range of the children in the home have all emerged as factors affecting children's development (Fosburg, 1982; Rosenthal, 1988).

NEED FOR A MORE COMPREHENSIVE STUDY

We have entered what Deborah Phillips (1988) has described as the "third wave" of child care research. Previously, studies attempted to discern how child care or family life, considered separately, affected children. Now some pioneering researchers have begun to probe the way family life and child care interact in influencing development (Howes et al.,1993; Kontos, 1994; McBride & Rubenstein, 1990).

In a study of children in centers, Howes and her colleagues (Howes et al., in press) found race to be a salient factor—in combination with family (especially maternal working conditions) and child care factors—in predicting child development outcomes. This research highlights the necessity of including children of different racial backgrounds in studies before generalizations about family and child care influence can be made.

The literature indicates that investigating family child care and relative care and its impact is a very important policy direction for new research, especially for those concerned about the lives of our youngest children. The growing public recognition that child care experiences are a part of children's education before school (Galinsky & Friedman, 1993) applies to family child care and relative care, not just to center care.

The impact that the National Child Care Staffing Study (Whitebook et al., 1989) had on policy and advocacy for staff and children in center-based child care suggested a timely need for a similarly large, multisite, observational study on multiple ecological levels (families, children, providers) of family child care and relative care. Policy issues dictated the inclusion of regulated and nonregulated, as well as relative and nonrelative, providers of family child care, even though many of them would not describe themselves as family child care providers and/or do not charge for their services.

In response to these needs, the Study of Quality in Family Child Care and Relative Care was designed to investigate the following questions:

- Who is providing family child care and relative care? What are their characteristics? Why are they doing this work?
- What is the overall quality of family child care and relative care?
- How do regulated, nonregulated, and relative providers differ in quality?
- Does the quality of care differ for children from low-income and minority families?
- What differentiates good from custodial or inadequate care?
- What are mothers looking for when they select family child care and relative care for their children?
- How do mothers locate family child care or relative care and how do they describe it?
- What are the characteristics of children in family child care and relative care?
- What do children do during their day in care?
- How does quality in child care affect children's development?
- Do state regulations or compliance with regulations relate to quality?

- How much do mothers pay for care and are they willing to pay more? Are cost and quality related?
- What is the rate of turnover among providers after one year and how do the providers still offering care differ from those who are not?

Each of these questions will be addressed in subsequent chapters. First, the methodology of the study will be explained in some detail. Next, the characteristics of the providers who participated in the study will be described, followed by a detailed treatment of how we measured quality in family child care and relative care. The three chapters that follow examine quality of care from three perspectives. Mothers' and children's experiences with family child care and relative care are then addressed in chapters 8 and 9. Data regarding the relationship of quality to regulation, cost, and turnover are reported in the latter half of the book. We end the book by reviewing key findings, suggesting implications, and making recommendations.

2

Methodology for the Study

The purpose of this chapter is to provide detailed information regarding the selection of the sample for the study and procedures for gathering the data. Sources for the sample of mothers and providers will be discussed first. Then sample biases will be examined. Finally, the measures and procedures for administering the measures will be described, as well as the regulatory context in the states selected for study.

HOW WERE MOTHERS SAMPLED?

Mothers who use family child care or relative care for a child under 6 years old were sampled in three communities in different states chosen because they are sites of Family-to-Family training programs for child care providers: Charlotte, North Carolina, Dallas-Fort Worth, Texas, and the San Fernando Valley, California. Family-to-Family is a national initiative sponsored by Dayton Hudson (in partnership with its Mervyn's, Target Stores, and Department Store Divisions) to promote quality in family child care through training, accreditation, provider associations, and local consumer education. Mothers were eligible for the study if they worked at least 15 hours per week and if their major form of care was family child care (including care by a relative). The children could also participate in other forms of care if they were in family child care at least 10 hours per week more than in any other form of care.

Mothers were sampled in four ways in an effort to attain a reasonably representative group who used family child care from both regulated and nonregulated providers, consistent with budgetary constraints. Because of concerns about the quality of care received by children from low-income and from minority families, we designed the sample to contain sufficient numbers of low-income families in addition to middle-income families, and sufficient numbers of African American and Latino families in addition to whites, to permit separate analyses for these groups. The first three methods, which generated the community sample of 739 mothers, identified families who used family child care or relative care. These mothers were then asked to refer their child care providers. The fourth method sampled child care providers who, in turn, referred families in their care. This "provider referral" sample includes 81 mothers. All mothers were interviewed by interviewers from Mathematica Policy Research, Inc.

1. Fifty-nine families were obtained by random-digit dialing to telephone exchanges with higher than average proportions of low-income and of minority families. This method is most representative of families with phones in the neighborhoods selected, but also most expensive and thus represents the smallest sampling group: 11,058 phone numbers were screened in order to identify 84 eligible households and complete 59 interviews (many phone numbers were for business rather than households, or were for households without any children under age six). The response rate for families identified as eligible was 70%.

2. The bulk of the sample, 529 families, came from families located from a list of names of families with children under the age of 6 that was purchased from a commercial vendor. In all, 10,503 numbers were screened in order to identify 662 eligible households and complete 529 interviews. This method was most successful in Texas. In California and North Carolina, fewer eligible families, and fewer low-income families and minority families, were identified with this method. The response rate among eligible families was 80%.

3. Birth records were used to locate 151 additional low-income and minority households in California and North Carolina. In North Carolina, African American children below the age of 6 were sampled from county records of births. In California, records were sampled from the UCLA Medical Center, a site with a high proportion of births to low-income families. In the two states combined, 4,579 families were sought, 43% were located, 200 eligible families were identified, and 151 interviews were completed, for a 76% response rate among eligible families.

4. Provider referral sample: In California, family child care providers were identified from state licensing lists. In North Carolina and Texas, providers were identified both from licensing

lists (two thirds) and from newspaper advertisements (one third), and were asked to identify parents who would be interested in the study. Eighty-one mothers were interviewed after both they and providers had agreed to participate in the study. The response rate was 78%.

Overall, 739 interviews with mothers of age-eligible children were generated by the first three methods. With the additional 81 interviews obtained from mothers in the provider referral sample, the final sample size is 820. Table 2.1 shows the number of interviews by state and sampling method.

Families were defined as low income if they had incomes under 165% of the poverty rate for their family size, and otherwise as high income. (Note that, for purposes of analyses, low income is defined as under $20,000 per year, without regard for family size.) Response rates for the sample were virtually identical for the two groups (low income: 78%, $n = 204$; high income: 79%, $n = 525$). Respondents who declined to answer the income question in the screening interview ($n = 12$) replied at a lower rate (33%).

Respondents in the sample were first screened for eligibility and then administered an interview that focused on their perceptions of quality, characteristics of their family child care setting, their search for family child care, their working conditions, and other related issues (see Table 2.2). At the end of the interview, mothers were requested to refer their child care provider to the study, and to grant permission for study staff to observe their child (hereafter referred to as the "target child") in the child care home. (Families were informed that the provider would receive a gift certificate if she agreed to participate.) Fifty percent of the 741 respondents interviewed referred their providers. Referral rates were 56% in North Carolina, 51% in Texas, and 44% in California. In order to assure adequate samples of child care providers for both low-income and minority families, low-income and minority mothers who did not initially refer their provider were offered a financial incentive of $35 to do so.

TABLE 2.1. SOURCES OF SAMPLE OF MOTHERS, BY STATE

Source of sample	North Carolina	Texas	California	Total
Random digit dial	12	20	27	59
Commercial list	125	248	156	529
Birth records	48	—	103	151
Reverse sample	28	25	28	81
Total	213	293	314	820

TABLE 2.2. MEASURES USED IN TELEPHONE INTERVIEWS WITH 820 MOTHERS

Purpose	Source	Description	Alpha/ Interobserver reliability
Demographics		Age, education, income, ethnicity, marital status, household composition, number and ages of children.	
Child care arrangement	Adapted from Hofferth et al., 1991	History, cost, assistance with cost, and hours of target child's child care arrangement, number of previous arrangements.	
Mothers' willingness to pay more	Galinsky & Shinn, 1994	Willingness to pay more if provider asks, and amount of payment.	
Importance of features of child care to high-quality care	Galinsky & Shinn, 1994	Mothers' assessment of how important each feature is to high-quality care. Features include: (1) regulatable aspects of child care (number and ages of children, provider training, group size, and adult–child ratios; (2) quality of the relationship between provider and child; (3) factors that affect parents (cost, location, hours, frequency of closings, parent opportunity for input); and (4) safety and cleanliness.	
Satisfaction with features of child care	Galinsky & Shinn, 1994	Satisfaction with size and ratio (2 items); satisfaction with parental needs, including hours, schedule flexibility, costs, and continued availability day in and day out (4 items); satisfaction with the provider, including her licensure and training, the home-like atmosphere, the way the provider taught the children to get along, and teaching of cultural or religious values (5 items); satisfaction with warmth, including warmth, attention to children, experience, and openness to mothers' visiting (4 items); satisfaction with shared values, including cleanliness, safety, attention to nutrition, the degree the provider shares the mother's values, her style of discipline, her communication with parents, and her relationship to the child's family (7 items).	$\alpha = .79$ $\alpha = .72$ $\alpha = .65$ $\alpha = .74$ $\alpha = .78$

16

Measure	Source	Description	
Maternal assessment of features of care	Galinsky & Shinn, 1994	Mothers' reports of regulatory statutes, whether the provider is a relative, weekly cost, ratios, relationship with provider, communication with provider, encouragement to drop in to visit child, tours of care, and frequency of breakdown of arrangements (9 items).	$\alpha = .73$
Process of finding child care	Adapted from Hofferth et al., 1991	Ease and difficulty in finding care, reasons for choosing current arrangement, process for finding, amount of choice, preference for type of care.	
Overall satisfaction with child care	Adapted from Quinn & Staines, 1979	Overall satisfaction with child care, willingness to recommend provider to a friend, and willingness to make same choice of care again (3 items).	
Job conditions			
Number of hours worked	Quinn & Staines, 1979		
Job autonomy	Piotrkowski & Katz, 1983	Amount of say that parent has about her job (4 items).	$\alpha = .73$
Job demands	Karasek, 1979	Degree to which job is hectic and demanding (5 items).	$\alpha = .66$
Work–family outcomes			
Spillover	Hughes, 1988 Galinsky &	Assessment of ways in which job affects parents' mood, energy, and relationships at home (5 items).	$\alpha = .68$
Absenteeism	Hughes, 1985	Amount of time missed for various reasons (square-root transformation).	
Work–family conflict	Quinn & Staines, 1979	Assessment of conflict in balancing work and family responsibilities (1 item).	

(cont'd.)

TABLE 2.2 (CONT'D.)

Purpose	Source	Description	Alpha/ Interobserver reliability
Personal outcomes			
Perceived stress	Cohen, Karmarch, & Mermelstein, 1983	Frequency of feeling stressed and unable to cope (6 items).	$\alpha = .74$
Maternal separation anxiety	Hock, Gnezda, & McBride, 1983	Highest-loading items from maternal separation anxiety subscale (11 items).	$\alpha = .83$
Child benefits	Hock et al., 1983	Child benefits subscale from maternal separation anxiety measure (6 items).	$\alpha = .65$

HOW WERE FAMILY CHILD CARE PROVIDERS RECRUITED?

As indicated above, providers were recruited slightly differently, depending on the method by which their name was received. Because all providers except one were female, female pronouns will be used throughout the book when referring to providers.

Community Sample

Mathematica obtained the name of the provider, her telephone number if she had one, the parent who referred the provider, and the parents' telephone number. Providers who had telephone numbers were contacted directly by the respective site coordinator whose job it was to recruit providers and coordinate data collection. Providers who spoke only Spanish were contacted by a bilingual staff member (due to staffing limitations, only providers who spoke English or Spanish were able to be included in the study). Site coordinators explained to providers that a parent of a child in her care (both referred to by name) had participated in a national telephone survey regarding family child care and that the mother had given the provider's name because she agreed to allow her child to participate in the observational component of the study if the provider was willing. The procedure to be followed if the provider agreed was explained, including the fact that the visit would take two to three hours while the target child was awake and playing, that she (the provider) would be interviewed and asked to complete some questionnaires, and that the provider would receive a $20 gift certificate in appreciation for her participation.

Rate of agreement to participate by providers across the three sites was 40% (357 providers referred; 144 providers observed). Thirty-one percent of the referred providers refused to participate, and 28% were ineligible. The percentage of providers observed, refused, and ineligible varied somewhat by state (see Table 2.3). The highest refusal rate and lowest ineligible rates were in Texas.

The primary reason for ineligibility was the target child leaving care between the time of the parent interview by Mathematica and contact

TABLE 2.3. PARTICIPATION RATES OF PROVIDERS, BY STATE

State	Completed	Ineligible	Refused	Total
North Carolina	47 (45%)	31 (30%)	26 (25%)	104
Texas	50 (37%)	26 (19%)	60 (44%)	136
California	47 (40%)	44 (37%)	26 (23%)	117

with the providers by the site coordinator. It should be noted that contact with the provider typically took place within 48 hours of the interview with the mother. During the difficult economic period in which the study was conducted, many mothers moved in and out of the labor market, often looking for jobs. We also assume that, in some cases, mothers reported on child care arrangements that they were no longer using but had used recently. Reasons for ineligibility by site and for the total sample are indicated in Table 2.4. Of the *eligible* providers, 56% participated in the study. In all, 47 providers from North Carolina and California and 50 providers in Texas participated from the community sample.

Provider Referral Sample

After all eligible community sample referrals who agreed to participate had been observed, a decision was made to increase the total number of participating providers per site to 75 by recruiting the "provider referral sample." The provider referral sample (25 in Texas; 28 in North Carolina and California) was recruited by contacting additional providers and obtaining a parent referral. To locate additional providers, site coordinators attempted to gather 100 non-duplicate telephone numbers of providers from newspaper advertisements and other sources of family child care advertising (e.g., grocery store and laundromat bulletin boards). The rationale for this approach was that it might generate additional nonregulated providers for the sample. This turned out to be the case in North Carolina and Texas. Thus, the North Carolina and Texas site coordinators called each of the 100 telephone numbers of

TABLE 2.4. REASONS FOR INELIGIBILITY OF PROVIDERS, BY STATE

| Reason | *Percentage of Providers Ineligible* | | | |
	Total	North Carolina	Texas	California
Child no longer in care	64	20	16	28
Center-based care	13	4	9	0
In-home care	7	2	0	5
Third-shift care	1	1	0	0
Not enough hours	7	3	0	4
Duplicate provider	5	1	1	3
Provider did not speak English or Spanish	2	0	0	2
Child too young	1	0	0	1

providers and, for those who were reachable and still in business, informed them about the study. If they expressed any interest, a letter was sent to them providing additional details and substantiating the credibility of the study. An additional telephone contact was made by the site coordinator to solicit the provider's participation in the study. This process resulted in approximately half the desired number of additional providers in North Carolina and Texas.

The next step was to utilize the lists of regulated family child care providers available from the state in Texas and North Carolina and from Child Care Resource and Referral in California. In Texas and North Carolina, the provider referral sample was completed by randomly selecting providers from the regulated family child care list who had not been previously referred by mothers for the community sample. Letters were sent to each of the randomly selected providers and then a follow-up telephone call was made to solicit their participation. This process continued until the target number of providers was reached.

In California, because there was virtually no advertising of non-regulated family child care, the entire provider referral sample was generated from the regulated family child care list. A random list of regulated caregivers was generated by the Resource and Referral agency serving the target area. Providers were mailed a letter explaining the study along with three return postcards addressed to the researchers. The first postcard was used by the provider to indicate her interest in participating in the study. The other two postcards were to be given to parents that the interested providers believed met study criteria and might be willing to give permission for their child to be observed, as well as agree to participate in the phone survey. This postcard briefly described the study, what involvement would entail for parents and child, and requested that interested parents return the postcard to the researchers. The visit was scheduled after receiving a postcard from both a provider and a parent. Mothers were then interviewed by Mathematica (in most instances, the visit occurred following the interview).

SAMPLE VARIATION AND BIAS

Characteristics of the Mothers' Sample

An important question, in a study such as this, is the extent to which the sample differs by state and by sampling method, and the extent to which observed differences reveal biases due to sampling method. We knew before beginning the study that the ethnic composition of the mothers' sample would differ considerably by state because of differences in the three communities studied. The North Carolina sample was almost evenly split between African Americans and whites; in both California and Texas, the sample was nearly evenly split between Latinos and whites, with a substantial minority, especially in Texas, of African Americans. Asian Americans and respondents of other ethnicity were almost all in the California sample.

The multiple sampling methods mean that, strictly speaking, the mothers' sample is not representative of any population. The random-digit dialing and birth record samples were chosen to overrepresent low-income families and minority families. Not surprisingly, respondents from the commercial list were less likely to be members of minority groups, had higher incomes, and were better educated; yet even these respondents, chosen from areas with concentrations of minority group members, were only 46% white. The provider referral sample was more likely to be white and middle income than was the commercial list sample in these respects, but may still not be unrepresentative of child care users. Thus, although the full sample is not formally representative of family child care and relative care users, we met our goal of obtaining substantial numbers of both low income and minority respondents. The demographic characteristics of the full sample of 820 mothers are presented in Table 2.5. We are also encouraged by the high response rates among families who were identified as eligible for the study, and by the comparable response rates for white and African American families and for low- and high-income respondents. More details about differences in mothers and providers by state and sampling method are provided in Appendix A.

Bias in the Provider Referral Process

Although the community sampling strategy succeeded in reaching mothers who reported that their providers were not regulated, it did not guarantee that mothers would in fact refer these providers to the study or that the providers would participate. Thus it is important to investigate biases at these two stages of the process. As noted above, we offered a $35 incentive to mothers in low-income families and in minority families if they would refer their providers to us. Not surprisingly, in view of these incentives, referral rates differed by income group $[\chi^2 (2) = 21.33, p < .001]$ and by ethnicity $[\chi^2 (2) = 6.67, p < .05]$. Mothers with household incomes below $20,000 were more likely to refer providers (65%) than were households in the middle- (48%) and upper-income (43%) groups, and African Americans were more likely to refer providers (58%) than were whites (48%), and Latinos and others (46%). The additional incentives were not successful in increasing referral

TABLE 2.5. DEMOGRAPHIC CHARACTERISTICS OF MOTHERS

Characteristics of Mothers	n	Percentage
Education		
Less than high school	47	6
Some high school	56	7
Diploma or GED	225	27
Some college, AA degree	251	31
BA degree	170	21
Graduate work or degree	71	9
Family income		
Under $20,000	165	21
$20,000–$39,999	287	36
≥$40,000	349	44
Ethnicity*		
White, non-Latino	347	42
African American	190	23
Latino	254	31
Other	29	3
Marital Status		
Single	102	12
Married, living with partner	664	81
Divorced, separated	49	6
Widowed	4	—
Child is first-born	407	50
Age	30.6 years	5.6 standard deviation

n = 820
*Ethnicity is defined somewhat differently in the full sample of mothers and in the subsample of children observed.

rates among Latino families. As a consequence of these differential referral rates, mothers who referred providers had lower levels of educational attainment than those who did not [t (737) = –4.00, $p < .001$]. High school was the mean education level of those who referred providers, and some college was the mean level for those who did not.

Referral rates also differed by state and sampling method [χ^2 (7) = 23.64, $p < .01$], with respondents in California and in the commercial list sample least likely to refer providers. These differences diminished after controlling for ethnicity, but among African American families there was still an effect by sampling method, and among Latino and other families there was still an effect by state, in the same directions as for the overall sample.

Referral rates did not differ by characteristics of care, in particular whether the provider was or was not a relative [χ^2 (1) = 1.79, n.s.], or whether the mother believed the provider to be regulated [χ^2 (1) = 05, n.s.]. There was also no difference by the number of children the provider cared for, as reported by the mother [t (735) = 0.31, n.s.] or by the mother's overall satisfaction with the child care home [t (737) = 1.35, n.s.].

Bias in the Providers' Willingness to Participate in the Study

Of the 366 providers referred by mothers to the study, 142 (or 39%) could be located and agreed to participate in the study. There were several differences in characteristics of the families served by referred providers who did and did not participate [χ^2 (2) = 9.07, p < .05]. Acceptance rates by referred providers were 46% for providers who served families with incomes of $40,000 and above, 40% for those who served families with incomes in the middle group, and 28% for those who served families with incomes below $20,000. These biases counterbalanced the greater tendency for low-income families to refer providers, so that the final sample on whom we have data from both mothers and providers is similar with respect to income compared with the full community sample of mothers. Providers for more educated mothers were also more likely to participate than were those for less educated mothers [t (364) = 2.20, p < .05], again counterbalancing the opposite bias that appeared in the referral process. Providers for white and African American families agreed to participate with similar rates (45% and 42%, respectively) but only 24% of providers for Latino families and 29% of providers for the small group of Asian American and other families participated [χ^2 (2) = 14.37, p < .001]. A loglinear analysis found no differences in participation rates either by state [χ^2 (2) = 2.87, n.s.] or by sampling method [χ^2 (2) = 1.19, n.s.] among providers who were referred to the study.

There were a few important differences in characteristics of care arrangements between providers who did and did not agree to participate. Providers whom the mother believed to be regulated were much more likely to participate (51%) than were providers whom the mother thought nonregulated (35%). Interestingly, there were no differences in participation rates by relatives or nonrelatives [χ^2 (1) = 0.23, n.s.] and no differences according to the number of children cared for [t (363) = 1.18, n.s.). Mothers' overall satisfaction with the child care home was slightly (though not statistically significantly) higher for providers who participated than for those who did not [t (343) = 1.95, p < .06]. Because mothers' satisfaction with nonparticipating providers was more variable than with participating providers [F (Levene's test) = 1.53, $p < .01$], the latter analysis was conducted using a separate variance estimate.

Cumulative Effects of Provider Sample Bias at the Two Stages of the Selection Process

To determine the cumulative effects of the two-stage selection process (whether mothers referred their providers and whether referred providers agreed to participate), we compared providers from the community sample who ultimately participated in the study with those who did not participate (either because the mother refused to refer them or because they refused to participate after they were referred), using mothers' reports of their own and their providers' characteristics (see Chapter 8 for a discussion of the accuracy of mothers' reports of their providers). Families served by participating and nonparticipating providers were comparable in income [χ^2 (2) = 0.28, n.s.] and education [t (737) = .08, n.s.]. Providers who served Latino families and families of other ethnicities were less likely to participate (12%) than were providers who served African American (24%) and white (23%) families [χ^2 (2) = 14.01, $p < .001$].

Participating providers were no more or less likely than were the other providers to be relatives [χ^2 (1) = .02, n.s.] but, according to mothers' reports, participating providers were more likely to be regulated (40%) than were nonparticipating providers (30%) [χ^2 (1) = 5.22, $p < .05$]. Participating providers served similar numbers of children to the nonparticipating providers [t (737) = 1.15, n.s.] and mothers were equally satisfied with the care they provided [t (737) = –1.07, n.s.].

A loglinear analysis showed that ultimate participation rates were higher in North Carolina (25%) than in Texas (18%) or California (16%) [χ^2 (2) = 6.26, $p < .05$], but did not differ by sampling method [χ^2 (2) = 2.16, n.s.].

Summary

The providers who ultimately participated in the study were quite similar in most respects to the providers described by the community sample of mothers. In some cases, biases at the two stages of sampling canceled each other out. For example, participating providers served families who were almost identical in income and education to the full sample of providers because incentives for low-income families to refer providers were counterbalanced by a greater tendency for providers to high-income families to participate. In the case of ethnicity, however, biases at the two stages of sampling were in the same direction. Latino mothers (and those of other ethnic groups) were less likely than were white and African American mothers to refer their providers, and their providers, in turn, were less likely to participate.

Because referral rates differed by state, so did the ultimate participation rates, but there were no differences by state in participation rates among providers who were referred to the study, nor were there differences at either stage of recruiting providers by the sampling method used to recruit mothers. A larger proportion of providers from North Carolina than from other states participated in the study. This is probably because North Carolina had almost no Latino families or providers in the sample—the group least likely to participate.

Referral rates did not depend in any way on characteristics of care, but unregulated providers were less likely than were regulated providers to participate in the study. Interestingly, mothers were as likely to refer relatives as nonrelatives, and the providers who were relatives were equally likely to participate. There was no difference by either referral status or participation rates in the number of children served. Overall, there were no differences in maternal satisfaction ratings among mothers whose providers did and did not ultimately participate in the study.

We were initially very concerned that mothers using care they believed was regulated would be more likely to refer their providers. Since this was not the case, and since mothers referred providers with whom they reported varying degrees of satisfaction, we can have confidence that the referral process was not a screen to eliminate care that was underground or of poorer perceived quality.

There were some differences by sampling method. The provider referral sample, in particular, is quite different from the community sample. Providers from the referral sample were more likely to be regulated, and because this sample is over one third of the provider sample (36%), the provider sample is biased toward regulated care. Because previous research has shown that regulated providers offer better quality care, our sample procedures may overestimate the quality of care provided. The reverse sample is only 10% of the mothers' sample, however, so it is less of a biasing factor in the mothers' reports of care.

PROCEDURES FOR PROVIDER OBSERVATIONS

Providers were visited for approximately 3 hours, usually between 8:30 and 11:30 in the morning. Timing of the visit was designed to cover periods during which the target child was awake and engaging in typical daily activities. The provider was asked to carry on as usual, despite the presence of the observer.

Observations were conducted by trained female observers who lived in the communities where they worked. Training consisted of five days learning to reliably administer the observational instruments and to be sensitive to the unique aspects of family child care and relative care as child care settings. Cultural sensitivity was also included in the training. All observers initially involved in the study were trained together to maximize consistency across sites. The observers represented a culturally diverse group (African American, Latino, and Asian—in addition to white—observers were trained). Spanish-speaking providers were always observed by a bilingual observer.

On arrival, the observer identified the target child and made an initial count of children (related and unrelated) and adults (providers and nonproviders) in the home. Changes that occurred in number of children or adults during the observation, and the timing of those changes, were noted for later calculation of adult–child ratio and group size. Four 5-minute, time-sampling observations of the target child were conducted during the first 60 to 75 minutes of the visit, at approximately equal intervals. The time-sampling observations focused on children's cognitive and social play, type of play activities, and level of adult involvement. In between time-sampling observations, observers took notes for later scoring of the Arnett Scale (Arnett, 1989), the Waters-Deane Attachment Q-set (Waters & Deane, 1985), and the Family Day Care Rating Scale (FDCRS) (Harms & Clifford, 1989).

Beginning in the second hour of observation, the observer asked the provider questions as her responsibilities allowed. These questions focused on aspects of the FDCRS that were unable to be observed, such as business practices, formal and informal training experiences, etc.. Some providers preferred to respond to the questions in writing rather than in an interview format. During this time, when not talking to the provider, observers continued to observe and take notes for later scoring of the Arnett, Waters-Deane, and FDCRS instruments. The visit ended when the observer had completed the time-sampling observations and had obtained sufficient information through observation and interview to complete the scoring of the instruments.

At the end of the visit, providers were given a 12-page questionnaire to complete and return to the researchers (assistance was given to providers with literacy problems, although this was a rare occurrence). Providers were given a stamped, self-addressed envelope in which to return the questionnaire to the researcher, but some of the envelopes (for those who failed to put them in the mail) were retrieved by observers. The questionnaire consisted of eight different measures: Caregiving Daily Hassles (Kontos & Riessen, 1993; Block Childrearing Practices Report—Revised (Rickel & Biasetti, 1982); Job Satisfaction,

Job Commitment, Job Attitudes, Questionnaire on Social Support (Crnic, Greenberg, Ragozin, Robinson, & Basham, 1983); Family Child Care Support; and Features of High Quality Family Child Care. If the target child was at least 30 months of age, providers were also asked to complete the Adaptive Language Inventory (Feagans & Farran, 1979) and Preschool Behavior Questionnaire (Behar & Stringfield, 1975) on the child. Providers were given a $20 gift certificate when all questionnaires were completed and returned.

The measures used in the study with providers and children are described in Tables 2.6 and 2.7. Measures without citations were developed by the authors. This description of the measures is elaborated in the following chapters as results are introduced.

REGULATORY CONTEXT

An important factor affecting studies of child care, in general, and of family child care in particular, is the regulatory context in the geographic area selected for study. State child care regulations can address issues of child health and safety, group size, allowable number of infants, number of children per adult, discipline, parent relationships, and many other aspects of child care. In addition to licensing, other inspectors approve homes or centers for building safety, fire safety, and sanitation.

Each state is responsible for establishing its own laws, systems of inspection, and regulations for child care in centers and in family child care homes. Policies determining which programs and providers are subject to regulation and which are not are set by each state. Parents and relatives are not subject to regulation for care of their related children. All states license full-day child care centers, although some states exempt certain types of centers, such as those that operate part-time or that operate under the auspices of the public schools or religious organizations.

Regulations for family child care vary from state to state. One variation concerns who is required to be regulated. These definitions depend on the number of unrelated children the provider accepts, whether the provider's own preschool children are counted in the total number, and the number of infants and/or school-age children in care. Thus, there are some homes that are not required to be regulated and that operate legally without it. Another variation concerns the way different states define "regulation." It may or may not include inspection, health and safety requirements, annual training, or other requirements. Some of these differences in the definition of regulation are reflected in the different terminology chosen by states to refer to regulated providers: for example, some states choose the term *licensing*, while others choose *registration*.

Family child care regulations for the three states involved in this study are listed in Table 2.8. These regulations reveal the extent to which the three states are similar (e.g., fire safety) and different (e.g., group size, training). We began the study with the assumption that the regulatory climate would affect the quality of family child care (but probably not relative care) in each state. The regulatory differences among these three states are numerous but not dramatic. The effects of regulation on quality are presented in Chapter 10.

The remainder of the book will report findings of the study. We begin by describing the characteristics of the providers in the study and then examine the quality of care they are providing. We examine quality in four ways: overall, by type of provider, by family characteristics (income and ethnicity), and by comparing providers offering different levels of quality. We then turn to the mothers' experiences in finding child care and their perceptions of family child care and relative care. Next we focus on children's experiences in family child care and relative care and how quality affects their development. Finally, the effects of regulation on quality, the relation between cost and quality, and provider longevity are addressed.

(Tables 2.6–2.8 follow)

TABLE 2.6. MEASURES USED IN INTERVIEWS, OBSERVATIONS, AND SELF-REPORT ASSESSMENTS WITH PROVIDERS

Purpose	Source	Description	Alpha/ Interobserver reliability
Provider background		Age, sex, marital status, employment history, family income.	
Description of family child care and relative care home		Hours of operation, number and ages of children, hours children spend in care, presence of assistants, openings for more children.	
Motivation		Primary motivation for providing care (16 items); self description of job (4 items).	
Social support			
General social involvement	Crnic et al., 1983	Availability of, and satisfaction with, social support in community, with friends, and with intimate relationships (16 items).	Involvement $\alpha = .52$ Satisfaction $\alpha = .77$
Family child care involvement	Kontos, based on form used by Crnic et al., 1983	Involvement in, and satisfaction with, social support from other family child care and relative care providers (16 items).	Involvement $\alpha = .79$ Satisfaction $\alpha = .78$
Presence of providers' children, family members		Reports of providers' own children, presence of children.	
Business and safety practices		Insurance, benefits, specific business practices, including depreciating cost of child care and reporting income on taxes, providing Social Security number to parents, having doctor's phone number, daytime phone number for children's parents, emergency authorization form and immunization records (14 items).	$\alpha = .91$
Activities		Observational scheme for coding predominant activities for children.	$k = .91$

Measure	Source	Description	Reliability
Process quality ratings			
Arnett Scale of Caregiver Sensitivity	Arnett, 1989	Assessment of three aspects of provider-child relationship: sensitivity, restrictiveness, and detachment (26 items).	$k = .93$ Sensitivity $\alpha = .91$ Harshness $\alpha = .83$ Detachment $\alpha = .81$
Process quality observation Howes Involvement Scale	Howes & Stewart, 1987	Ratings of six levels of adult-child involvement: The Adult Involvement Scale (Howes and Stewart, 1987) was used to rate the intensity of adult-child involvement. This scale has six levels ranging from (1) ignoring the child; (2) routine caregiving in which the provider gives routine care, e.g., blowing nose; (3) minimal caregiving when the provider talks to or touches the child in order to discipline the child, to answer direct requests for help, or to give verbal directives with no reply encouraged; (4) answering the child's social bids in a positive but brief manner; (5) extending and elaborating on the child's social bids; and (6) intense caregiving, including holding or hugging the child to provide comfort, engaging the child in prolonged conversation, or playing interactively with the child. Can be summed to low-level involvement and responsive involvement.	$k = .86$
Limit-Setting Measure	Dunn, 1990	Observational scheme for coding predominant activities for children.	$k = .83$
Process quality self-report Block and Block Child-Rearing Attitudes Scale revised	Adapted from Rickel & Biasatti, 1982	Extent to which providers endorse flexible child-rearing attitudes and practices (nurturance), and attitudes and practices intended to control children's behavior (restrictiveness) (40 items).	Nurturant $\alpha = .79$ Restrictive $\alpha = .80$

(cont'd.)

TABLE 2.6 (CONT'D.)

Purpose	Source	Description	Alpha/ Interobserver reliability
Structural quality			
Group size		Observed number of children present at 15-minute intervals across observation period.	
Ratio		Observed number of children for each adult present who is providing care.	
Formal education of provider		Level of schooling completed.	
Family child care training		Conferences and workshops attended.	
Years of Experience		Years of experience in providing family child care and relative care.	
Adult work environment			
Hassles	Kontos & Riessen, 1993	Frequency of occurrence of 25 issues that are unpleasant or stressful about job.	$\alpha = .92$
Work satisfaction		Provider's satisfaction with her work (10 items).	$\alpha = .73$
Job commitment		Commitment to providing family child care and relative care (6 items).	$\alpha = .63$
Family child care income		Providers reporting their rates from family child care and relative care.	
Global quality: Family Day Care Rating Scale (FDCRS)	Harms and Clifford, 1989	Observational measure focusing on the six areas of caregiving practice: space and furnishings, basic needs, language and reasoning, learning activities, social development, and adult needs (33 items).	$k = .89$
Providers' descriptions of quality	Adapted from Galinsky and Shinn, 1994	Provider ratings of 30 aspects of quality that factor into parents as partners, cost and convenience, cleanliness and safety, school-like and/or home-like environment, warmth, structure, ratio, and group size.	

TABLE 2.7. MEASURES USED IN ASSESSING CHILD OUTCOMES

Type of Measure	Source	Description	Alphal Interobserver reliability
Attachment Security	Waters & Deanne, 1985	Q-set based on 2–3 hour observation; differentiates between a secure, an anxious/avoidant, and an anxious/resistant attachment to provider (90 items).	$k = .85$
Howes Peer Play Scale	Howes, 1980	Observation of four, 5-minute time samples over 2–3 hours measures aimless wandering, onlooker behavior, and the complexity of play with peers (6 scale points).	$k = .87$
Object Play	Adaptation of Smilansky, 1968	Frequency of play coded into six categories: (1) noncognitive play; (2) functional play without objects; (3) functional play with passive use of objects; (4) functional play with active use of objects; (5) constructive play; and (6) dramatic play.	$k = .87$
Adaptive Language Inventory	Feagans & Farran, 1979	18-item rating scale assessing children's functional communication skills.	$\alpha = .94$
Preschool Behavior Questionnaire	Behar & Stringfield, 1975	30-item rating scale assessing children's aggression, anxiety, and hyperactivity.	$\alpha = .86$

TABLE 2.8. COMPARISON OF STATE REGULATORY CLIMATES

Regulatory Item	California	Texas	North Carolina
Definitions of homes not covered by licensing	Providers caring for children from one unrelated family in addition to the provider's own family are legally exempt from licensure.	Providers caring for three or fewer unrelated children in addition to the provider's own children are legally exempt from registration.	Providers caring for two or fewer unrelated children in addition to provider's own children or providing care less than four hours each day are legally exempt from licensure.
Regulatory policy for subsidized homes	All providers who care for children receiving subsidies must be licensed.	All subsidized providers must be registered, except for self-arranged care.	All nonregistered subsidized (except for grandparents, aunts, and uncles) providers and the parent they serve are required to complete a self-certifying basic information and health and safety checklist.
Group size			
Family child care home	6 maximum	12 maximum (under 14 years old) including the caregiver's own children	8 maximum; no more than 5 (including the children of the provider) can be preschool-age
Large or group family child care home	12 maximum	12 maximum	15 maximum
Ratio			
Family child care home	1:6 No more than 3 infants, including provider's own children; no more than 4 infants only	Set by the age of youngest child— 1:12 maximum Up to 4 infants 0–17 months (i.e., 1:4 + 2 school-age children)	1:8 No more than five preschool-age

	Large or group family child care home		
	2:12 No more than 4 infants, including provider's own children	1:12 4 infants with one provider; no other children; 10 infants with two providers	Infants: 1:6 0–4 yrs.: 1:6; 0–12 yrs.: 1:8; 2–12 yrs.: 1:10; 3–12 yrs.: 1:12; school-age: 1:15 1:15 when all school-age (1:12 if any child is preschool-age)
Training requirements prior to becoming a provider	Applicant needs to attend an "Orientation" given by Community Care Licensing.	Providers must attend 6 hours of orientation prior to registration	None
Yearly training required	None	20 hours per year; first-aid and CPR required	None
Inspection	Once every three years	30% a year, random—all new applications are inspected prior to issuance of the registration	Once every two years
Unannounced parental access	Yes	No	Yes
Liability insurance required	Is not required, but parents must sign an "Affidavit Regarding Liability Insurance."	No	No

3

The Characteristics of Providers

As discussed in Chapter 1, previous research on family child care tended to be affected by one or more of several limitations, including outdatedness, small sample size and/or single site, omission of nonregulated and relative providers, and/or lack of observational data. One purpose of our study was to obtain up-to-date answers to a series of basic questions regarding the providers of family child care and relative care using a diverse, multisite sample:

- What are the characteristics of family child care and relative care providers?
- What are their motivations for providing care?
- To what extent are providers integrated into social support networks?
- How do providers organize their service?
- How do providers relate to families?

Throughout the study, as we recruited families and providers to participate and completed our interviews and observations, it became clear that it is difficult and, in fact, incorrect to treat these providers as a homogeneous group. At least three very different groups of people provided care for the children in our study:

1. *Relatives of the child who are not regulated providers:* There are 54 nonregulated providers in the sample, of whom approximately two thirds are grandmothers, one fourth are aunts, and the remainder are other relatives of the target child. Forty-nine percent take care of children in addition to the target child and their own children. For the most part, these additional children

are also relatives. The mean number of children they care for is 1.88. Fifty-two percent of them charge for providing care.

2. *Nonregulated family child care providers who are not relatives:* There are 60 nonregulated providers in the sample. All are unrelated to the target child. Sixty-four percent take care of children in addition to the target child in our study and their own children. The mean number of children they care for is 2.94. Ninety-six percent of them charge for providing care.

3. *Regulated family child care providers:* There are 112 regulated providers in the sample (verified by lists of regulated providers maintained in each state). Of these, 106 are not related to the target child and 6 are related. Ninety-nine percent of these providers take care of other children in addition to the target child and their own children. The mean number of children they care for is 5.39. All of them charge for providing care.

There were no differences among our three sites in the proportion of children in each group of providers [χ^2 (4) = 6.09, n.s.]. There were, however, differences among these groups in terms of demographic characteristics of the providers and of the families that select their care, motivations for providing care, integration into social networks, in the organization of their child care service, and in relations with the families whose children are in their care. These will be discussed in the subsequent sections of this chapter.

DEMOGRAPHIC CHARACTERISTICS OF PROVIDERS IN EACH GROUP

Ethnographic research on a small sample of family child care and relative care providers suggests that regulated, nonregulated, and relative providers differ in demographic characteristics (Nelson, 1990). The three groups of providers in our study differed in age, ethnicity, marital status, employment history, and family income.

Age. The providers ranged in age from 18 to 81 years. As shown in Table 3.1, their average age was 42.4 years (*SD* = 13.6). Their median age was 36 years. Only 1% of the providers was under 20 years, but 10% were 65 years and older. Relative providers were older than either regulated or nonregulated family child care providers (Scheffe = .05). Approximately two thirds of the relatives were grandmothers, one-fourth were aunts, and the remainder were other relatives of the target child.

TABLE 3.1. DEMOGRAPHIC AND SOCIAL CHARACTERISTICS OF PROVIDERS

Provider Characteristics	Total (n = 226)	Regulated (n = 112)	Nonregulated (n = 60)	Relative (n = 54)	χ^2 or F-Test (Scheffe)
Age	42.4 yrs.	40.5 yrs.	35.9 yrs.	52.9 yrs.	29.16***
Ethnicity					47.93**
White	57%	71%	59%	28%	
African American	22	17	18	37	
Latino	16	5	21	33	
Other	5	7	2	2	
Education					56.11**
<High school	22%	6%	33%	46%	
High school	22	24	19	23	
Some college, AA degree	38	46	33	25	
BA degree +	18	24	15	6	
Family income					36.41***
<$20,000	40%	23%	50%	65%	
$20,000–$39,999	34	39	35	23	
≥$40,000	26	38	15	13	
Marital Status					27.38**
Married/living with partner	73%	72%	75%	61%	
Never married/divorced/widowed	27	28	25	39	

Years of experience as provider	5.7 yrs.	6.1 yrs.	4.1 yrs.	6.6 yrs.	2.00 ns
Previous employment history					8.06*
Yes	92%	97%	87%	87%	
No	8	3	13	13	
Type of previous job					31.84**
Unskilled	12%	6%	11%	26%	
Other	88	94	89	74	
General social support[a]	-.17	.68	-.17	-1.33	5.30**

* p < .05; ** p < .01; *** p < .001; ns = not significant
[a]Standardized scores— the lower the score, the less social support.

Ethnicity. Fifty-seven percent of the providers were white, 22% African American, and 16% Latino, as seen in Table 3.1. The remaining 5% of the providers were Asian American, Native American, or biracial. Ethnicity was associated with provider group. White providers tended to be regulated, whereas Latino and African American providers were more likely to be relatives.

Education. The median education for all providers was some college or an associate degrees (see Table 3.1). Nonregulated and relative providers were more likely to have less than a high school diploma than were regulated providers.

Family Income. For most (82%) of the providers, a second adult contributed to their family income. There were no differences between provider groups in whether or not a second adult contributed to the family income [$\chi^2 (2) = 1.74$, n.s.]. Median family income for the providers in our sample was between $20,000 and $29,000.

Family income varied by provider group (see Table 3.1). Regulated family child care providers had higher family incomes than did relative or nonregulated providers. The median family income for regulated providers was between $30,000 and $39,000 and for relatives and nonregulated providers it was between $10,000 and $19,000.

Marital Status. Seventy-three percent of the providers were married and another 16% were divorced. The remaining providers were either never married (5%) or widowed (6%). Marital status was associated with provider group. Relative providers were less likely to be married or living with a partner and more likely to be single (primarily widowed), as shown in Table 3.1.

Years of Experience as a Provider. On average, the providers in our study had been providing care for nearly six years. The nonregulated providers reported the least experience, but there were no statistically significant differences in years of experience as a function of provider group.

Employment History. Most (92%) of the providers had been employed outside of the home prior to becoming a family child care provider. Relatives and nonregulated providers were less likely than were regulated family child care providers to have had previous outside employment, as indicated in Table 3.1.

Table 3.1 describes the previous employment of the different groups of providers. There was a significant association between previous job and provider group. Relatives were more likely to have been unskilled service workers, whereas regulated family child care providers were more likely to have been skilled, clerical, or professional workers.

Associations Between Family and Provider Income and Ethnicity. Child care professionals suggest that family child care provides for continuity between the culture of the family and the culture of child care because it is often provided by neighbors and friends of the family. To test this assumption, we examined the income level and ethnicity of the families served by the provider and associations between family (target child) race and class and provider race and class.

The child care arrangements families select for their children are influenced by their social class and race. Using census bureau statistics, Hayes, Palmer, and Zaslow (1990) concluded that low-income and Latino families were more likely to select informal child care arrangements, whereas better educated and high-income white and African-American families were more likely to select formal arrangements. Family child care is generally considered an informal arrangement and center care a formal arrangement. However, within family child care, regulated care is a more formal child care arrangement than is relative or nonregulated care. Consistent with these findings, in our study there were significant associations between family income and family ethnic background and the group of provider selected. As shown in Table 3.2, families with incomes over $40,000 tended to select regulated care, whereas families with incomes below $20,000 tended to select relative care. As shown in Table 3.3, white families tended to select regulated care whereas African American and Latino families were more likely to select relative care.

TABLE 3.2. DISTRIBUTION OF TARGET CHILDREN BY FAMILY INCOME IN EACH PROVIDER GROUP

Family Income $\chi^2 = 25.97^*$	*Percentage of Children in Provider Group*			
	Total	Regulated	Non-regulated	Relative
Less than $20,000 $n = 34$	15	27	29	44
$20,000 to $40,000 $n = 85$	38	39	30	31
Over $40,000 $n = 107$	47	65	23	12

* $p < .001$

TABLE 3.3. DISTRIBUTION OF TARGET CHILDREN BY FAMILY ETHNICITY IN EACH PROVIDER GROUP

Family Ethnicity $\chi^2 = 27.70*$	Percentage of Children in Provider Group			
	Total	Regulated	Non-regulated	Relative
White n = 137	62	60	25	15
African American n = 53	24	36	24	40
Latino n = 25	11	16	36	48

* $p < .001$

Families with higher incomes tended to select providers with higher family income [χ^2 (4) = 30.81, $p < .0001$]. Seventy-five percent of the families with incomes lower than $20,000 selected providers with family incomes of less than $20,000. Forty percent of families with incomes greater than $40,000 selected providers with incomes greater than $40,000.

There were also significant associations between family and provider ethnicity [χ^2 (4) = 232.63, $p < .001$]. Eighty-seven percent of African American families selected African American providers. Eighty-six percent of white providers selected white providers. Eighty-three percent of Latino families selected Latino providers.

Summary

In general the providers in our study were women approaching middle age and the end of their child-bearing years. They tended to be married or living with a partner. Slightly over half were white, almost one quarter African American, and almost one fifth Latino. Most of the providers had been employed outside of the home prior to providing child care. The median family income of the providers was between $20,000 and $29,000. Most of the providers had a second adult in the household who contributed to the family income. Providers who contributed a larger percentage of the family income tended to have lower family incomes.

There were three distinct groups of providers in our study. Relative providers were most likely to serve African American and Latino children, to serve families with annual incomes of $20,000, and to themselves be African American or Latino. Relative providers were older; they were often the grandmother of the target child in our sample, and more likely than other providers to be widowed. They were also more likely to have worked at unskilled service jobs prior to caring for children, and their median family incomes were between $10,000 and $19,000.

Regulated family child care providers, in contrast, tended to serve more affluent white families and to themselves be white. They were more likely to be married, living with a partner, or divorced. Their prior jobs were more likely to have been skilled, clerical, or professional. Their own median family incomes were between $30,000 and $39,000.

Nonregulated family child care providers fell somewhere in-between relative and regulated providers in these demographic characteristics. They more often cared for children from middle-income as opposed to low-income families, but they were not as often selected by high-income families. Latino families were more likely to select nonregulated as opposed to regulated providers, but nonregulated providers were less likely to be selected than were relative providers. The nonregulated providers themselves were the youngest of the providers and more likely than were regulated providers to have never been married or divorced. They were also more likely than were relative providers to have held prior skilled jobs but were less likely to have been professionals. Their median family income was similar to that of relative providers.

MOTIVATIONS OF PROVIDERS

Ethnographic studies of family child care suggest that motivation to become a provider is based on wanting to be able to stay home and care for their own children (Eheart & Leavitt, 1989; Nelson, 1990). We examined whether this was the motivation of the providers in our study and whether the three provider groups differed in their motivations for becoming providers.

Rank Ordering of Reasons for Becoming a Provider

Providers were asked to indicate on a prepared list their primary motivation for becoming a provider. The rank ordering of their reasons for becoming a provider is shown in Table 3.4 The most highly ranked reasons are personal rather than professional in nature: to stay home with their own children and to help out the mothers of the children in their care.

Providers in the three different provider groups differed in their reasons for becoming a provider [χ^2 (6) = 51.16, $p <$ .0001]. Only the four highest ranked reasons were considered, to minimize small cells. Table 3.5 presents the distribution of reasons by the three provider groups.

TABLE 3.4. REASONS FOR BECOMING A PROVIDER

Reason	Percentage of Providers Selecting Reason as Primary (n = 211)
Stay home with own children	49
Want to help the mothers of the children I care for	21
Want to work with children	13
Want to work at home	12
The mothers asked me	4
Only job I can do	1

Regulated and nonregulated family child care providers were most likely to want to stay home with their own children; relative providers were most likely to want to help the mothers of the children in their care.

Providers' Characterizations of Their Work

To further examine motivations, we also asked providers to characterize their jobs by selecting from four alternative descriptions. Over half of the providers (52%) described child care as their chosen profession. There were differences among the three provider groups in their self-descriptions [χ^2 (6) = 49.95, $p < .0001$]. As shown in Table 3.6, regulated providers were most likely to see their caregiving as their chosen occupation, whereas relative and nonregulated providers were most likely to see their caregiving as good only while their own children (or grandchildren) were young.

Summary

The primary motivation for becoming a provider for those studied was to stay home with their own children. However, over half of the providers described family child care as their chosen occupation, as opposed to 30% who described it as a good way to work while their children are young. This suggests that most of the providers in our study enjoy the actual work as opposed to feeling it a duty to stay home with their children.

Additionally, relatively few providers described selecting family child care as an occupation because they wanted to work with children or as a stepping stone to related work. This suggests that the providers we interviewed did not see family child care as a step on a career ladder in the general field of children's services.

Likewise relatively few providers merely wanted to work at home or felt that family child care was their only job choice. The fact that

TABLE 3.5. DISTRIBUTION OF REASONS FOR PROVIDING CARE BY PROVIDER GROUPS

	Percentage of Providers		
Reason	Regulated (n = 105)	Nonregulated (n = 56)	Relative (n = 50)
Stay home with own children	63	56	22
Want to help mothers	9	15	60
Want to work with children	13	19	7
Want to work at home	15	10	11

TABLE 3.6. DISTRIBUTION OF SELF-DESCRIPTIONS OF WORK BY PROVIDER GROUP

	Percentage of Providers			
Self-description	Regulated (n = 106)	Non-Regulated (n = 54)	Relative (n = 40)	Total (n = 200)
Chosen occupation	69	43	23	52
Stepping stone to related work	13	11	8	12
Good while my children are young	18	41	48	30
Temporary employment	0	2	21	6

most had some prior outside employment provides external validity to these sentiments.

There were differences in the motivations of the three provider groups. Not surprising given their age and status differences, relative providers were most likely to want to help the mothers of the children they cared for, whereas regulated and nonregulated family child care providers were more likely to want to stay home with their own children. Regulated providers were more likely to see family child care as a chosen profession than were nonregulated or relative providers. This suggests that regulation is associated with the perception of oneself as a professional.

INTEGRATION OF PROVIDERS IN SOCIAL SUPPORT NETWORKS

Prior research on family child care reports paradoxical findings on the involvement of family child care providers in social support networks (Kontos & Riessen, 1993, Zinsser, 1991). In these studies, family child care providers report that they are well integrated into familial and neighborhood social networks. Furthermore, nonregulated and relative providers, and to a lesser extent regulated providers, get referrals for children to care for from these networks. These reports stand in contrast to informal knowledge of family child care and relative care indicating that, during the actual hours of offering care, providers are often alone; isolated from other adult contacts. Despite the efforts of service agencies, individual family child care providers are often unaware of other providers or of networks and services available to them.

In order to examine these issues further, we asked the providers about their general social involvement with others, including their spouse or partner, and about their involvement with the family child care community. We also asked the providers to rate their satisfaction with the involvement and support received from each of these sources.

General Social Support

To measure general social support we used the Questionnaire on Social Support (Crnic et al., 1983). This instrument assesses the availability and satisfaction with three levels of social support: the community (e.g., organizations); friendships (e.g., neighbors); and intimate relationships (e.g., spouse). It consists of 16 items, 4 for community support, 8 for friendship support, and 4 for intimate support.

Providers in this study described themselves as only "somewhat" involved in their neighborhoods ($M = 1.89$ on a 3-point scale) and with organized community groups ($M = 1.65$ on a 3-point scale). They averaged almost 4–7 phone calls and 3.5 visits with relatives and friends per week. Only 1.9% had no phone contacts with relatives and friends and 26% had no visits with friends and relatives. Most (96%) felt that there was someone in their social network with whom they could share anger and happiness.

We created a composite variable for general social involvement from these individual items (alpha = .52). Scores on general social involvement were standardized and thus could vary from +1 to −1. Because this composite score and all others were derived from this sample of providers, in addition to a sample of providers obtained as part of an accompanying study, the mean for general social involvement is not zero. The average score, −.17 (reported in Table 3.1) suggests that the providers are typically slightly uninvolved. The three groups of providers differed in their general social involvement. Regulated providers had higher general social involvement scores than did either relative or nonregulated providers.

Individual ratings of satisfaction with these social support items were used to create a composite representing satisfaction with general social involvement (alpha = .77). Scores on satisfaction with general social involvement could vary from +1 to –1. The average score was –.01. This score suggests that providers were, on average, neither satisfied nor dissatisfied. There were no differences among the provider groups in the area of satisfaction with general social involvement.

Social Integration into the Family Child Care Community

An instrument to assess social integration into the family child care community was developed for this study. The item format was identical to the Questionnaire on Social Support (Crnic et al., 1983) with content specific to family child care and relative care providers.

Twenty-five percent of the providers in our study knew no other family child care providers and 42% had no contact with other providers in the average week. Fifty-four percent had no contact with organized groups of family child care providers. Item responses for family child care community involvement were used to create a standardized, composite variable (alpha = .79) for involvement with the family child care community. Scores on family child care community involvement could vary from +1 to –1. The average score was –.80, suggesting that providers were typically rather uninvolved.

There were differences among the provider groups in their involvement with the family child care community [F (2, 212) = 69.22, $p <$ .0001, Scheffe = .01]. Regulated providers had more involvement than did either nonregulated providers or relatives. Nonregulated providers had more involvement than did relatives.

Individual item ratings of satisfaction with family child care community involvement were used to create a satisfaction with family child care involvement composite (alpha = .78). Scores on satisfaction with family child care community involvement could vary from +1 to -1. The average score was –.09, indicating a slight tendency toward dissatisfaction. There were differences among the provider groups in satisfaction with family child care involvement [F (2, 212) = 3.33, $p <$ .04, Scheffe = .05]. Regulated providers were more satisfied than were either nonregulated providers or relatives with their involvement in the family child care community.

Summary

Providers in our study were consistent with previous studies of family child care providers (Kontos, 1992) in perceiving themselves to be well integrated into general social networks and reporting satisfaction with their social involvement. However, the average provider in this study had relatively little contact with the family child care community.

Regulated family child care providers had more social involvement in general and more involvement with the family child care community than did relatives or nonregulated providers. Relative providers were the most socially isolated of the three provider groups. Although we would expect regulated providers to be more involved in the family child care community than were the other provider groups, it is surprising to also find more general social involvement in this group.

Providers reported that they are satisfied with their social involvement in general and with their family child care community involvement. At times, intervention programs have been based, in part, on the premise that family child care providers are socially isolated and would prefer more social contact (e.g., Sale & Torres, 1973). However, if, as in this study, providers perceive themselves as socially integrated and if they are satisfied with their social support, they may not see a need to participate in such programs. This may mean that seeking social support is not a strong motivator for providers to join training programs (Sales & Torres, 1973).

PROVIDERS' ORGANIZATION OF FAMILY CHILD CARE SERVICE

Family child care providers at times may appear to the general public, parents, and even to themselves to be simply women who are staying home with their children and simultaneously caring for some other children. The reality of family child care is more complex. Providers organize their family child care service in diverse ways. Some of the factors that can vary in the family child care infrastructure are whether the providers' own children are present, and if so, how many and of what ages; the number and ages of the other children; whether she does housework when children are present and/or plans activities for them, whether the provider uses an assistant or works alone; and her rates and various business practices. We interviewed and observed the providers in our study in order to describe variations in the organization of child care services.

Providers' Own Children

Most studies of family child care providers have found that providers have a child living at home but not necessarily cared for during family child care hours (Kontos, 1992). In our study, most of the providers (71%) had a child of their own living at home. Regulated and nonregulated providers had more of their own children living at home than did relative providers [$F\,(2,\,216) = 6.50$, $p < .002$, Scheffe = .01]. This is understandable because the relative providers were typically past their own child-bearing years.

Over half of the providers (54%) had preschool age and younger children living at home. The age of the providers' own children also differed within the three provider groups [χ^2 (12) = 13.7, p < .05]. As seen in Table 3.7, nonregulated providers were most likely to have preschool age children (76%), followed by regulated (59%) and relative providers (20%). Nonregulated providers were most likely of all the provider groups to have infants of their own. Regulated and nonregulated providers were more likely than were relative providers to have preschoolers and school-age children of their own. Relative providers were most likely to have their young-adult children living at home.

Thus, while over half of all providers had to consider their own children when they organized their child care service, the nonregulated providers most clearly fit the picture of women who have decided to stay home with their own children and then perhaps, not knowing that they should be regulated, helped out a friend by caring for another child. The regulated providers were more likely than were the nonregulated providers to care for other people's children, whether or not they had children of their own. The relative providers were less likely to have young children at home but more often have their adult children living with them as well as caring for the child in our study, who was most often a grandchild (these were not three-generational families; the grandchildren in our sample were in out-of-home relative care).

Number of Children Enrolled in Care

The average number of children enrolled by providers in our study was 3.98 (SD = 2.8). This is comparable to the 3.5 children reported by the NDCHS and the 3 reported by the Profile of Child Care Settings (PCS)

TABLE 3.7. DISTRIBUTION OF PROVIDERS BY GROUP WITH AT LEAST ONE CHILD IN THE SPECIFIED AGE RANGE

	Percentage of Providers			
Age range	Regulated (n = 112)	Non-Regulated (n = 60)	Relative (n = 54)	Total
Under 12 months	4	13	6	7
12–29 months	23	30	4	20
30–59 months	32	33	10	26
60–71 months	16	4	0	8
6–12 years	44	38	18	42
13–19 years	33	25	22	27
Over 20 years	33	15	63	37

(Hofferth & Kisker, 1992) but less than most recent smaller studies report (Kontos, 1992). In our study, as in the NDCHS, regulated family child care providers enrolled more children ($M = 5.8$, $SD = 2.6$) than nonregulated providers ($M = 2.6$, $SD = 1.7$) or relative providers ($M = 1.9$, $SD = 1.5$) [F (2, 216) = 73.60, $p < .0001$, Scheffe = .01]. Providers in the three groups also varied in the number of children enrolled in each age group, as shown in Table 3.8. Regulated providers enrolled more infants, toddlers, preschoolers, and school-age children than did nonregulated and relative providers.

Openings for More Children

Twenty-four percent of the providers reported that they had openings for more full-time children. In contrast, the Profile of Child Care Settings found that 46% were willing and able to accept more children (Hofferth & Kisker, 1992). More regulated (30%) and nonregulated (28%) providers were willing to take additional full-time children than were relatives (8%) [χ^2 (2) = 10.55, $p < .005$]. The number of openings for full-time children ranged from 0–12 ($M = .83$, $SD = 1.8$).

Thirteen percent of the providers reported that they would take more part-time children. More regulated (14%) and nonregulated (22%) providers were willing to take more part-time children than were relatives (2%) [χ^2 (2) = 9.55, $p < .008$]. The number of openings for part-time children ranged from 0 to 12 ($M = .46$, $SD = 1.43$).

TABLE 3.8. DIFFERENCES AMONG PROVIDER GROUPS IN NUMBER OF CHILDREN ENROLLED BY AGE GROUP

	Number of Children in Provider Group			
Age Range	Regulated (n = 112)	Non-Regulated (n = 60)	Relative (n = 54)	Total
Under 12 months	.92	.40	.27	11.09** Reg > Nonr,Rel
12–29 months	2.60	1.04	.78	38.76** Reg > Nonr,Rel
30–59 months	2.29	.94	.65	20.90** Reg > Nonr,Rel
Over 60 months	.85	.56	.24	3.72* Reg > Nonr,Rel

*$p < .05$; **$p < .001$

Formal/Planned Versus Informal/Not Planned Activities

We asked providers two questions about how they organized their child care days: whether they felt able to do housework while they were caring for children, and how often they planned activities.

Overall, 83% of the providers responded that they were able to do their housework while they cared for the children. However, providers in the three groups differed on this dimension [χ^2 (2) = 7.29, $p < .03$]. Relative providers (92%) and nonregulated providers (88%) were more likely to do housework than were regulated providers (76%).

Fifty-nine percent of all the providers said that they planned activities for the children at least once a week. The extent of planned activities is presented in Table 3.9. Within the group of providers who planned activities, the majority said that they either planned several activities daily (20.2%) or that they planned two to four activities per week (18.3%).

The extent of planned activities varied by provider groups [χ^2 (8) = 60.50, $p < .0001$]. The distribution of planning by provider groups also is presented in Table 3.9. Regulated providers were more likely to frequently plan activities than were relative providers or nonregulated providers. Nonregulated providers were more likely than were relatives—but less likely than were regulated providers—to plan activities.

Use of a Paid Assistant

Only 22% of the providers paid an assistant to help them provide child care. Regulated family child care providers (32%) were more likely than were nonregulated providers (13%) or relative providers (13%) to use assistants [χ^2 (2) = 12.93, $p < .002$]. Similarly, the Profile of Child Care Settings Study found that 38% of regulated and 25% of nonregulated providers have helpers (Hofferth & Kisker, 1992).

TABLE 3.9. SELF-DESCRIBED PLANNED ACTIVITIES BY PROVIDER GROUP

	Percentage of Providers			
Planned Activities	*Regulated*	*Non-Regulated*	*Relative*	*Total (n = 208)*
None	20	46	80	40.9
1 per week	6	9	8	7.2
2-4 per week	23	25	2	18.3
1 per day	18	11	6	13.5
Several per day	33	9	4	20.2

Business Practices

Although some providers think of themselves as "mother-substitutes," others see themselves as running a small business out of their home. As family child care has become more formal and apparent to the public eye, there is increasing interest in the ways in which providers handle the business aspects of caring for children. We asked providers about their fees for children of varying age groups, and to indicate whether or not they engaged in various business practices.

Weekly Rates. The weekly rates charged by providers varied by the age of the child and by whether the provider was regulated, nonregulated, or a relative. Infant, toddler, and preschool care was more expensive than was school-age care. Regulated providers charged more than did nonregulated providers, and nonregulated providers charged more than did relative providers. Table 3.10 describes the average weekly rates charged by providers, based on both those who charge and on those who do not charge. Relative providers (48%) were more likely than were nonregulated (4%) or regulated providers (0%) not to charge [χ^2 (2) – 82.64, $p < .0001$].

Weekly rates only for providers who charged for care are presented in Table 3.11. Only the rates for relative providers are substantially changed. Using these recalculated rates, providers charged less for school-age care than for the care of younger children, and regulated providers charged more for infant, toddler, and preschool care than did nonregulated or relative providers.

Providers with higher family incomes also charged more for infant care ($r = .35$, $p < .01$), toddler care ($r = .35$, $p < .01$) and preschool care ($r = .42$, $p < .01$). Providers were less likely to charge for care if they themselves had family incomes of less than $20,000 (19%) rather than high incomes (10%) [χ^2 (2) = 9.10, $p < .01$].

Chapter 11 examines child care costs from the mother's perspective. It was important to examine child care rates separately from parental costs for child care because we found that providers and mothers of the same target child do not always agree on whether payment is made, or on how much.

Annual Earnings. In a companion study, *The Economics of Family Child Care Study,* conducted by Kathy Modigliani, Suzanne Helburn, Mary Culkin, and John Morris (unpublished), 124 providers from our study who charged fees for their services were interviewed extensively about their income and expenses. The researchers determined these providers' yearly gross income from child care (including parent fees, income from the Child and Adult Care Food Program, and government subsidies) as well as their costs of providing child care (IRS allowable direct out-of-pocket costs, such

TABLE 3.10. Average Weekly Rates by Age of Child and Provider Group for All Providers

Age of Children	Average Rate of Provider Groups					
	Regulated (n = 112)	Non-Regulated (n = 60)	Relative (n = 54)	Total (n = 208)	Range	F-test Scheffe
Under 12 months	$80.42	$54.03	$23.21	$68.68	0–$130	37.60** Reg > Nonr > Rel
12–29 months	$80.01	$51.28	$31.04	$65.95	0–$130	59.10** Reg > Nonr > Rel
30–60 months	$75.59	$47.43	$26.67	$62.07	0–$125	58.48** Reg > Nonr > Rel
School-age	$42.97	$27.89	$15.71	$35.07	0–$110	6.98* Reg > Rel

$*p < .01; **p < .001$

TABLE 3.11. WEEKLY RATES BY AGE OF CHILD AND PROVIDER GROUP WHEN PROVIDERS CHARGED FOR CARE

| Age of Children | Average Rate of Provider Groups | | | | | F-test Scheffe |
	Regulated (n = 112)	Non-Regulated (n = 52)	Relative (n = 31)	Total	Range	
Under 12 months	$80.42	$54.03	$40.63	$71.82	$35–$130	19.43* Reg > Nonr, Rel
12–29 months	$80.01	$51.28	$38.80	$67.89	$15–$130	45.01* Reg > Nonr, Rel
30–60 months	$75.59	$47.43	$37.33	$64.60	$15–$125	40.89* Reg > Nonr, Rel
School-age	$42.97	$27.88	$31.43	$37.77	$7–$110	2.93

*p < .001

as food, toys, equipment). From these data, they calculated providers' net income. The average annual net income for the 124 providers was $12,707.51. There were significant differences in net annual earnings for all three provider groups [F (2, 122) = 17.38, $p < .01$, Scheffe < .01]. Regulated providers earned more ($15,648.81 annually) than did nonregulated providers ($8,025.51 annually) who, in turn, earned more than did relative providers who charged ($2,993.44 annually).

Only 10% of providers enrolled in their homes children whose parents' fees were subsidized by governmental funding. Regulated (11%) and nonregulated (12%) providers were more likely than were relative providers (4%) to have subsidized children [χ^2 (2) = 8.56, $p < .05$]. These low numbers suggest that children eligible for child care subsidies are more likely to be served in center-based rather than in home-based care.

Insurance. Only 20% of the providers had family child care liability insurance. Regulated providers (34%) were more likely to have liability insurance than were nonregulated (9%) or relative providers (2%) [χ^2 (2) = 29.21, $p < .0001$]. Seventy-one percent of the providers had property insurance. Regulated (83%) providers were more likely to have property insurance than were nonregulated (61%) or relative (58%) providers [χ^2 (2) = 14.61, $p < .0007$].

Benefits. Workers employed outside of their homes often receive vacation, health, and retirement benefits as part of their compensation packages. We asked the providers if they were covered by any of these plans. These findings are described in Table 3.12. Almost three

TABLE 3.12. PERCENTAGE OF PROVIDERS IN EACH PROVIDER GROUP RECEIVING BENEFITS

	Percentage of Providers				
Benefits	Regulated (n = 112)	Non-Regulated (n = 60)	Relative (n = 54)	Total (n = 226)	χ^2
Paid vacation or holidays	54	24	4	35	40.35**
Unpaid vacation or holidays	55	67	76	63	6.40*
Health insurance (from any source)	80	67	70	74	4.30
IRA or retirement plan	36	23	38	33	3.57

*$p < .05$; **$p < .001$

quarters of the providers were covered by health insurance, but only 33% had a retirement plan. These health and retirement plans may have been connected to their husband's employment. There were no differences among the three groups of providers in receiving these benefits. Relatively few providers received paid vacations and those who did were most likely to be regulated providers. Over half of the providers took unpaid vacations; of those who took unpaid vacations, relatives and nonregulated providers were most likely to do so.

Specific Business Practices for Family Child Care. In addition to the more general business practices described above, we asked providers about nine business practices recommended by experts for family child care. These are described in Table 3.13. We created a composite variable to represent business practices by summing these nine individual items (alpha = .91). Scores could range from 0 to 9. The average business practices score was 7.48, suggesting that providers typically engage in a number of these practices. There were significant differences among the three groups of providers [$F(2,181) = 156.01$, $p < .0001$; Scheffe = .01]. Regulated providers had higher scores than nonregulated or relative providers. Nonregulated providers had higher scores than relatives.

Summary

The average provider in our study cared for her own preschool child and four other children. These enrollment figures are similar to the 3.5 children reported in the NDCHS (Divine-Hawkins, 1981) and the three enrolled children reported by Hofferth and Kisker (1992) in the National Child Care Survey and the Profiles of Child Care Settings. In our study, regulated providers enrolled more children than did nonregulated or relative providers. This finding is also consistent with prior research (Kontos, 1992).

The regulated and nonregulated family child care providers in our study almost all charged for their services. This finding is also consistent with the NCCS and PCS. When providers charged, the average hourly rate for preschool and younger children (across all age groups, and assuming a 40-hour work week) was $1.96 for regulated and $1.27 for nonregulated providers. These are similar figures to those reported in NCCS and PCS two years earlier (regulated, $1.61; nonregulated, $1.48).

Regulated providers were more likely to plan activities and less likely to do housework when caring for children than were nonregulated and relative providers (although the majority of providers did do housework). Activity planning appeared to occur with a similar frequency as that reported by a sample of midwestern regulated providers

TABLE 3.13. PERCENTAGE OF PROVIDERS USING SPECIFIC FAMILY CHILD CARE BUSINESS PRACTICES

Business Practice/ Provider Group	Didn't Know About (%)	Don't Want to Do (%)	Planning to Do (%)	Currently Doing (%)
Depreciate the costs of child care on income tax forms				
Regulated (n = 52)	9	23	9	59
Nonregulated (n = 111)	25	44	14	17
Relative (n = 37)	30	70	0	0
Total (n = 200)	17	37	8	38
Report child care income on taxes				
Regulated (n = 111)	1	0	5	94
Nonregulated (n = 52)	4	32	22	42
Relative (n = 36)	17	78	0	5
Total (n = 201)	4	22	8	65
Report child care expenses on taxes				
Regulated (n = 112)	0	4	6	90
Nonregulated (n = 52)	10	46	17	27
Relative (n = 35)	17	80	0	3
Total (n = 199)	6	28	8	58
Provide social security number to parents				
Regulated (n = 109)	1	1	6	92
Nonregulated (n = 54)	6	35	13	46
Relative (n = 33)	15	70	3	12
Total (n = 196)	5	22	7	66
Have parent–provider contract				
Regulated (n = 110)	0	14	12	74
Nonregulated (n = 53)	15	55	8	22
Relative (n = 37)	14	84	0	2
Total (n = 200)	6	38	8	22

(cont'd.)

TABLE 3.13 (CONT'D.)

Business Practice/ Provider Group	Didn't Know About (%)	Don't Want to Do (%)	Planning to Do (%)	Currently Doing (%)
Keep doctor's phone numbers for each child				
Regulated (n = 112)	0	2	2	96
Nonregulated (n = 55)	2	20	4	74
Relative (n = 47)	11	38	0	51
Total (n = 214)	3	14	2	81
Have emergency authorization forms				
Regulated (n = 112)	0	1	1	98
Nonregulated (n = 55)	7	27	20	46
Relative (n = 47)	11	47	4	38
Total (n = 214)	4	18	6	72
Have parent's daytime phone numbers for each child				
Regulated (n = 112)	0	0	1	99
Nonregulated (n = 56)	0	0	3	97
Relative (n = 50)	6	8	2	84
Total (n = 218)	1	2	2	95
Keep immunization records				
Regulated (n = 112)	1	9	7	83
Nonregulated (n = 55)	7	45	16	32
Relative (n = 49)	12	71	0	17
Total (n = 216)	5	32	8	55

(Kontos & Riessen, 1993). It makes sense that the providers caring for the most children are most likely to think ahead about what the children are going to do during the day. Most providers in our sample expected to combine taking care of the house with taking care of the children. Linked with the finding that 41% of the providers planned no activities for the children, and that most of those who did plan activities did so less than daily, these data suggest that most of the providers in our sample perceived family child care as a home-like, informal, unstructured child care arrangement.

Regulated providers were more likely than were nonregulated or relative providers to organize their family child care home as a small business. They were the most likely to have family child care liability and property insurance, take paid vacations, and to use business practices recommended by experts. Relative providers were the least likely to do these things. For example, 51% of relatives did not have a doctor's phone number, 16% had no day-time phone number for the child's parents, and only 5% reported their child care income to the IRS.

Nonregulated providers presented a mixed picture regarding business practices. They were unlikely to have insurance, only one quarter took paid vacations, and less than half reported their family child care income to the IRS or gave their social security numbers to the parents of the children in their care. Therefore, the charge that nonregulated providers are part of the underground economy appears to have some merit. However, most of the nonregulated providers did keep parents' and doctor's phone numbers, and almost half had emergency authorization forms.

RELATIONS WITH PARENTS

Ethnographic studies of family-based providers suggest that parent–provider relations are intense and, at times, difficult (Nelson, 1990). We asked the providers a series of questions to examine parent–provider relations from the providers' perspective. Over half of all providers believed that children were better off being cared for by parents. Regulated providers were more likely than were relative and nonregulated providers to believe that children should be cared for by their mothers, as shown in Table 3.14. There was evidence, however, of positive and friendly interactions between parents and providers. Most providers socialized with the parents of the children they cared for, and about one third of the nonrelative providers considered the parents their friends. Relative providers were more likely to socialize with the parents of the child, and to do so more frequently, than were regulated

TABLE 3.14. RELATIONS WITH PARENTS, BY PROVIDER GROUP

	Providers			
Relations with Parents	*Regulated (n = 112)*	*Nonregulated (n = 56)*	*Relative (n = 54)*	*F-test/χ^2*
Think it is best for children to be with parents	65%	44%	44%	9.22**
Socialize with parents	58%	67%	93%	20.34***
Mean number of times	2.19	3.00	10.93	22.48***
				Rel > R, N
Are criticized by parents	83%	89%	96%	5.55
Mean number of times	.49	.15	.25	.91
Share feelings with parents	68%	75%	79%	2.76
Mean number of times	6.21	4.95	10.20	2.65
Argue over child-rearing	92%	94%	98%	2.56
Mean number of times	.49	.05	.05	6.34
Talk about children	99%	100%	100%	.98
Mean number of times	16.02	15.01	17.28	1.04
Friends with parents	38%	21%	NA	2.78
Argue over money	93%	89%	98%	3.56
Mean number of times	.21	3.11	0	1.42
Argue about lateness	90%	95%	94%	1.55
Mean number of times	.45	.07	.07	3.09*

*p < .05; **p < .01;***p < .001; NA = not asked

and nonregulated family child care providers. Most providers had shared feelings with the parents, and almost all providers had talked with the parents about their children.

Almost all providers also reported some negative interactions with parents. Almost all providers had argued with parents about child rearing, money, and being late to pick up their child. Most providers had felt criticized by parents. These interactions tended to be infrequent. There were no differences among the three groups of providers in negative interactions with parents.

Summary

Provider reports of their interactions with parents are consistent with previous accounts (Nelson, 1990). Providers report that they have both friendly and negative interactions. Except for increased socialization with the parents, relative providers, as a group, do not report more intense interaction, either positive or negative, than do regulated and nonregulated providers. Regulated providers are surprisingly strong in their belief that children should be home with their parents. Perhaps this is explained by the relatively large percentage of these providers who are motivated to work at family child care as a way to stay home with their own children.

CONCLUSIONS

These data confirm the existence of three distinctively different types of providers: regulated providers, nonregulated providers, and relative providers. Each group of providers varies consistently in demographic characteristics as well as in the types of families they served. For instance, low-income families and Latino families were more likely to be using relative providers. More important, perhaps, is the fact that the provider groups had different motivations for offering child care and that they organized their services differently. Thus, it makes little sense to look at these 226 providers as members of one group. Rather, they are three distinct groups of providers who differ in their perceptions of who they are and what they are doing. An inkling of this finding emerged during observer training and data collection, when observers were reminded repeatedly that using the term *family child care provider* was foreign to many nonregulated providers, and to most relative providers. Likewise, inquiring about their family child care "business" with these two groups made no sense to them. In light of these findings, the remainder of the book will take provider group into consideration when discussing results.

4

The Quality of Care

I t has been difficult for researchers and the family child care community to agree on a definition of quality in family child care (Modigliani,
1991; Perrault, 1992). This is partly because the care provided in family child care is extremely heterogeneous in structure, ranging from
arrangements that the naive observer could not distinguish from parental
care to arrangements best defined as small child care centers. In design-
ing the quality assessments for this study, we have been acutely aware
of the need to capture this variety and to focus on the nature of the care
provided for the target child rather than on the match between some ide-
alized family child care setting and the observed provider.

In this chapter, we examine how quality was measured in our
study, the relations between different components of quality, and
describe how the average provider compares to these quality standards.
In examining the quality of the average family child care and relative
care home we are, for the moment, ignoring the tremendous variety in
our sample. As can be seen in Chapter 3, the three provider groups
represented in this study (regulated and nonregulated family child care
providers and relative providers) differ in demographic characteristics,
in motivation for providing care, in the organization of their child care
services, and in the activities provided. In Chapter 5 we will examine
differences in quality among these three provider groups.

Following Bronfenbrenner's (1979) theory of human ecology, child
care researchers have divided quality into three components: *process*
quality, *structural* quality, and the quality of the *adult work environment* (Clifford, Harms, Pepper, & Stuart, 1992; Phillips & Howes, 1987).
These three components are theorized to be interrelated and ultimately
related to children's behavior and development in child care. *Process*

quality forms the base level of the model because it is most directly related to children's behavior. At the second level of the model are the *structural* and *adult work environment* quality components. These components influence *process* quality directly and children's behavior indirectly, through *process* quality.

Process quality, the first level in our model, is defined as the interactions the children have with their providers. More specifically, it includes: ratings of provider sensitivity, harshness, and detachment; observed provider involvement and limit-setting with children; and self-reported provider attitudes toward children.

Studies have found that *process* quality is directly linked to the behavior and the development of children in child care centers (Howes, Phillips & Whitebook, 1992). If the teachers are sensitive, attentive to individual needs, and involved in and facilitating of the children's activities, the children are found to behave and develop in a competent manner. In terms of the behaviors we measured in this study, we expect that in family child care and relative care homes that are high in *process* quality, the children will be relatively free from behavior problems, will use language appropriately, will have secure attachment relationships with providers, and will engage in complex play with peers and objects.

According to this model of child care quality, providers, as well as children, are influenced by their environments. Provider's ability to interact appropriately with children (*process* quality) is theoretically dependent on *structural* quality and the quality of the *adult work environment*. *Structural* quality includes components that could be, and sometimes are, subject to government regulation. These components are:

- Group size, or the number of children cared for
- Ratios, or the number of children per adult
- Caregiving experience of the provider
- Formal education of the provider
- Specialized training of the provider

More favorable *structural* quality is expected to enhance *process* quality. When the provider cares for fewer children, she is expected to be better able to respond to each child in a more sensitive and individualized manner. If a provider has more formal education and specialized training in child development, she is expected to be able to use this knowledge to influence her behaviors with children. She may, for example, understand that separations are difficult for toddlers and comfort the child who is inconsolable when her parent leaves rather than deciding that the child is spoiled by the parent and needs to be taught to be quiet and to be good.

Process quality is also expected to be influenced by the *adult work environment.* The *adult work environment* in this study is defined in terms of income and benefits (described in Chapter 3) and in terms of providers' self-reports of their job stress, work satisfaction, and work commitment. According to our model, the provider who is poorly compensated may be too preoccupied by the real demands of living in or close to the poverty line to be able to respond in a sensitive or appropriate way to the children. In reviewing literature on caregiving styles of low-income families, McLloyd (1990) suggests that poverty creates psychological distress in adults and that this distress interferes with the adults' ability to be sensitively involved with children. Strong relations between the *adult work environment*, particularly salary, and process quality have been found in center-based child care (Hofferth & Kisker, 1992; Whitebook, Howes, & Phillips, 1990). We expect to find similar relations in family child care.

In this study of family child care, we modified the theoretical model by introducing two other components of quality. We used a measure of *global* quality as a way of summarizing *process, structural,* and *adult work environment* components of quality. We also asked the providers to define quality and therefore used *provider perceptions* as a final quality assessment. The other components of quality—*process, structural, adult work environment,*—have been defined by experts. The inclusion of a *provider perception* of quality permits us to include the providers' own voices in the discussion of quality.

To ascertain whether the theoretical model of quality in child care is appropriate for family child care, we examined the relations among quality components. Furthermore, in order to maximize the reliability and validity of our observations, we needed to use several measures for each component, and therefore we also examined what the relations are among our various measures of each quality component. To accomplish these goals, we first treat each component of quality separately. Within each, we describe how it was measured, examine average scores of providers for each measure, and then examine relations among the various measures of that component. In the final sections of this chapter, we examine interrelations among the quality components and the providers' own definitions of quality. In Chapter 9 we examine relations between quality components and children's behaviors and development.

MEASUREMENT OF PROCESS QUALITY

As previously stated, *process* quality is defined and measured as rated provider sensitivity, harshness and detachment; observed provider involvement and limit setting with children; and self-reported provider attitudes toward children.

Sensitivity, Harshness, and Detachment

A warm and caring relationship between the provider and the child is high on most peoples' list of what they hope for in child care. Sensitive caregivers who are not harsh or detached are the most likely to be capable of these relationships (Howes & Hamilton, 1992). Observers in this study rated provider sensitivity, harshness, and detachment to the target child at the end of their 2–3 hour observations in the providers' homes, using the Arnett Scale of Provider Sensitivity (Arnett, 1989). (Interobserver reliability range = .88 to .97, median = .93.) This scale was designed for use within child care settings and distinguishes among providers with different levels of training (Arnett, 1989) and different attachment relationships with children (Howes & Hamilton, 1992a). It consists of 26 items, each rated on a 4-point scale. Three composite measures were derived based on previous work with the scale. These are provider sensitivity (alpha = .91), harshness (alpha = .83), and detachment (alpha = .81).

We can best understand the meaning of these measures with an example. If a child is crying, the provider observed as *sensitive* (warm, attentive, engaged) would go over to the child, find out what the problem was, and comfort the child. In contrast, the provider observed as *harsh* (critical, threatens, punishes) would tell the child to stop crying using an angry tone, might tell the child he or she couldn't play with anything until the crying stopped, and/or within the child's earshot complain about him or her in front of others. The provider observed as *detached* (low level interaction, interest, and supervision) would ignore the child's crying, letting the crying persist over a long period of time.

In our sample of providers, sensitivity scores averaged 2.86 (*SD* = .60, range = 1.4 to 4.0); harshness scores averaged 1.52 (*SD* = .46, range = 1 to 3.78); and detachment scores averaged 1.61 (*SD* = .66, range = 1 to 3.75). These scores mean that the average provider was somewhat sensitive and not very harsh or detached in her interactions with the children. Note that there was considerable variation in all of these scores.

The National Child Care Staffing Study (NCCSS) (Whitebrook, et al., 1990) also used this scale to rate teachers, albeit in centers. In the NCCSS, sensitivity scores averaged 3.2; harshness scores 1.6; and detachment scores 1.5. Using the NCCSS scores as a comparison, the family child care providers in this study were less sensitive, but similar in harshness and detachment to center providers.

Provider Involvement

As discussed in Chapter 2, a researcher observed each child and provider for at least two hours in the child care setting. During this period, the observer coded four 5-minute time samples of the social behavior of the child. The time samples were spaced evenly throughout the observation period. Each 5-minute time sample was broken into fifteen 20-second intervals. Within each 20-second interval, the child's proximity to the adult was coded. The child was considered to be in proximity if he or she was within 3 feet of the adult. If the child was in proximity, the adult–child involvement was rated on the Adult Involvement Scale.

Interobserver reliability on the adult–child interaction measures was established to an 82% agreement (agreements/agreements+disagreements) for all behaviors in an interval prior to data collection. Interobserver reliability was reestablished at midpoint of the data collection. Median reliability scores from these reliability checks ranged from kappa = .81 to kappa = .92 (median = .86).

The Adult Involvement Scale (Howes & Stewart, 1987) was used to rate the intensity of adult–child involvement. This scale has six levels: (1) ignoring the child; (2) routine caregiving, for example, provider wipes the child's nose but says nothing; (3) minimal caregiving when the provider talks to or touches the child in order to discipline the child, to answer direct requests for help, or to give verbal directives with no reply encouraged; (4) answering the child's social bids in a positive but brief manner; (5) extending and elaborating the child's social bids, and (6) intense caregiving including holding or hugging the child to provide comfort, engaging the child in prolonged conversation or playing interactively with the child.

Composite scores were created from the frequency counts of adult involvement. *Total time near adult* was the sum of all intervals in which the child was within 3 feet of the provider. *Percent low level* involvement was the percentage of intervals in which the child was within 3 feet of the provider and ignored (1) or the adult involvement was routine (2) or minimal (3). *Percent responsive caregiving* was the percentage of intervals in which the child was within three feet of the adult and the adult involvement was responsive (4), elaborate (5), or intense (6).

The children in our study were within three feet of the provider an average of 45% of the observation period (*SD* = .28, range = 0 to 100%). Forty-six percent (*SD* = .25, range = 0 to 100%) of the time that children were within 3 feet of the provider, either the provider ignored them (20%) or she engaged with them at a low level (26%). On the average, providers engaged with the children in a responsive manner 54% of the time they were within 3 feet of her (*SD* = .31, range = 0 to 100%).

In sum, children stayed near the provider less than half of the time they were observed and providers responded in a positive manner to the children slightly more than half of the time they were close by. The average provider was thus nonresponsive or inappropriate slightly less than half of the time the child was near by. This means that providers were responsive to the target children for about 30 minutes and ignored or responded in an inappropriate manner for about 30 minutes out of the 2-hour observation period. In the remaining hour, the providers were more than 3 feet away from the target children. As the providers were aware of the identity of the target children, our estimates are probably an overstatement of average positive involvement. It would be inappropriate for a child to spend all of his or her time either being ignored or in intense interaction with an adult. In an ideal situation, children would spend some time in high-level adult involvement, some time playing alone, and some time playing with peers. Therefore the average child in our study is receiving sufficient responsive care. We are concerned, however, that the average child is receiving as much unresponsive care as responsive care.

Provider Limit Setting

A measure of provider limit setting was developed based on a measure used by Dunn (1990). Limit setting has been reported to be an important dimension of family child care in other research studies (Cochran, 1977; Howes, 1983).

We recorded each instance of the provider verbally putting limits on the child's behavior. Limit-setting could vary from asking a child to stop or change a behavior ("Get off the couch.") to threatening a consequence ("If you don't stop that, I'll put you in time out."). The median interobserver reliability was kappa = .83. Limit-setting occurred on the average 2.02 times per 2-hour observation period ($SD = 3.31$, range 0 to 25). This is lower than the 3 times per hour reported in toddler-age, mother–child interaction (Minton, Kagan, & Levine, 1971), and much lower than a study of center-based providers (Kontos & Dunn, 1993).

Provider Child-Rearing Attitudes

We asked the providers to report on their child-rearing attitudes on a modified version of the Block and Block Child Rearing Attitudes Scale (Rickel & Biasatti, 1982). This questionnaire consists of 40 items scored on a 7-point Likert scale (7 = very characteristic). Items on the *nurturant* subscale concern the extent to which respondents endorse flexible child-rearing attitudes and practices (e.g., "I tell the children they can always discuss things with me.") whereas those on the *restrictive* subscale relate to the extent to which respondents endorse attitudes and practices designed to control children's behavior (e.g., "Children should be seen and not heard."). As this measure was designed for parents, we reworded it, substituting "the children I care for" for "my child" to make it applicable to family child care and relative care providers. Ratings on items belonging to each subscale were summed to create two scores: nurturant (alpha = .79) and restrictive (alpha = .80).

In our sample of providers, *nurturant* scores averaged 5.33 (*SD* = .79, range = 1 to 7). *Restrictive* scores averaged 2.75 (*SD* = 1.43, range = 1 to 7). This means that the average provider was relatively nurturant and not very restrictive.

Interrelations Among Process Quality Measures

In order to examine the consistency of the process measures, we created a table of intercorrelations (see Table 4.1). This tells us whether our observations were consistent with our ratings and whether our ratings and observations were consistent with the provider's self-ratings.

The process measures were moderately interrelated, giving us confidence in our measurement of process quality. It is important that we found convergence between our observations and ratings and the providers' self-assessments. This means that the providers see themselves similarly to the way we saw them.

Specifically, providers rated as more sensitive were also rated as less harsh and detached, observed to be more responsive, and reported themselves to be more nurturant and less restrictive. Providers rated as more harsh were also rated as more detached and reported themselves to be more restrictive. Providers rated as more detached were observed to be less responsive and rated themselves as more restrictive and less nurturant. Providers observed to have more low-level involvement also were observed to have less responsive involvement and engaged in more limit setting and reported themselves to be restrictive. Providers observed to have more responsive involvement reported themselves to be less restrictive.

MEASUREMENT OF STRUCTURAL QUALITY

As noted earlier, structural quality is defined as group size (the number of children cared for), the number of children per adult provider, the experience of the provider, the formal education of the provider, and the specialized training of the provider.

Group Size

To assess group size we counted the number of children present at 15-minute intervals across our observation. These counts were averaged to create a group size measure. This observed group size is different from enrollment because it reflects the number of children present on the day we observed. As revealed in Chapter 3, the observed group size is comparable to the self-reported group size found in the PCP and NCCS

TABLE 4.1. INTERCORRELATIONS AMONG PROCESS QUALITY MEASURES

	Ratings		Observations			Self-report	
	Restrictiveness	Detachment	Low Involvement	Responsive Involvement	Limit-Setting	Restrictiveness	Nurturant
Ratings							
Sensitivity	-.39**	-.61**	-.33**	.35**	-.07	-.44**	-.27**
Harshness		.30**	.09	-.05	.08	.18**	-.11
Detachment			.14*	-.30**	-.12	.22**	-.20**
Observations							
Low involvement				-.62***	.29**	.27**	-.01
Responsive involvement					-.05	-.27**	.13
Limit setting						.09	.04
Self-report							
Restrictiveness							.04
Nurturant							

*p < .05; **p < .01; ***p < .001

studies (Hofferth & Kisker, 1992). Group size averaged 3.98 (*SD* = 2.65, range = 1 to 13).

The number of the children present varied by age level, as can be seen in Table 4.2. Providers had more toddlers and preschoolers than they did infants or school-age children. Only 36% of the homes we visited had at least one infant present. This is surprising since family child care is often considered to be the care arrangement of choice for infants. The small number of school-age children present is not surprising since our visits were usually in the morning, when the older children were in school.

The providers own children were included in observed group sizes if they were present during the observation. The number of the providers' own children present also varied, as presented in Table 4.3.

Ratio of Children to Adults

In order to calculate the ratio or the number of children cared for by each adult, we noted the number of adults present during the observation and the number of adults actually caring for children; that is, a husband might be counted as being in the house but not as caring for children. Only 46% of the providers were the only adult in the house during our observation. However, 72% of the providers were the only adult taking care of children during the observation. We also noted if a teenage child (age 13–18) was present and helping to care for the children. Five percent of the providers had a teenage helper.

The ratio of children to adults was calculated by dividing the number of children by the number of adults actually providing care. The average ratio was 3.3 children per adult (*SD* = 2.0, range = .4 to 10.7).

Therefore, the average provider in our sample worked alone and cared for 3.3 children. In somewhat more than half of the homes,

TABLE 4.2. NUMBER OF CHILDREN IN CARE, BY AGE LEVEL

Age	Mean	Range	Percentage of Homes with at Least One in Age Range (n = 226)
Under 12 months	.51	0–3	36
Toddlers (12–29 months)	1.61	0–8	76
Preschoolers (30–59 months)	1.27	0–7	62
School-age (6–12 years)	.42	0–5	22

another adult who was not caring for the children was physically present. This observed ratio is comparable to the self-reported ratio found in the PCP and NCCS studies (Hofferth & Kisker, 1992).

Background of Providers

Experience. The providers averaged 5.7 years providing child care ($SD = 6.7$, range = 1 to 48). The distribution of years of experience was skewed; that is, most of the providers were relatively inexperienced. The modal number of years of experience was one and the median was three years. Twenty-two percent of the providers were in their first year of providing care.

Formal Education. The formal education of the providers in our study ranged from less than high school to a graduate degree. Although the median level of schooling was some college or an AA degree, 36% of the providers had a high school education or less and only 17% had college degrees or higher. Table 4.4 presents the proportion of providers at each level of schooling.

The PCP and NCCS studies report that about half the providers in their sample had some education after high school (Hofferth & Kisker, 1992). The providers in our sample were somewhat better educated. In California, workshops on family child care are given through the community college system and count as college courses and thus as formal education past high school. This may have elevated the formal schooling level of some of the providers in the sample.

TABLE 4.3. NUMBER OF PROVIDER'S OWN CHILDREN IN CARE, BY AGE LEVEL

Age	Mean	Range	Percentage of Homes with at Least One in Age Range (n = 226)
Under 12 months	.09	0–2	8
Toddlers (12–29 months)	.21	0–2	19
Preschoolers (30–59 months)	.22	0–4	18
Kindergarten (60–71 months)	.04	0–1	4
School-age (6–12 years)	.15	0–3	11
Teenage (13–17 years)	.04	0–2	2

TABLE 4.4. FORMAL SCHOOLING OF PROVIDERS

Level of Schooling	Percentage of Providers (n = 218)
Less than high school	9
Some high school	13
High school graduate	22
Some college or AA degree	38
Four-year degree	10
Some graduate school	4
Graduate degree	3

Training. Most of the providers (98%) reported that they had some specialized training in child care. This is much higher than the 64% for regulated providers and the 34% for nonregulated providers found in the PCP and NCCS studies (Hofferth & Kisker, 1992). The elevated training level in our sample may be attributed to the fact that the three states represented in our sample (North Carolina, California, and Texas) have all emphasized training of family child care providers. To understand these training figures, it is important to examine where the training occurred.

Specialized training can occur as part of the formal education system and/or as informal workshops, conferences, and the like. Our measure of training via the formal education system appeared to be flawed (levels of formal education and formal training did not match). Thus, our focus is on training outside the formal education system.

Table 4.5 presents the proportion of providers who received specialized training within the informal training network known as family child care training. Providers were most likely to have attended a child and adult care food program workshop. It is noteworthy that almost one quarter of the providers had taken a course on family child care. The number of different workshops and the number of times attending them was used to create a standard composite score for informal training (alpha = .57). This score could range from −1.0 to 1.0. The average score was −.77 (SD = 7.35). Because this score, like the other standard composite scores (e.g., social support), was derived from a larger sample that included providers from the companion training study, the mean is not 0.

Interrelations Among Structural Components of Quality

In order to examine interrelations among structural components of quality, we calculated a table of intercorrelations. These are represented in Table 4.6. It was important to do this in order to examine whether or not the measures of structural quality were consistent with each other.

TABLE 4.5. FAMILY CHILD CARE TRAINING

Training	Percentage of Providers (n = 226)	Average Number of Training Sessions Attended (in past 2 yrs.)
Child care food program	36	1.53
Family child care association meetings	28	3.35
Local or state family child care conference	10	.25
Local or state general child care conference	16	.51
National conference	3	.09
15-hour or more course in family child care	24	1.4

TABLE 4.6. INTERCORRELATIONS AMONG STRUCTURAL MEASURES OF QUALITY

	Group Size	Number of Children per Adult	Years of Experience	Formal School	Informal Training
Group size	.82***	-.01	.19**	.54**
Number of children per adult			-.05	.17*	.50**
Years of experience				-.17*	.16
Formal school					.20
Family child care training					

*p < .05; **p < .01; ***p < .001

Based on findings from prior child care research, we hypothesized that high levels of formal education and training would be associated with lower group sizes and ratios (Phillips & Howes, 1987). This was not true in this study. In fact, providers who cared for more children (that is, had larger group sizes) also had more children per adult (higher ratios), had more formal schooling, and had attended more family child care training.

Prior child care research also suggests that more experience is associated with less schooling and training (Phillips & Howes, 1987). This finding was partially supported in our study. Providers with more experience had less formal schooling.

Finally, prior child care research suggests that more formal schooling is associated with more specialized training. We also found this relationship. Providers with more formal schooling had more family child care training.

RELATIONSHIP BETWEEN STRUCTURAL AND PROCESS QUALITY

According to our theoretical model of quality in family child care, measures of structural quality should be related to measures of process quality. We assume that a provider with more advantageous structural components will be able to provide more sensitive and responsive caregiving. To test this assumption we created a correlation matrix between structural and process quality measures. The results are presented in Table 4.7.

Structural measures of provider education and training were positively related to process quality measures. Providers with more formal schooling were rated as more sensitive and less detached, observed as more responsive and reported more nurturant and less restrictive child rearing attitudes. Providers with more family child care training were rated as more sensitive and less detached and rated themselves as less restrictive.

The structural measures of group size and ratio also were related to process quality but in the opposite direction of that predicted by research (see Chapter 1), by our theoretical model, and by most child care advocates. In our study, providers with more children (larger group sizes) were rated as more sensitive and perceived themselves to be more nurturant and less restrictive than did providers with fewer children. Providers with more children per adult (higher ratios) perceived themselves as less restrictive than did providers with fewer children per adult. These were unexpected findings, albeit consistent with the findings reported earlier that providers who cared for more children also had more children per adult, more formal schooling, and attended more family child care training. It is important to note, however, that the group sizes and ratios described as large in this study would be small in the context of most child care centers. This might partially explain our counter-intuitive results for these variables.

MEASUREMENT OF THE ADULT WORK ENVIRONMENT

The adult work environment is defined in terms of income and benefits (described in Chapter 3) and in terms of providers' perceptions of their job stress, work satisfaction, and work commitment.

TABLE 4.7. RELATIONS BETWEEN STRUCTURAL AND PROCESS QUALITY

Process Quality	Structural Quality				
	Group Size	Ratio	Years of Experience	Formal School	Family Child Care Training
Ratings					
Sensitivity	.17*	.09	-.08	.29**	.28**
Harshness	.08	.13	.20**	-.05	.02
Detachment	-.10	-.03	.19**	-.18**	-.18**
Observations					
Low-level	-.12	-.07	-.02	-.16*	
involvement	-.11				
Responsive	.08	.01	-.07	.20**	
involvement	.12				
Limit-setting	-.04	.01	-.10	.09	.07
Self-report					
Nurturant	.04	.08	-.13	.16*	.10
Restrictiveness	-.31**	-.24**	.16*	-.41*	.19**

*p < .05; **p < .01

We assessed job stress with a newly created measure based on providers' descriptions of the things that are unpleasant or stressful about their jobs (e.g., continually cleaning up messes, hard to manage children in public, parents coming late, parents with late payment). Providers rated each of the 25 items twice, once for frequency of occurrence and again for the magnitude of the stress or unpleasantness of the item. The items were summed to form a hassles score (alpha = .92). The score could range from 1 to 4. The providers' average score was 1.74 (SD = .42, range = 1.04 to 3.12). Therefore the average provider reported low levels of job stress.

Work satisfaction (alpha = .73) was based on 10 items rating the providers' satisfaction with their work (e.g., "I enjoy my work rather than feeling miserable when I work." "I find my work worthwhile rather than useless."). Work satisfaction scores could range from 1 (low) to 7 (high). The average work satisfaction score was 5.63 (SD = .95, range 2.7 to 7). Therefore, the average provider was satisfied with her work.

Work commitment (alpha = .63) was based on six items describing commitment to the job (e.g., "I feel committed to child care." "I feel stuck in family child care."). Work commitment scores could range from 1 (low) to 5 (high). The average work commitment score was 4.29 (SD = .71, range = 1.8 to 5.0). Therefore, the average provider was committed to her job.

Interrelations Among Adult Work Environment Measures

Interrelations among adult work environment components of quality were computed to assess the consistency of these variables. These are presented in Table 4.8. There was moderate consistency. Providers who reported more hassles also reported lower work satisfaction. Providers with higher family child care income reported more work commitment. This is consistent with the NCCSS, which found provider compensation to be related to job commitment (Whitebook et al., 1990). However, providers with higher incomes also reported more hassles.

RELATIONSHIP BETWEEN PROCESS QUALITY AND ADULT WORK ENVIRONMENT

Our theoretical model assumes that process quality will be related to the adult work environment. Providers who are committed and satisfied and have adequate family child care incomes are expected to be higher in process quality. To test this assumption, we created a correlation matrix between process quality and adult work environment variables (see Table 4.9).

The relations found in our sample support the theoretical model. Providers who were better compensated were also rated as more sensitive and less detached, observed to be more responsively involved, and reported themselves to be more nurturant and less restrictive. Providers who reported higher job satisfaction also described themselves as more nurturant. Providers who reported more job commitment were rated as more sensitive and described themselves as more nurturant and less restrictive.

There was one unexpected finding. Providers who reported more hassles were also rated as more sensitive and less detached, observed

TABLE 4.8. INTERCORRELATIONS AMONG ADULT WORK ENVIRONMENT COMPONENTS OF QUALITY

	Family Child Care Income	Hassles	Work Satisfaction	Work Commitment
Family child care income		.24*	-.10	.34*
Hassles			-.50*	-.07
Satisfaction				.25
Commitment				

*$p < .01$

TABLE 4.9. RELATIONS BETWEEN PROCESS QUALITY AND ADULT WORK ENVIRONMENT

	Adult Work Environment			
Process Quality	*Family Child Care Income*	*Hassles*	*Work Satisfaction*	*Work Commitment*
Ratings				
Sensitivity	.29**	.23**	-.07	.18*
Harshness	.07	.09	-.03	.09
Detachment	-.20**	-.16*	.03	-.13
Observations				
Low-level involvement	-.20*	-.17*	.10	-.07
Responsive involvement	.19*	.11	.02	.06
Limit-setting	-.11	-.03	-.009	.04
Self-report				
Nurturant	.09	-.03	.24**	.24**
Restrictiveness	-.37**	-.24**	.06	-.24**

$*p < .05; **p < .01$

as having less low-level involvement, and described their child rearing attitudes as less restrictive.

MEASUREMENT OF GLOBAL QUALITY

Process quality, structural quality, and the adult work environment theoretically can be summarized into a single score by using a measure of global quality. There are several instruments designed to measure global quality in family child care (for reviews of these measures see Clifford et al., 1992; Modigliani, 1991). From the measures available, we selected the Family Day Care Rating Scale (FDCRS) (Harms & Clifford, 1989). This scale is a 33-item measure that focuses on six areas of caregiving practices: space and furnishings, basic needs, language and reasoning, learning activities, social development, and adult needs. Each item is rated on a 1–7 scale with 1 indicating inadequate practices and 7 excellent practices (3 = adequate/custodial; 5 = good). The assessment is conducted after at least a 2-hour observation in the family child care and relative care home and an interview with the provider. A total score is created by summing the individual items and dividing by the total number of items. If providers were scored on both the infant/toddler and preschool versions of the same item, these were averaged before summing. The FDCRS has been shown to have high interobserver reliability and high internal consistency (Clifford et al., 1992; Howes & Stewart, 1987). In previous research, scores were associated with observed level of home stimulation (Goelman et al., 1990), provider involvement with children, and children's competence (Howes & Stewart, 1987). In our study, interobserver agreement was kappa = .89.

The average FDCRS score for the providers in our study was 3.39 (*SD* = 1.08), or minimally adequate. Scores ranged from 1.14 to 6.68. Thirty-five percent of the providers received ratings in the inadequate range, 56% in the adequate/custodial range, and 9% in the good range.

INTERRELATIONS AMONG THE GLOBAL QUALITY MEASURE AND OTHER MEASURES OF QUALITY

In order to test our theoretical assumption that the FDCRS global quality measure captures the three components of quality (process, structural, and adult work environment), we examined relations between these quality components and global quality scores.

Global Quality and Process Quality

We first examined the relations between global quality and measures of process quality. As shown in Table 4.10, there were significant relations in the expected direction between 7 of the 8 process measures and global quality. Specifically, providers with higher global quality scores also were rated as higher in sensitivity and lower in harshness and detachment. They were observed to be more responsive and to have less low-level involvement. Providers with higher global quality scores reported higher nurturant and lower restrictive child-rearing attitudes. There was no significant association with limit setting. This is strong evidence for the ability of our global quality measure to represent process quality.

Global Quality and Structural Quality

We next examined relations between global quality and structural quality. As presented in Table 4.11, all six structural quality measures were significantly related to global quality. Four of these measures were in the theoretically expected direction. Providers with higher global quality scores also had fewer years of experience as providers, more formal education, and more family child care training.

Two of the significant relations were in the theoretically opposite

TABLE 4.10. RELATIONS BETWEEN GLOBAL AND PROCESS QUALITY

Process Quality	Global Quality
Ratings	
Sensitivity	.69**
Harshness	-.32**
Detachment	-.55**
Observations	
Low-level involvement	-.15*
Responsive involvement	.28**
Limit-setting	.12
Self-report	
Nurturant	.24**
Restrictiveness	-.47**

$*p < .05; **p < .01$

TABLE 4.11. RELATIONS BETWEEN GLOBAL AND STRUCTURAL QUALITY

Structural Quality	Global Quality
Number in group	.34*
Number of children per provider	.27*
Years of experience	-.17*
Formal school	.51*
Family child care training	.46*

$*p < .01$

direction. Providers with higher global quality scores also cared for more children and had more children per provider. However, recall that smaller group size and ratios also were negatively related to both higher process quality and the other structural quality measures. Therefore, despite this unexpected finding, the FDCRS global quality measure appears to well represent structural quality.

Global Quality and the Adult Work Environment

Finally, we examined relations between global quality and the adult work environment (see Table 4.12). Three of the four adult work environment measures were significantly related to global quality. Two of these were in the expected direction. Providers with higher global quality scores reported more family child care income and more job commitment. The discrepant relation was that providers with higher global quality scores reported more hassles. It is important to note that there is some ques-

TABLE 4.12. RELATIONS BETWEEN GLOBAL QUALITY AND THE ADULT WORK
ENVIRONMENT

Adult Work Environment	Global Quality
Family child care income	.42*
Hassles	.24*
Job satisfaction	-.03
Job commitment	.27*

*$p < .01$

tion about the meaning of hassles: Providers with more hassles were
also rated as more sensitive and less detached, observed to have less
low-level involvement, and described their child rearing attitudes as less
restrictive. Therefore the FDCRS global quality measure appears also to
represent the quality of the adult work environment.

Summary

In this section we examined the assumption that the FDCRS global
quality scores could stand for, or represent, three components of quality: process, structural, and adult work environment. The analysis supported the assumption. Therefore, either the single global quality score
or the inadequate (average item scores of 1–2.99), adequate/custodial
(average item scores of 3–4.99), and good (average item scores of 5–7)
categories of global quality will be used to represent family child care
and relative care quality throughout the rest of this book. "Inadequate
quality" was defined as potentially harmful to children's development.
"Adequate/custodial" was defined as having potentially neutral effects
on children's development, neither enhancing nor harmful. "Good" was
defined as potentially enhancing to children's development.

PROVIDERS' DEFINITIONS OF QUALITY

In the final section of this chapter, we examine providers' definitions of
quality. During our interviews, we asked providers to rate the importance
of 30 aspects of quality in child care. These aspects were rated on a 6-
point scale, with 6 representing "extremely important." These individual
item ratings were subjected to a principal components analysis with vari-
max rotation. An 8-factor solution accounted for 63% of the variance.

The resulting grouping of provider definitions of quality measures
are displayed in Table 4.13. The average rating assigned to each fac-

TABLE 4.13. PROVIDER DEFINITIONS OF CHILD CARE QUALITY (*N* = 206)

Definition	Factor loadings
Parent/provider relationships	
Parents influence the child's care	.75
Open to parents dropping in	.69
Provider supports working parents	.74
Provider shares parents' values	.68
Provider communicates with parents	.52
Cost and convenience	
Cost is reasonable	.76
The care covers the hours needed	.75
The hours and schedule are flexible	.65
Convenient location	.61
Care is available day in and day out	.47
Safe environment	
Attention to nutrition	.76
Cleanliness	.74
Attention to child's safely	.72
Nice play area	.55
School-like	
Children are prepared for school	.73
Children's day-to-day activities	.63
Religious or cultural values are taught	.57
Good equipment, toys, and materials	.52
Home-like	
Provider who is a friend or neighbor	.89
Provider is related to child	.87
Home-like environment	.37
Warmth	
Provider's warmth to children	.71
Attention children receive	.71
Provider's style of discipline	.57
Way provider teaches kids to get along	.41
Professional	
Provider's experience	.68
Provider is regulated or registered	.64
Provider has received training	.56
Ratio and group size	
Number of children in group	.81
Number of children for each adult	.81

tor is in Table 4.14. Providers gave the highest rating to warmth and to clean and safe aspects of quality. Interrelations among provider definitions of quality are presented in Table 4.15. Factors were modestly related, except for "home-like."

TABLE 4.14. AVERAGE RATING GIVEN BY PROVIDERS TO ASPECTS OF QUALITY (N = 206)

Aspect	Average Rating
Parent/provider relationships	4.37
Cost and convenience	3.90
Safe environment	4.49
School-like	3.83
Home-like	3.96
Warmth	4.57
Professional	3.93
Ratio and group size	3.96

To find out how providers' definitions of quality fit with our measures of global quality, we correlated the FDCRS score with the providers' scores for the eight factors comprising their definitions of quality. Providers with higher global quality scores were less likely to assign high ratings to the "home-like" and "school-like" factors and more likely to assign high ratings to the "warmth" factor (see Table 4.16.)

Summary

The providers in our sample reported that they valued warmth, cleanliness, and safety in assessing the quality of family child care homes. Providers who valued warmth also had high global quality scores. This represents considerable consistency between child care experts and family child care providers in their assessments of quality.

CONCLUSIONS

The theoretical model that shaped this research assumes that process quality, the most important component of quality in terms of children's development, is influenced by structural and adult work environment quality components. By and large, the model was supported. The measures selected to assess each component of the model were consistently interrelated and relations between quality components were as predicted.

There are two exceptions to this generalization. In this sample, group size and adult–child ratio were positively rather than negatively related to other structural quality measures and to process quality. One

TABLE 4.15. INTERRELATIONS AMONG PROVIDER DEFINITIONS OF QUALITY ($N = 206$)

	Cost and Convenience	Clean and Safe	School-like	Home-like	Warmth	Structure	Ratio and Group Size
Parents as partners	.60*	.48*	.37*	.09	.41*	.46*	.40*
Cost and convenience		.47*	.26*	.14	.31*	.44*	.36*
Clean and safe			.48*	.06	.41*	.49*	.29*
School-like				.24*	.33*	.36*	.24*
Home-like					-.09	.04	.05
Warmth						.23*	.27*
Structure							.30*

*$p < .01$

TABLE 4.16. RELATIONS BETWEEN GLOBAL QUALITY AND PROVIDER DEFINITIONS OF QUALITY

Provider Definitions	Global Quality
Parents as partners	-.007
Cost and convenience	.001
Clean and safe	.001
School-like	-.16*
Home-like	-.30**
Warmth	.17*
Structural	.02
Ratio and group size	.09

*$p < .05$; **$p < .01$

explanation for this finding was that most of the family child care homes in our sample were in compliance with child care experts' recommendations for group size and ratio. This issue will be discussed in some detail in Chapter 10. Perhaps having three or four children present requires providers to be more intentional in their interactions with each child, while providers who have only one or two children in their care find it easier to become occupied with tasks other than caregiving.

The second discrepancy between our sample and the model was that providers who reported more hassles (our measure of job stress) were also rated and observed to be more sensitive and responsive and described themselves as less harsh. These data are consistent with those of Kontos and Riessen (1993). Recall that the level of hassles was, on the average, low. It may be that providers high in process quality take the problems of their jobs more seriously, are more honest in their job descriptions, or have larger groups of children and thus a more complicated job .

Similar to child care experts, providers valued warmth as an important component of quality. Providers' ratings of warmth, however, were unrelated to structural or global quality. We can only speculate as to the reason for these results. One possibility is that providers have different notions of warmth than do the "experts," or the researchers.

5

Comparisons of the Quality of Care Among Regulated, Nonregulated, and Relative Providers

T he purpose of this chapter is to compare family child care and relative care quality as defined in Chapter 4 among the three groups of providers identified in Chapter 3: regulated, nonregulated, and relative. The three groups of providers were distinct in demographic, motivational, and organizational features. Therefore we also thought they might vary in level of quality or, alternatively, the components of quality might differ among the three groups. Thus, the questions addressed in this chapter are:

- How do regulated, nonregulated, and relative providers compare in quality of care?
- Are the components of quality different for regulated, nonregulated, and relative providers?
- How do regulated, nonregulated, and relative providers differ in their definitions of quality?

COMPARISONS OF GLOBAL QUALITY AMONG PROVIDER GROUPS

We began by comparing the global quality of the regulated, nonregulated, and relative providers. Recall from Chapter 4 that global quality well represents process, structural, and adult work environment quality.

The three groups of providers had different global quality scores [F (2, 222) = 34.13, p = .0001; Scheffe = .01]. Regulated providers had higher scores (M = 3.92, SD = .94, range = 1.88–6.67) than either non-regulated providers (M = 3.06, SD = 1.04, range = 1.14–6.16) or relative providers (M = 2.64, SD = .79, range = 1.33–5.23; Scheffe = .01). The average regulated and nonregulated provider fell into the "adequate/custodial" range. The average relative provider fell into the "unacceptable" range. Within each provider group there were some providers in each category of global quality.

When providers were categorized into "inadequate," "adequate/custodial," and "good" global scores, there also were significant differences among provider groups [χ^2 (4) = 57.80, p = .0001]. The modal regulated provider category was "adequate/custodial," while the modal nonregulated and relative provider category was "unacceptable" (see Table 5.1).

DIFFERENCES IN COMPONENTS OF QUALITY BETWEEN PROVIDER GROUPS

In order to determine whether the components of quality are different for regulated, nonregulated, and relative providers, we also compared the three provider groups on structural, process, adult work environment, and provider definitions of quality. To examine whether the components of good quality were the same for all three provider groups, we used a 3 (provider group) by 3 (quality group: inadequate, adequate/custodial, and good) multivariate analysis of variance strategy for each quality component. All of the analyses presented in the subsequent section had significant multivariate main effects for quality group. If we were to find, and we did not, significant interactions between provider group and quality group, we could conclude that the components of quality are different within the three groups of providers.

TABLE 5.1. PERCENTAGE OF EACH PROVIDER GROUP IN EACH GLOBAL QUALITY CATEGORY

Global Quality	Regulated (n = 112)	Nonregulated (n = 60)	Relative (n = 54)
Inadequate	13	50	69
Adequate/custodial	75	47	30
Good	12	3	1

Comparisons of Process Quality

There was a significant multivariate main effect for provider group for process quality [F (16, 362) = 4.59, p = .0001]. Descriptive statistics, univariate F-tests, and Scheffe post hoc tests are presented in Table 5.2. Regulated providers were rated as more sensitive, and observed to be more responsive, than were relative and nonregulated providers. Relative providers were rated as more detached than regulated and nonregulated providers and observed to engage in more low-level involvement than regulated providers did. Relative providers reported more restrictive child-rearing attitudes than did nonregulated providers who, in turn, reported more restrictive attitudes than did regulated providers. The multivariate interaction of provider group and quality group was not significant [F (24, 780) = 1.18, n.s.]. Therefore, relationships between provider group and process quality variables did not depend on overall quality.

TABLE 5.2. COMPARISONS OF PROCESS QUALITY AMONG PROVIDER GROUPS

Process Quality	Regulated (n = 112)	Non-regulated (n = 60)	Relative (n = 54)	F-test/ Scheffe
Ratings	M	M	M	
Sensitivity	3.03(.53)	2.79(.61)	2.57(.54)	12.19** Reg > Rel, Nonr
Harshness	1.58(.49)	1.46(.49)	1.48(.34)	1.56
Detachment	1.46(.55)	1.65(.68)	1.86(.76)	7.09** Rel > Nonr, Reg
Observation				
Low-level involvement	.20(.20)	.28(.24)	.35(.30)	5.04* Rel > Reg
Responsive involvement	.60(.28)	.49(.32)	.47(.32)	4.46* Reg > Rel, Nonr
Limit-setting	2.11(3.82)	1.72(2.12)	2.16(3.30)	.56
Self-report				
Nurturance	5.37(.67)	5.26(.73)	5.31(.72)	.08
Restrictiveness	2.22(1.16)	2.80(1.43)	3.77(1.35)	23.51** Rel > Nonr >Reg

*p < .01; **p < .001

Comparisons of Structural Quality

There was a significant multivariate main effect for provider group for structural quality [$F(12, 412) = 2.65$, $p = .003$]. Descriptive statistics, univariate F-tests, and Scheffe post hoc tests are presented in Table 5.3. Regulated providers cared for more children, had more children per provider, and had more informal training than did nonregulated or relative providers. Nonregulated providers had more children and more children per provider than did relative providers. Differences in amount of formal schooling among the three groups were not statistically significant. The multivariate interaction of provider group and quality group was not significant [$F(12, 329) = 1.22$, n.s.]. Therefore, the relationship between provider group and structural quality did not depend on overall quality.

Number of Children. We examined whether, in any of the provider groups, caring for just one child versus two or more children influenced global quality ratings. There were no significant main effects or interactions. To further explore differences among provider groups in number of children present during the observation and their range of ages, we computed the percentage of providers in each provider group with at least one child present in several age groups (e.g., infant, toddler, preschool, school-age). These findings are presented in Table 5.4. Nonregulated providers were most likely to have at least one infant present. Regulated providers were most likely to have at least one toddler and at least one preschooler present.

TABLE 5.3. COMPARISONS OF STRUCTURAL QUALITY AMONG PROVIDER GROUPS

Process Quality	Regulated (n = 112)	Non-regulated (n = 54)	Relative (n = 52)	F-test/ Scheffe
Number of children	5.39(2.47)	3.24(2.34)	1.88(1.24)	9.68* Reg > Nonr > Rel
Number of children per provider	4.29(1.76)	2.94(1.98)	1.63(1.00)	6.66* Reg > Nonr > Rel
Years of experience	6.11(7.09)	4.13(4.42)	6.61(7.88)	2.00
Formal school	4.00(1.11)	3.26(1.33)	2.67(1.44)	1.32
Family child care training[a]	2.14(7.97)	-4.28(5.61)	-6.11(3.09)	9.75* Reg > Nonr, Rel

*$p < .01$
[a]Family child care training is a standardized composite score.
Note: Formal schooling categories: 1 = less than high school; 2 = some high school; 3 = high school graduation; 4 = some college or AA degree; 5 = four-year degree; 6 = some graduate school; 7 = graduate degree

TABLE 5.4. PERCENTAGE OF PROVIDERS IN EACH PROVIDER GROUP WITH AT LEAST
ONE CHILD PRESENT IN EACH AGE GROUP

Age Group	Regulated (n = 112)	Non-regulated (n = 60)	Relative (n = 54)	χ^2
Infant (under 12 months)	46	70	28	9.60*
Toddler (12–29 months)	91	64	58	27.11**
Preschooler (30–59 months)	74	54	45	14.42*
School age (over 60 months)	24	25	13	3.14

*$p < .01$; **$p < .001$

TABLE 5.5. PERCENTAGE OF PROVIDERS IN EACH PROVIDER GROUP WHO HAD
ATTENDED EACH TYPE OF FAMILY CHILD CARE TRAINING

Workshop	Regulated (n = 112)	Non-regulated (n = 56)	Relative (n = 54)	χ^2
Food program	63	14	0	76.70***
Family-based child care association	52	9	0	62.01***
Local or state family-based child care conference	16	5	4	8.02*
Local or state general child care conference	25	11	2	16.14**
National conference	4	4	0	1.89
15-hour or more family-based child care course	39	14	4	29.16***
15-hour or more course in child care	58	14	8	46.94***

*$p < .05$; **$p < .01$; ***$p < .001$

Family Child Care Training. To further understand the differences
among provider groups in family child care training, we computed the
percentage of providers in each group who had attended various types
of workshops. These findings are presented in Table 5.5. Each type of

workshop, with the exception of those held at national conferences, was most likely to be attended by regulated providers.

Comparisons of the Adult Work Environment

There was a significant multivariate main effect for provider group for adult work environment [F (8, 440) = 9.36, p = .0001]. Descriptive statistics, univariate F-tests and Scheffe post hoc tests are presented in Table 5.6. Regulated and nonregulated providers reported more child care income, more hassles, and more job commitment than did relative providers. Nonregulated providers reported more child care income than did relative providers. The multivariate interaction of provider group and quality group was not significant [F (9, 528) = .93, n.s.]. Therefore, relationships between provider group and adult work environment variables did not depend on overall quality.

COMPARISONS AMONG PROVIDERS' DEFINITIONS OF QUALITY

There was a significant multivariate main effect by provider group for providers' definitions of quality [F (16, 308) = 1.86, p = .02]. Descriptive statistics, univariate F-tests and Scheffe post hoc tests are presented in Table 5.7. Relative providers are more likely to endorse home-like as an element of quality than are nonregulated or regulated providers. Nonregulated providers are more likely to endorse home-like as an element of quality than are regulated providers. Regulated providers are more likely to endorse structure than are nonregulated providers. It is

TABLE 5.6. COMPARISONS OF ADULT WORK ENVIRONMENT AMONG PROVIDER GROUPS

Adult Work Environment	Regulated (n = 112)	Non-regulated (n = 56)	Relative (n = 51)	F-test/ Scheffe
Child care income ($ per week)	400.88	136.62	41.84	23.93* Reg > Nonr > Rel
Hassles	1.85(.39)	1.70(.43)	1.45(.32)	11.99* Reg, Nonr > Rel
Job satisfaction	5.52(.96)	5.59(.95)	5.91(.90)	1.30
Job commitment	4.49(.54)	4.30(.71)	3.87(.86)	13.21* Reg, Nonr > Rel

*p < .01; **p < .001

TABLE 5.7. COMPARISONS OF SELF-DEFINITIONS OF QUALITY AMONG PROVIDER GROUPS

Quality	Regulated (n = 110)	Non-regulated (n = 56)	Relative (n = 51)	F-test/ Scheffe
Parents as partners	4.45(.53)	4.35(.49)	4.22(.83)	.14
Cost and convenience	3.96(.68)	3.84(.66)	3.86(1.04)	.54
Clean and safe	4.54(.49)	4.43(.46)	4.47(.49)	1.54
School-like	3.75(.70)	3.83(.66)	3.99(.64)	.01
Home-like	2.92(.85)	3.26(.76)	4.08(.78)	10.32** Rel > Nonr > Reg
Warmth	4.65(.38)	4.56(.45)	4.40(.49)	.06
Structure	4.08(.77)	3.71(.79)	3.86(.90)	3.93* Reg > Nonr
Group size and ratio	3.95(.98)	4.12(.67)	3.80(1.20)	.26

*$p < .01$; **$p < .001$

worth mentioning, however, that for 6 of 8 dimensions of quality, the provider groups did not differ. The multivariate interaction of provider group and quality group was not significant [$F (32, 624) = 1.06$, n.s.]. Therefore, the relation between provider group and providers' definitions of quality did not depend on the level of global quality.

SUMMARY AND CONCLUSIONS

The results of these analyses are clear and consistent. Regulated providers offer higher quality care than do nonregulated or relative providers. Nonregulated providers offer higher quality care than do relative providers. The quality components were similar for different provider groups.

Understanding the reasons for these results requires a look at the demographic characteristics of the providers, their motivations for being providers, as well as their training for what they do (reported in Chapter 3). Compared to the other two provider groups, relative providers are most likely to be low income (65% have family incomes of less than $20,000) and report the smallest social network. They are more likely to be caring for children for adult-focused reasons (helping mothers as opposed to children) and are least likely to see providing care as their chosen occupation. They are also the least likely to have training for what they do. This is the reverse of regulated providers, who are more affluent, report greater social support, care for children for child-focused reasons, and are more likely to see family child care as their chosen occupation and to be trained for their work. It is conceivable that relative providers are leading more stressed lives due to poverty, social isolation, and providing care out of a sense of obligation rather than commitment. Without training in responsive caregiving that might compensate for the need to work in these adverse conditions, it is no wonder children may not receive the quality of care that parents and policymakers assume they will receive from relatives.

The stark differences in quality of care found between these provider groups must also be interpreted in light of income and ethnic differences in the families using these types of care. It is to these differences that we turn in the following chapter.

6

Relationship of the Quality of Care to Family Income and Ethnicity

A prime purpose of this study was to determine whether families' economic status and race predict the quality of their family child care or relative care arrangement. Little is known about the characteristics of families who use family child care or relative care and only three studies have examined associations between family child care quality and family characteristics (Howes & Stewart, 1987; Kontos, 1994; Goelman & Pence, 1987; to our knowledge, there are no such studies for relative care). Although Kontos (1994) found no associations in a midwestern sample of families and providers, Howes and Stewart (1987) found that more stressed families used lower quality family child care in an urban setting. Pence and Goelman (1991) reported that urban Canadian mothers using lower quality, unlicensed family child care were less educated than were mothers using licensed family child care and center care. These data appear to suggest that, at least in urban settings, there is reason to be concerned about the quality of family child care for stressed, less educated families who are more likely to be low income.

Studies of child care supply and demand also indicate that concern regarding the quality of family child care for low-income families is warranted (once again, no data are available on relative care). For instance, Sonenstein and Wolf (1988) found that families on AFDC were more likely to use family child care than were families in the general population. Researchers have also found that child care is in shorter supply in low-income neighborhoods (Culkin et al., 1991; Hill-Scott, 1989). The need for research that directly focuses on the linkages of family child care and relative care quality with family income is evident in the paucity of studies that directly speak to this issue. Because members of racial minorities are disproportionately low income, it is important that both income and race be considered. Therefore, the following questions are addressed in this chapter:

- How does quality of care vary by income of families?
- How does quality of care vary by ethnicity of families?

These questions become even more urgent when we consider the sample of providers and target children who participated in this study. As noted earlier, regulated providers were more affluent than were the other providers and more likely to be white and to care for more affluent children of white families. Relative providers, on the other hand, were less affluent and were more likely to be African American or Latino and to care for less affluent children of African American or Latino families. Nonregulated providers fell in-between regulated and relative providers on these characteristics. Thus, provider type, quality of care, and income and ethnicity of providers and families are completely intertwined. Due to small cell sizes, it was not possible to compare quality of care by taking into account income of children's families and ethnicity simultaneously with provider group. Therefore, this set of analyses comparing quality by family income and ethnicity is designed to complement those of Chapter 5, which compared quality by provider group.

QUALITY OF CARE AND FAMILY INCOME

Income for our sample of families using family child care varied considerably, with a low of under $5,000 and a high of $150,000 or more. The median income was $40,000–$50,000 per year, compared with a median of $35,353 for all American families in 1990 (U.S. House of Representatives Committee on Ways and Means, 1992). The higher income in our sample is presumably a consequence of the requirement that mothers in the sample work. Similarly, the National Study of the Changing Workforce conducted by the Families and Work Institute found that the median household income of U.S. wage and salaried workers was $42,500 in 1991–92 (Galinsky et al., 1993).

Families were divided into three groups, according to their income. The low-income group consisted of families whose household income was less than $20,000 per year. The upper-income group consisted of families whose household income was $40,000 or more. The remaining families, whose household income was between $20,000–$39,000 per year, comprised the middle-income group. The upper-income group ($n = 107$) was assumed to earn above the median national income, whereas the middle-income ($n = 85$) and low-income ($n = 34$) groups were assumed to earn at or below and far below, respectively, the median national income. Income groups were evenly distributed across the three sites.

Quality of care was compared across the three family income groups for process, structural, and global quality, quality of the adult work environment, and providers' definitions of quality. The amount that families were charged for care (as reported by providers, pro-rated to a weekly, full-time rate) was also compared by income group. Because income and maternal education co-vary, and it is likely that better educated mothers selected better quality care, income group comparisons were also made controlling for maternal education.

Family income and type of care co-varied, as reported in Chapter 3 (refer to Table 3.3). Upper-income families were more than twice as likely to be using regulated providers than were low-income families, and were infrequent users of relative providers. The middle-income families were approximately evenly divided across the three types of care. Low-income families were most likely to use relative providers (nearly half) and the remaining low-income families were divided between regulated and unregulated nonrelatives.

Process Quality

There was a significant multivariate main effect for family income on process quality variables (see Table 6.1). Providers for low-income children exhibited significantly more low-level involvement and less sensitivity than did providers for high-income children. Providers caring for children in higher income families were rated as less detached than those caring for children in low-income families. Although there were no family income differences in restrictiveness of the providers as rated by observers, the providers themselves reported differences in their restrictive child-rearing attitudes by family income. Restrictiveness was significantly different for providers in the three family income groups; providers for low-income children reported themselves to be most restrictive, whereas providers for high-income children reported themselves to be the least restrictive. Providers' responsive involvement, restrictiveness (ratings), limit setting, and nurturant child-rearing attitudes were no different by family income level.

Family income effects for detachment and low-level provider involvement disappeared when maternal education was controlled. Ratings of the provider on sensitivity varied by family income, regardless of maternal education [$F (2, 197) = 6.96$, $p = .001$], as did provider restrictive child-rearing attitudes [$F (2, 168) = 7.84$, $p = .001$].

TABLE 6.1. PROCESS QUALITY BY FAMILY INCOME

| | Family Income Level | | | |
	< $20,000 (n = 34)	$20,000– $39,000 (n = 85)	> $39,000 (n = 107)	F-statistic/ Scheffe
Process Quality				2.95**
Ratings				
Sensitivity	2.38	2.8	2.99	13.12** H, M > L
Restrictiveness	1.68	1.51	1.51	1.50
Detachment	1.91	1.62	1.50	4.24* L > H
Observations				
Low involvement	.39	.25	.22	5.16** L > M, H
Responsive involvement	.45	.52	.58	2.34
Limit-setting	3.04	1.79	2.14	1.24
Self-report				
Restrictiveness	4.87	3.85	3.30	15.50** L > M > H
Nurturant	6.44	6.34	6.32	.34

*p < .01; **p < .001

Structural Quality

A multivariate analysis was not conducted for structural variables because the amount of missing data on several variables rendered the sample size too small. There were no differences in ratio, provider experience, or provider family child care training as a function of family income. Differences emerged, however, on group size, and formal education (see Table 6.2). Group sizes and formal education were highest for providers of higher income children (no two pairs were significantly different, however).

When maternal education was controlled, there was only one difference in structural quality as a function of family income: provider formal schooling [$F (2, 171) = 4.03$, $p < .05$].

Adult Work Environment

There was a significant multivariate main effect for family income on adult work environment (see Table 6.3). Providers' daily hassles and job

TABLE 6.2. STRUCTURAL QUALITY BY FAMILY INCOME

| | Family Income Level | | | |
Structural Quality	< $20,000 (n = 34)	$20,000– $39,000 (n = 85)	> $39,000 (n = 107)	F-test/ Scheffe
Ratio	2.88	3.13	3.56	1.95
Experience	6.58	5.72	5.4	.36
Group size	3.24	3.7	4.43	3.27*
				Scheffe ns
Formal school	2.67	3.29	3.89	12.18**
				H > M < L
Family child care training	-4.21	-2.05	-.94	1.41

*p < .05; **p < .001

TABLE 6.3. ADULT WORK ENVIRONMENT BY FAMILY INCOME

| | Family Income Level | | | |
	< $20,000 (n = 34)	$20,000– $39,000 (n = 85)	> $39,000 (n = 107)	F-test/ Scheffe
Adult work environment				3.72*
Hassles	1.69	1.69	1.80	1.51
Job Satisfaction	5.71	5.63	5.5	.65
Job Commitment	3.90	4.29	4.46	7.27*
				H > M > L

*p < .001

satisfaction were no different as a function of family income. On the other hand, providers of higher income target children were more committed to their jobs than were providers of medium-income target children who were, in turn, more committed than were providers of low-income children. This effect approached significance when maternal education was controlled ($p = .07$).

Global Quality

There was a significant difference in global quality as a function of family income [$F(2, 227) = 27.05$, $p < .001$; Scheffe = .01]. Each income group differed significantly from the others. Low-income families were using care that was inadequate in quality ($M = 2.57$), whereas the middle-income families were using care that was adequate/custodial ($M = 3.12$). The higher income families were using care in the upper range of adequate/custodial ($M = 3.8$). These differences held when maternal education was controlled [$F (2, 171) = 8.59$, $p < .000$]. In other words, regardless of maternal education, the lower the child's family income, the lower the quality of the family child care home in which he or she is enrolled.

Providers' Definitions of Quality

There was a multivariate main effect for family income on provider definition of quality care (see Table 6.4). The effects were modest. Providers perceived just 2 of the 8 aspects of quality differently as a function of family income. Providers of higher income children rated how school-like and how home-like the family child home is as more important to quality than did providers of middle- and low-income children (although no two pairs of means for "school-like" were significantly different). Neither of these two effects was significant when maternal education was controlled.

TABLE 6.4. PROVIDER DEFINITIONS OF QUALITY, BY FAMILY INCOME

	Family Income Level			
	< $20,000 (n = 34)	$20,000– $39,000 (n = 85)	> $39,000 (n = 107)	F-test/ Scheffe
Providers' definitions of quality				2.21**
Parents as partners	1.48	1.53	1.67	1.43
Cost and convenience	1.94	1.98	2.15	1.24
Clean and safe	1.48	1.45	1.55	.82
School-like	2.03	2.05	2.30	3.12* Scheffe ns
Home-like	2.28	2.58	2.99	7.62** H > M, L
Warmth	1.46	1.46	1.32	2.44
Structure	1.99	2.07	2.07	.12
Ratio group size	1.78	2.09	1.98	.90

*$p < .05$; **$p < .001$

Weekly Rates

The multivariate main effect for family income on weekly rates for family child care and relative care (including providers who did not charge) approached significance ($p < .06$; see Table 6.5). Three of the four univariate tests were significant, however. For care for infants, toddlers, and preschoolers, higher income families were charged more than were lower income families. There were no differences in rates for school-age child care as a function of family income.

Including providers who do not charge in the comparisons of rates by family income makes it difficult to determine what typical rates are for providers who *do* charge. Consequently, a similar analysis was conducted after eliminating providers from the sample who did not charge. A multivariate analysis was not conducted because these sample restrictions combined with missing data rendered the sample too small. Results of the univariate analyses can be seen in Table 6.6. Once again, there were main effects for family income on three of the four weekly rates variables. Only rates for school-aged children did not vary significantly by family income. Rates for infants of higher income families were higher than for middle- and low-income families; rates for infants of middle-income families were higher than for low-income families. Rates for toddlers and preschoolers of higher income families were higher than for middle- and low-income families.

TABLE 6.5. WEEKLY RATES BY FAMILY INCOME FOR ALL PROVIDERS

	Family Income Level			
	< $20,000 *(n = 34)*	*$20,000– $39,000* *(n = 85)*	*> $39,000* *(n = 107)*	*F-statistic/ Scheffe*
Weekly rates				1.92
Infant rates	$39.231	54.97	68.88	4.62* H > L
Toddler rates	$35.77	55.26	68.00	5.97* H > L
Preschool rates	$36.54	52.47	68.15	6.86* H > L
School-age rates	$31.15	32.85	35.78	.71

*$p < .01$

TABLE 6.6. WEEKLY RATES BY FAMILY INCOME FOR PROVIDERS WHO CHARGED

| | Family Income Level | | | |
Weekly Rates	< $20,000 (n = 34)	$20,000–$39,000 (n = 85)	> $39,000 (n = 107)	F-statistic/ Scheffe
Infant rates	$52.50	$70.74	$84.46	15.44* H > M > L
Toddler rates	$52.00	$63.02	$79.62	17.10* H > M, L
Preschool rates	$49.72	$58.35	$76.26	17.73* H > M, L
School-age rates	$36.58	$46.04	$50.03	1.49

*$p < .001$

Summary

Results of these analyses revealed that children from low-income families were cared for in family child care and relative care homes that were significantly lower in process and global quality (and cared for by providers who were less educated) than were children from more well off families. Commitment to family child care work was lowest for providers of children from low-income families and a priority for more school-like and home-like family child care settings was greatest for providers of children from higher income families. Low-income families were charged less for the care of young children than were higher income families. Viewed in the context of the type of family child care (regulated, relative, unregulated) most frequently utilized by the three family income groups, these results reflect the differences in quality among the three types of care presented in Chapter 5. In other words, lower income families seem to be significantly more likely to purchase unregulated or relative care, and they receive lower quality care for their children as a result. In light of the rate differentials by family income, it appears that affordability of care is a factor in the type of care a family chooses. The analyses of covariance suggest that maternal education may mediate the family income effect on quality. Maternal education did not moderate the effect of family income on provider sensitivity or global quality—two important quality indicators.

The higher priority of providers of children from higher income families for both school-like and home-like characteristics in family child care appears to be a contradiction. However, these results may reveal that some providers are concerned both about nurturing and learning—two characteristics of child care settings that are not necessarily mutually exclusive.

QUALITY OF CARE AND FAMILY ETHNICITY

As indicated in Chapter 2, the sample included families from a number of ethnic groups (as determined by maternal ethnicity). The largest group was whites, accounting for 62.3% of the sample ($n = 137$). African American families accounted for 24% of the sample ($n = 53$). The remaining families were identified as Latino (11%; $n = 25$), Asian American (1.8%; $n = 4$), and Native American (0.5%; $n = 1$). Families were divided into three groups according to their ethnicity (ethnicity for families in the provider sample was determined slightly differently than for the larger sample of mothers who were interviewed by phone). White and African American families were two of the groups. The third group was composed of the non-African American families of color: Latino, Asian American, and Native American families ($n = 30$). Although this third group does not represent a homogeneous ethnic group, it was necessary to combine these three ethnic groups for purposes of analyses due to their small size and the pattern of missing data. The alternative, deemed less desirable, would have been to drop the third group completely.

The families in these three groups were not evenly distributed across the three sites [$\chi^2 = 39.78$; $df = 4$]. African American families were located primarily in North Carolina (62.3%) and in California (28.3%). The group comprised mostly of Latino and Asian American families was approximately evenly divided between California (56.7%) and Texas (43.3%). White families were approximately evenly divided across sites, although there were more in California (38.75%) than in Texas (31.4%) or North Carolina (29.9%).

Family ethnicity co-varied with type of family child care (refer to Table 3.3). White families were most likely to used regulated providers, whereas the other two groups of families were most likely to use relative providers. The use of unregulated providers was similar across the three ethnic groups.

Quality of care was compared across the three ethnic groups of families for process, structural, and global quality, in addition to quality of the adult work environment and providers' definitions of quality. Because ethnicity co-varied with income and education, and because it is likely that more well off, better educated mothers chose higher quality care, the comparisons were also made controlling for family income and maternal education.

Measures selected for this study were carefully selected from existing measures to ensure their sound psychometric properties and their relevance to predicting children's development among groups of varying backgrounds. To the extent that our measures of family child care and relative care quality represent middle class, white values, the ethnic differences in quality could be a reflection of different child-rearing preferences.

Process Quality

There was a multivariate main effect for family ethnicity on process quality (see Table 6.7). Family ethnicity differences were present for providers' low-level involvement, sensitivity, detachment, and restrictive attitudes. Providers of children from white families received higher sensitivity ratings than did the other two groups of providers. Restrictive child-rearing attitudes were higher for providers of children from

TABLE 6.7. PROCESS QUALITY BY FAMILY ETHNICITY

	White (n = 137)	African American (n = 53)	Latino/Asian/ Native American (n = 30)	F-test/ Scheffe
Process quality				2.90**
Ratings				
Sensitivity	2.98	2.58	2.62	10.42** W > A, L
Restrictivenss	1.51	1.64	1.47	1.61
Detachment	1.52	1.67	1.86	3.29* Scheffe ns
Observation				
Low involvement	.25	.32	.18	3.03* Scheffe ns
Responsive involvement	.56	.50	.50	.74
Limit-setting	2.02	3.03	1.13	2.58
Self-report				
Restrictiveness	3.44	4.15	4.42	8.47** A, L > W
Nurturant	6.38	6.33	6.2	.65

*$p < .05$; **$p < .001$

African American families and other families of color. Providers of white children exhibited more high involvement and less detachment, but no two pairs of means were significantly different. There were no differences in providers' high level involvement, restrictiveness ratings, nurturing attitudes, or amount of limit setting by family ethnicity.

When family income and maternal education were controlled, just one family ethnicity effect on process quality remained: sensitivity [F (2, 189) = 3.95, p = .02].

Structural Quality

A multivariate analysis was not conducted for structural variables because the amount of missing data on several variables rendered the sample size too small. There were significant family ethnicity univariate differences for ratio, group size, and formal education (see Table 6.8). Children from Latino/Asian/Native American families were in family child care homes or relative care with significantly fewer children per adult than were children from white families. A similar effect was present for group size, although the Scheffe test indicated that no two pairs of means were significantly different. Providers of white children had more formal education than did providers of Latino/Asian/Native American children. There were no differences in any aspect of structural quality of family child care or relative care for children of white versus African American families. There were no differences in provider experience or family child care training as a function of family ethnic-

TABLE 6.8. STRUCTURAL QUALITY BY FAMILY ETHNICITY

Structure	White (n = 137)	African American (n = 53)	Latino/Asian/ Native American (n = 30)	F-test/ Scheffe
Ratio	3.64	2.96	2.47	5.41* W > L
Experience	5.61	7.21	3.50	2.80
Group size	4.43	3.40	3.31	4.53* Scheffe ns
Formal school	3.74	3.25	2.70	8.37* W > L
Family child care training	-2.19	-.03	-3.75	1.77

*p < .01

ity. When family income and maternal education were controlled, there were no differences in structural quality of family child care or relative care as a function of family ethnicity.

Adult Work Environment

There was a significant main effect for family ethnicity on the adult work environment (see Table 6.9). Provider hassles and job satisfaction—but not job commitment—varied as a function of family ethnicity. Providers of children from white families reported more hassles than did providers of children from Latino/Asian/Native American families. Job satisfaction was higher for providers of African American children than for providers of white children. When family income and maternal education were controlled, the family ethnicity differences for job satisfaction remained [$F (2, 193) = 7.11$, $p = .001$].

Global Quality

Global quality of care varied as a function of family ethnicity [$F (2, 219) = 20.58$, $p < .001$]. Quality for white families was significantly higher ($M = 3.72$) than for African American ($M = 2.99$) or Latino/Asian/Native American families ($M = 2.63$). This effect was present even when family income and maternal education were controlled [$F (2, 163) = 4.36, = .008$].

Providers' Definitions of Quality

There was no multivariate main effect for family ethnicity on providers' definitions of quality (see Table 6.10). Providers differed in

TABLE 6.9. ADULT WORK ENVIRONMENT BY FAMILY ETHNICITY

	White (n = 137)	African American (n = 53)	Latino/Asian/ Native American (n = 30)	F-test/ Scheffe
Adult work environment				5.88**
Hassles	1.79	1.71	1.56	3.36* W > L
Job satisfaction	5.36	6.03	5.83	8.79** A > W
Job commitment	4.38	4.27	4.08	2.13

*$p < .05$; **$p < .001$

TABLE 6.10. PROVIDER DEFINITIONS OF QUALITY, BY FAMILY ETHNICITY

	White (n = 137)	African American (n = 53)	Latino/Asian/ Native American (n = 30)	F-test/ Scheffe
Definitions of quality				1.23
Parents as partners	1.59	1.60	1.55	.04
Cost and convenience	3.0	2.00	1.88	.71
Clean and safe	1.54	1.43	1.38	1.33
School-like	2.24	2.07	1.96	1.88
Home-like	2.87	2.53	2.5	2.65
Warmth	1.36	1.41	1.47	.67
Structure	2.15	1.96	1.63	3.69* W > L
Ratio/group size	2.07	1.93	1.73	.95

*$p < .05$

their perceptions of what constitutes quality care by family ethnicity on only one characteristic: home-like. Providers of children from white families rated this characteristic higher than did providers of children from Latino/Asian/Native American families. When family income and maternal education were controlled, this difference disappeared.

▬▬▬▬
Summary

These data reveal that white children tend to be in higher quality family child care or relative care than either African American children or children of other ethnic backgrounds. The differences in quality are strongly reminiscent of the differences present as a function of family income. Controlling for family income and maternal education eliminated most, but not all, quality differences. Global quality, provider sensitivity, and job satisfaction still varied as a function of family ethnicity. The robustness of the results for global quality and provider sensitivity may be due to the family ethnicity differences in the type of care used. Recall that white families were over-represented in the regulated providers group, whereas the other two groups of families were more likely to use relative providers—which has been shown to be, on average, of lower quality than regulated providers.

CONCLUSIONS

It is important that these data do not become the basis for "blaming the victim"—low-income parents and providers who have selected or are providing child care of less-than-ideal quality for the target children in the study. The differences in quality observed were related primarily to income. Research has shown us that the stresses of poverty lead to psychological distress that may interfere with parents' and providers' best intentions for the children in their care (McLloyd, 1990). In Chapter 8 we will report parents' perceptions of their child care choices and their financial constraints in finding care. Choices available to low-income families appear to be few and far between. The family income differences found in family child care and relative care quality speak to the need for new policies and practices that will make high-quality child care available to all families.

7

Comparisons of Providers Offering
Different Quality Levels of Care

L ittle is known about differences among providers who are offering care that differs in level of quality. Assuming that no provider
operates with the intent to provide inadequate or even ade-
quate/custodial care, the dynamics of providing good versus poor quality care may be easier to comprehend if we can begin to develop profiles
of providers who fall into these quality categories. Thus, the intent of
this set of analyses was to compare a number of quality components—
the personal and family background characteristics; state, regulatory
status, and type of provider; motivations to provide family child care
and relative care; involvement in the family child care community; the
adult work environment; definitions of quality; organization of child
care services; business practices; professional activities; and relations
with families served—for providers shown to offer good, adequate/cus-
todial, and inadequate quality care.

Providers were divided into three groups according to their Family
Day Care Rating Scale (FDCRS) average item score. Those whose average score was 5 or above were placed in the good quality care group.
Providers whose average score was less than 3 were placed in the inadequate quality care group. The remaining providers with scores from
3–4.99 were placed in the adequate/custodial quality care group.
Twenty-one providers (9%) were in the good quality group, 126
providers (56%) were in the adequate/custodial quality group, and 80
providers (35%) were in the inadequate quality care group.

The differences between the three quality groups of providers can be
made more graphic by examining item descriptors on the FDCRS
(Harms & Clifford, 1989). For instance, for "informal use of language," a
provider is considered to be inadequate if she does little or no talking

to infants and toddlers and talks to children 2 years and older primarily to maintain "control of children's behavior and manage routines." A provider who engages in some socializing with the older preschool children, who asks children mostly "yes/no" or short-answer questions, and who talks to infants and toddlers mainly to control behavior is considered to be adequate/custodial in informal use of language. A provider who is doing a good job with informal use of language, however, talks to infants and toddlers, encourages children to talk, responds to what they say, and uses language for enjoyment (e.g., songs and rhymes).

COMPONENTS OF QUALITY
FOR THE THREE GROUPS OF PROVIDERS

We first compared the structural, process, and adult work environment quality for providers in the three groups. We used three multivariate analyses of variance, one for each quality component. There were multivariate main effects for quality group for all components of quality [structural: $F(12, 382) = 1.98$, $p = .04$; process: $F(16, 362) = 8.81$, $p = .0001$; adult work environment: $F(6, 360) = 4.97$, $p = .001$]. This indicates that providers classified as inadequate, adequate/custodial, or good in global quality differed significantly in process, structural, and adult work environment quality.

Descriptive statistics, univariate F tests and Scheffe post hoc tests are presented in Table 7.1. Providers with good global quality scores had more family child care training, higher sensitivity ratings, and higher child care incomes than did providers with adequate/custodial scores. Providers with adequate/custodial global quality scores had more family child care training, higher sensitivity scores, and higher child care income than did providers with inadequate scores. Providers with good and adequate/custodial global rating scores had lower harshness and detachment scores, were observed to be more responsive, reported themselves to be more nurturant and less restrictive, and reported more hassles and more job commitment. These results were not surprising, given the results reported in Chapter 4 showing how the FDCRS, on which the quality groupings were based, well represent the components of quality.

Personal and Family Background Characteristics and Quality

We then turned to personal and family background characteristics to examine differences among providers offering good quality care and those who are not. There was a multivariate main effect for quality of

TABLE 7.1. COMPARISONS OF STRUCTURAL, PROCESS, AND ADULT WORK ENVIRON-MENT QUALITY AND DEFINITIONS OF QUALITY BETWEEN PROVIDERS WITH INADE-QUATE, ADEQUATE/CUSTODIAL, AND GOOD GLOBAL QUALITY SCORES

| Components of Quality | Providers by Global Quality | | | |
	Inadequate (n = 74)	Adequate/ Custodial (n = 126)	Good (n = 18)	F-test/ Scheffe
Structural quality				
Group size	3.00 (2.07)	4.38 (2.76)	5.82 (2.58)	.83
Number of children per adult	2.67 (1.79)	3.53 (2.00)	4.73 (1.94)	2.90
Years of experience	7.75 (9.56)	4.69 (4.44)	4.47 (3.11)	2.23
Formal school	2.60 (1.25)	3.91 (1.20)	4.35 (.93)	2.31
Family child care training	-4.62 (5.50)	-.90 (6.10)	6.91 (15.21)	4.28** G > A > I
Process quality				
Ratings				
Sensitivity	2.37 (.46)	3.07 (.46)	3.45 (.41)	59.61*** G > A > I
Harshness	1.72 (.58)	1.44 (.35)	1.35 (.27)	10.92*** I > A,G
Detachment	2.03 (.71)	1.41 (.51)	1.15 (.29)	27.66*** I > A,G
Observations				
Low involvement	.34 (.27)	.19 (.21)	.36 (.24)	10.17*** G,I > A
Responsive involvement	.40 (.32)	.63 (.27)	.54 (.25)	10.64*** A,G > I
Limit-setting	1.80 (2.61)	1.90 (3.14)	3.88 (6.04)	2.99*
Self-report				
Nurturant	5.13 (.78)	5.41 (.64)	5.63 (.36)	4.71** G,A > I
Restrictiveness	3.53 (1.41)	2.31 (1.28)	2.24 (.98)	21.15** I > A,G
Adult work environment				
Family-based child care income: $/wk	147.38 (139.34)	323.86 (260.90)	382.82 (238.52)	10.39** G > A > I
Hassles	1.59 (.45)	1.81 (.38)	1.86 (.39)	6.11** A,G > I
Job satisfaction	5.72 (1.03)	5.54 (.91)	5.85 (.86)	1.71
Job commitment	4.10 (.78)	4.36 (.66)	4.65 (.45)	6.48** A,G > I

*p < .05; **p < .01; ***p < .001

care on provider personal and family background characteristics (see Table 7.2). There were no significant differences in age, number of children, number of own children at home, or satisfaction with social support as a function of quality. Providers varied by quality on formal education, amount of social support, household income, child care earnings, and marital status. Providers offering inadequate quality care had less social support and smaller household income than did providers offering adequate/custodial care. They had less formal education and smaller child care earnings than did providers offering adequate/custodial and good quality care. Providers offering inadequate quality care were also less likely to be married or living with a partner than were providers in the other two groups.

TABLE 7.2. PERSONAL AND FAMILY BACKGROUND CHARACTERISTICS OF PROVIDERS, BY QUALITY RATINGS

	Providers, by Global Quality			
	Inadequate (n = 74)	Adequate/ Custodial (n = 126)	Good (n = 18)	F-Statistic/ Scheffe
Characteristics				4.40**
Age (yrs)	43.55	40.67	35.00	1.80
Amount of social support	-2.38	-.23	.332	3.62* A > I
Satisfaction with amount of social support	-1.25	-.45	-2.22	.47
Education	2.58	3.93	4.56	15.89** G,A > I
Household income	2.19	3.98	2.78	16.75** A > I
Number of children	1.81	1.92	2.11	.21
Number of own children at home	1.48	1.34	1.22	.20
Family child care earnings ($/week)	$123.27	267.58	375.78	8.07** G,A > I
Marital status (percent married or with partner)	63	80	72	25.50**

*p < .05; **p < .001

Distribution of Quality by State, Regulatory Status, and Type of Provider

Quality of care may differ by state (due to different child care regulations), regulatory status (regulated versus nonregulated), or by the number and relationship of children cared for. These comparisons are shown on Table 7.3. Our findings revealed that quality of care was not evenly distributed across states. Texas had the most good- and inadequate-rated quality care; North Carolina had the least good-rated quality care.

There was no relation between whether the provider's regulatory status was legal (i.e., regulated when stipulated by the state or legally exempt from regulation) and quality of care. There was, however, a relation between quality and whether a provider was regulated. The majority of providers providing inadequate quality care were nonregulated, whereas approximately two thirds of providers providing adequate/cus-

TABLE 7.3. SITE/REGULATORY STATUS/TYPE OF HOME, BY QUALITY RATINGS

	Providers, by Global Quality			
	Inadequate (n = 80)	Adequate/ Custodial (n = 126)	Good (n = 17)	χ^2
State				30.12*
California	26	40	24	
North Carolina	29	40	5	
Texas	45	20	71	
Regulatory status				53.61*
Nonregulated	82	34	18	
Regulated	18	66	82	
Legal status				NS
Illegally unregulated	30	20	12	
Regulated or legally exempt	70	80	88	
Home type				54.69*
Multiple families (unrelated)	32	77	100	
Child from one family (unrelated)	19	10	0	
Relative	49	14	0	

*p < .001

todial-rating quality care were regulated, and more than three fourths of providers providing good-rating quality care were regulated.

The number and relationship of children a provider cared for forms another category to relate to quality. Again, providers may be divided into three groups: those providing care for more than one family with one or more unrelated children; those providing care for only one child or siblings from one unrelated family; and a relative providing care for only one child or siblings from one related family. All providers giving good quality care were classified in the first group, whereas only a third of providers providing inadequate quality care were so classified. Most of the relative care was given by providers offering inadequate quality care. Providers providing adequate/custodial quality care were some-times relatives or were caring for children from just one family but were more typically providing care for children from more than one family.

Providers' Definitions of Quality and Quality Ratings

Because we know that type of care (defined by number and relationship of children in care), regulatory status, and quality of care co-vary, it is conceivable that providers vary in quality because they have different visions of what quality is. For instance, providers offering inadequate quality care who are more likely to be relatives may be more concerned about the "home-like" qualities of the child care setting than are the other providers. There was a multivariate main effect for quality of care on providers' definitions of quality (see Table 7.4). Contrary to expec-tations, providers offering adequate/custodial quality care rated "home-like" higher in importance to quality care than did providers offering inadequate quality care. Providers offering inadequate quality care rated "warmth" higher in importance to quality care than did providers offering adequate/custodial care. All of the other quality components were rated equally in importance to quality by the three groups of providers. Overall, the providers' definitions of quality were essentially similar, in spite of these two significant differences. These results sug-gest that differences in quality among the providers are not attributable to differences in their views of what quality is. In other words, the providers' definitions of quality were, by and large, not significantly associated with the level of quality they offered.

Provider Involvement in the
Family Child Care Community and Quality

There were differences in how involved the three groups of providers were in the family child care community. Providers offering good and

TABLE 7.4. PROVIDER DEFINITIONS OF QUALITY OF CARE, BY QUALITY RATINGS

	Providers, by Global Quality			
	Inadequate *(n = 76)*	*Adequate/ Custodial* *(n = 127)*	*Good* *(n = 17)*	*F-statistic/ Scheffe*
Definitions of quality				2.53*
Parent/provider relationship	1.66	1.56	1.54	.55
Cost and convenience	2.05	2.03	2.29	.71
Safe environment	1.51	1.50	1.48	.03
School-like	2.03	2.25	2.14	1.96
Home-like	2.34	2.97	2.67	9.11* A > I
Warmth	1.53	1.33	1.29	4.99* I > A
Professional	2.11	2.01	2.06	.61
Ratio/group size	2.20	1.90	1.82	1.91

*$p < .001$

adequate/custodial quality care were more involved than were providers offering inadequate quality care. There were no differences among the three groups with respect to their satisfaction with their level of involvement in the family child care and relative care community. In other words, providers were satisfied with their involvement in the family child care community, regardless of their amount of involvement in it (see Table 7.5).

Providers' Motivations and Quality

As explained in Chapter 3, we asked providers to indicate their primary and secondary reasons for working as child care providers from among seven choices. There were significant differences in providers' reasons by quality for two of the seven possible reasons: staying home with their own child and helping mothers. These results are presented in Table 7.6. Providers offering inadequate child care were less likely than were the other two groups of providers to report that staying home with their own child or grandchild was their primary motivation, and were more likely to indicate that helping mothers was their primary motivation. These data suggest that child-focused reasons for providing care are

TABLE 7.5 PROVIDER INVOLVEMENT IN THE FAMILY CHILD CARE COMMUNITY, BY QUALITY RATINGS

Providers in the Family Child Care Community	Providers, by Global Quality			
	Inadequate (n = 78)	Adequate/ Custodial (n = 124)	Good (n = 17)	F-statistic/ Scheffe
Involvement	-1.75	.054	.391	12.81 *G, A > I
Satisfaction with involvement	-.148	.015	-.72	.67

*p < .001

TABLE 7.6. MOTIVATION FOR BECOMING A PROVIDER, BY QUALITY RATINGS

Motivation	Providers, by Global Quality			
	Inadequate (n = 75)	Adequate/ Custodial (n = 120)	Good (n = 16)	χ2
Stay home with own child	35	55	56	10.9*
Work at home	11	12	19	1.59
Work with children	12	16	<1	.33
Help mothers	36	13	1	14.14**
Only job can do	3	< 1	< 1	7.14
Mother asked me	7	12	< 1	5.98
Recruited by training program	< 1	0	< 1	9.4

*p < .05; **p < .01

more typical of providers offering good quality care, whereas adult-focused reasons are more typical of providers offering inadequate quality care. This is not surprising, given our findings that relative providers who are older and caring for grandchildren or other relatives are more likely to be offering inadequate care, whereas regulated providers who are younger and more likely to be staying home with their own children are more likely to be offering good quality care.

Providers' perceptions of child care as a career varied by the quality of the care they were offering. These differences can be seen in Table 7.7. No providers offering good quality care considered their work temporary, and approximately two thirds reported that child care was their chosen job. Providers offering adequate/custodial care made similar

TABLE 7.7. PERSONAL VIEW OF JOB, BY QUALITY RATINGS

	Providers, by Global Quality		
	Inadequate (n = 76)	Adequate/ Custodial (n = 116)	Good (n = 17)
View			F = 15.09*
Chosen job	39	59	65
Stepping stone	10	12	12
Good while children at home	37	27	23
Temporary	13	3	0

*p < .05; **p < .01

choices. Providers offering inadequate quality care were nearly equally likely to report that child care was their chosen job (39%) or that it was good while their children or grandchildren were home (37%).

Providers' Organization of Child Care Services and Quality

Providers offering good and adequate/custodial quality family child care and relative care were more business-like than were providers offering inadequate quality based on the business practices scale created for this study (see Chapter 3). There were significant differences as a function of quality in the use of all nine business practices that make up the scale (see Table 7.8). In each case, the providers offering inadequate quality care were less likely to follow a particular practice than were providers offering either adequate/custodial or good quality care. The only business practices followed by a majority of providers offering inadequate quality care were keeping the phone numbers of the child's family physician and parents' daytime phone numbers (amazingly, 12% of them did *not* have parents' phone numbers). The only business practice not followed by the majority of providers offering good quality care was depreciating the costs of child care.

A higher proportion of providers offering good and adequate/custodial quality care had child care liability insurance, household property insurance, and health insurance than did providers offering inadequate quality care (see Table 7.9). Providers offering good and adequate/custodial quality care were more likely than were providers offering inadequate quality care to take paid vacations (but not unpaid vacations) or to have an IRA account. Providers offering good and ade-

TABLE 7.8. PERCENTAGE OF PROVIDERS CURRENTLY FOLLOWING BUSINESS PRACTICES, BY QUALITY RATINGS

Organizational Practice	Providers, by Global Quality			
	Inadequate (n = 55)	Adequate/ Custodial (n = 113)	Good (n = 16)	$\chi2$
Business practices score	25.00	31.65	34.19	F-statistic/ Scheffe: 30.17** G, A > I
Individual items				
Depreciate costs	21%	44%	47%	15.04*
Declare FCC income	32	78	88	51.96**
Declare FCC expenses	28	71	76	44.91**
Give parents' social security number	39	76	94	41.57**
Have parent contract	16	60	71	46.47**
Keep doctors' phone numbers	64	87	100	23.94**
Emergency authorizations	45	82	100	49.59**
Parent work phone numbers	88	98	100	12.65*
Immunization records	32	62	94	32.02**

*$p < .05$; **$p < .001$

quate/custodial quality care charged higher rates than did providers offering inadequate quality care for all ages except school-aged children. Providers offering inadequate quality care were less likely to hire a paid assistant. There were no differences among the three groups of providers in number of full-time or part-time openings.

Providers' Professional Activities and Quality

Providers offering good quality care were more likely to belong to the Child and Adult Care Food Program and to a family child care association than were providers offering adequate/custodial quality care who, in turn, were more likely to belong to these two types of organizations than were providers offering inadequate quality care. These data are consistent with our findings on providers' involvement in the family child care community.

Although the majority of all providers do housework during the day, fewer providers offering good quality care do this than providers offering adequate/custodial or inadequate quality care. The majority of providers offering good quality care planned several activities per day for the children, whereas the majority of providers offering inadequate quality care

TABLE 7.9 INSURANCE, FRINGE BENEFITS, ASSISTANTS, RATES, AND OPENINGS, BY
QUALITY RATINGS

Organizational Practice	Providers, by Global Quality			
	Inadequate (n = 52)	Adequate/ Custodial (n = 106)	Good (n = 16)	χ2
Child care liability insurance	7%	26%	33%	13.57**
Household property insurance	49	83	83	28.09**
IRA account	26	39	22	4.94
Health insurance	60	81	83	11.24**
Paid vacations	15	44	62	22.25**
Unpaid vacations	69	60	53	2.42
Paid assistant	13	27	22	5.98*
Weekly rates				F-statistic/ Scheffe
< 12 months	$44.85	$77.86	$69.41	16.55*** G, A > I
12–29 months	$46.36	$74.42	$73.06	20.19*** G, A > I
30–60 months	$40.24	$70.76	$65.47	22.34*** G, A > I
School-age	$27.30	$37.34	$43.92	1.88
Openings full-time	.81	.84	.80	.01
part-time	.49	.32	1.17	1.81

*$p < .05$; **$p < .01$; ***$p < .001$

never planned any activities. Providers offering adequate/custodial quality care were divided between those planning several activities daily, two to four activities per week, and no planned activities. A plurality of providers offering adequate/custodial quality care did not plan any activities for the children. These results are shown in Table 7.10.

Providers' Relations with Parents and Quality

As described in Chapter 3, providers were asked whether and how frequently (in the last three months) they socialized with parents; were criticized by parents; shared feelings with parents; argued over money, child rearing, or lateness; and talked with parents about the child. The

TABLE 7.10. PROVIDER PROFESSIONAL ACTIVITIES BY QUALITY RATINGS

	Providers, by Global Quality			
	Inadequate (n = 73)	Adequate/ Custodial (n = 19)	Good (n = 16)	χ2
Belong to Child and Adult Care Food Program	18%	59%	87%	38.70**
Belong to Family Child Care Association	15	31	69	16.79**
Do housework	88	83	59	8.39*
Activity planning				44.49**
Several daily	5	24	56	
One daily	11	17	0	
2–4 per week	10	23	19	
1 per week	10	7	0	
None	64	29	25	

*p < .05; **p < .001

multivariate effect for quality on the frequency items was not significant (see Table 7.11). In general, providers reported that negative interactions with parents were relatively infrequent but that most of these problems had occurred at some point. Providers offering inadequate and adequate/custodial quality care were more likely to report that they had argued with parents about child rearing than were parents offering good quality care, although the majority of all groups reported this. Providers were also asked to indicate whether they believed children were better off at home with their parents and whether they were friends with the parents. Providers offering inadequate quality care were less likely than were the other two groups of providers to believe that children were better off at home with their parents. However, approximately two thirds of providers offering adequate/custodial and good quality care responded affirmatively to this belief. In other words, they believed that children should be at home with their mothers. There was no relationship between relations with parents and the belief that children were better off at home with their parents.

Summary

We found many differences among providers who offer care that differs in level of quality. Process and structural quality varied as a function of level of quality, as did the quality of the adult work environment. The differences were in favor of providers offering good quality care.

TABLE 7.11. PROVIDERS' RELATIONS WITH PARENTS, BY QUALITY RATINGS

| | Providers, by Global Quality | | | |
	Inadequate (n = 78)	Adequate/ Custodial (n = 126)	Good (n = 17)	$\chi2$
Relations with parents				.82
Best for children to be with parents	42%	61%	67%	7.82*
Socialize with parents				
$M =$	7.35	3.20	.40	3.66*
% =	78%	64%	61%	4.67
Parents criticize				
$M =$	.32	.125	.40	.43
% =	90%	89%	78%	2.10
Share feelings				
$M =$	5.70	6.48	2.4	.27
% =	72%	71%	83%	1.15
Argue over childrearing				
$M =$	.08	.07	.00	.16
% =	92%	97%	82%	6.33*
Talk about children				
$M =$	15.54	15.89	13.80	.15
% =	99%	100%	100%	1.85
Friends with parents				
$M =$				
% =	81%	72%	67%	2.50
Argue about money				
$M =$	.08	.11	.00	.20
% =	93%	92%	100%	1.54
Argue about lateness				
$M =$	.95	.21	.00	.51
% =	96%	90%	89%	2.41

*$p < .05$

Providers offering differing levels of quality also varied in their personal and family background characteristics. Providers offering inadequate care were less well educated, less well off financially, had less social support, and were less likely to be married or to have a partner.

Regulated providers were more likely to offer good or adequate/custodial quality, whereas nonregulated providers were more likely to be offering inadequate quality care. Most of the relative care was classified as inadequate. All of the good quality care was by providers offering care to more than one unrelated family.

Providers offering good and adequate/custodial care were more likely to be involved in the family child care community and to be using standard business practices than were providers offering inadequate quality care. All providers were equally satisfied with their amount of involvement. Providers offering inadequate care were more likely to be offering care for adult-focused reasons, whereas the remaining providers were more likely to be motivated by child-focused reasons. Providers offering good quality care typically viewed their work as their chosen occupation.

There were no differences among the provider quality groups in relations with parents. Providers offering good and adequate/custodial care were more likely to believe that children were better off at home with their parents than were providers offering inadequate care. The latter group, however, were more likely to be relatives, which may explain that finding.

In spite of all the differences among providers who vary in the quality of care they provide, their definitions of quality are essentially the same. Thus, the differences do not appear to reflect different ideas of what quality care is.

CONCLUSIONS

These data present a consistent pattern of differences between providers offering good and inadequate quality care. By and large, providers offering adequate/custodial quality care were more often similar to those offering good quality than they were to those offering inadequate quality care.

Given the distribution of providers who are relatives versus regulated family child care providers across the levels of quality, it is not surprising that those offering good quality care were the more "professionalized" group. Providers offering inadequate quality care, many of whom are relatives, simply do not appear to perceive themselves to be engaged in child care as a profession. Rather, it seems they function more informally as custodial mother/baby-sitter in the midst of their other family responsibilities, but without the boundary clarity between roles provided by a more professionalized or intentional approach (Bollin, 1993), not to mention the satisfaction of knowing they are engaged in work they chose. We prefer to apply the term "intentional" to family child care and relative care providers rather than the term "professional" because it implies a career path distinct from other early childhood educators.

The indicators of professionalization or "intentionality" take several forms, including involvement in the family child care and relative care community, planning, as well as following standard business practices, including access to fringe benefits. Providers offering good and adequate/custodial quality care were more likely to have support for their work from the family child care community and their own family and were more involved in professional activities. Providers offering good quality care were less likely to do housework during caregiving hours (although the majority did) and were more likely to plan activities for the children daily. In other words, not only were providers of good quality care more involved with other providers, but by doing less housework and more activity planning, they were more intentionally child-centered than were the other providers. It makes sense that providers who are more child-centered in their practices would be observed to be more responsive in their interactions with children.

Providers offering good and adequate/custodial quality care were more likely to follow standard business practices, to be insured, and to have access to fringe benefits. Basic business practices, such as declaring one's child care income and expenses and having a contract with parents, were relatively uncommon among providers offering inadequate quality care. This is partially due to the fact that the latter group consists primarily of relatives who do not charge and would be unlikely to enter into a contractual agreement with a daughter. This would also explain the lower rates (except for school-age children) charged by providers offering inadequate quality care. The level of informality in these child care arrangements may be reflected in the number of providers who do not have a child's physician's telephone number, emergency authorization, or even the parents' work telephone number. Providers offering inadequate quality care were also less likely to be insured and rarely took paid vacations or paid an assistant. Because providers offering inadequate quality care were caring for small groups of children and were less likely to charge, it is not surprising that paid vacations and assistants were not the norm (paid assistants were not the norm for any group of providers). The lack of insurance is probably related to the lower household income of the inadequate quality group who were also less likely to be married or to have a partner.

Relations with parents were no different across the three groups of providers. Being related to the child does not improve or worsen parent-provider relations and offering good quality child care does not include enhanced parent–provider relations. Interestingly, a large proportion of providers believe that children are better off at home with their parents and, paradoxically, the proportion was largest for providers offering good and adequate/custodial quality care. We can only speculate as to the reasons for this difference. Two potential reasons stand out: motivation for becoming a provider and relationship with the mother. Providers offering good and adequate/custodial quality care were those most likely to have chosen family child care and relative care as a profession in order to stay home with their own children. These providers valued caring for their own children to the point of finding an occupation that would allow them to do so. The providers offering inadequate quality care, on the other hand, expressed different motivations for their work. They are caring for children in order to help mothers—a large percentage of whom we know are low-income and clearly need to work. We also know that a large percentage of those low-income mothers are the daughters of the providers. Thus, the discrepancy in beliefs about where children are best nurtured may have emerged from differing values regarding child rearing and closeness to the mother. In general, the belief that children are better off at home with their parents may be a reflection of our societal ambivalence about working mothers (McCartney & Phillips, 1988).

8

Mothers and Child Care

C hildren do not find their own way into child care arrangements. It is parents who select arrangements for their children and who remove children from arrangements that are inconvenient, which they cannot afford, or with which they are dissatisfied. Increasing the quality of care children experience involves not only understanding providers and what they do, but also understanding how parents think about quality, how they go about selecting care, and whether definitions of quality and processes of selecting care differ for different groups of parents. If different groups of parents select different types of arrangements, then we would find predictable combinations of family and family child care characteristics. Previous research conducted in urban settings suggests that families with the fewest resources may be unable to find or afford high quality care (Goelman & Pence, 1987; Howes & Stewart, 1987). Thus, children with the greatest needs often receive the worst quality care.

We need to understand how knowledgeable parents are about the characteristics of their provider and the care their children receive. And we need to know what features of both their beliefs about the child care situation and the actual situation as independently observed make them more or less satisfied with care.

Previous research has found few associations between quality of care and parental satisfaction with care (Kontos, 1994; Shinn, Phillips, Howes, Whitebook, & Galinsky, 1990). This may be due to the fact that parents are not privy to most of what happens during the day when their child is in care. Moreover, parents with very young, nonverbal children are unable to talk with them about their experiences in care and are reliant on indirect cues from children regarding the suitability of the setting—cues that have multiple interpretations. For example, is a mother to interpret a child's separation tears as normal separation anxiety or as a problem with the child care setting? This study provided a unique opportunity to learn more about what makes parents satisfied with family child care and relative care by examining the parents' perceptions of their child's child care setting as compared to independent observations of the setting.

Child care arrangements may affect not only children but the family system, including parents' levels of stress and their ability to hold jobs (Buchanan, 1993). The features of child care that have the greatest impact on parents' well being may well be features that have little influence on children, such as the cost of care or the frequency with which arrangements break down so that the parent must make some alternative plan. Thus, it is important to understand not only how child care affects children but also how it affects their parents.

In this chapter, our investigative lens turns toward parents of children in family child care and relative care, specifically their mothers, because mothers have traditionally been most involved in their children's care and because most children who live in single-parent families live with their mothers. Our assumption is that we must understand the family perspective on child care before we can fully understand the impact of child care on children. To this end, this chapter addresses several questions:

- According to mothers, what constitutes high quality child care? Do mothers who select different types of care define quality differently? Do different ethnic groups of mothers define quality differently?
- What do mothers believe about children's learning in child care and providers' training?
- How do mothers go about selecting care? What do they seek in care? How easy or difficult is it for them to find it?
- How accurate are mothers' perceptions of regulatable aspects of care?
- How do overall quality of care (as observed independently) and particular features of care (as reported by mothers) affect mothers' satisfaction with care and overall well being?

For the most part, this set of analyses uses data from the full sample of 820 mothers (described in Chapter 2). To investigate questions concerning the accuracy of mothers' knowledge of their child care situation and the effects of quality of care (as observed independently of mothers' reports) on their satisfaction with care, we use the smaller, matched subsample of 218 mothers and providers.

MOTHERS' DEFINITIONS OF QUALITY OF CARE

Although there has been debate and discussion in the child care community about what constitutes quality care for children, parents are not necessarily a part of the discussion and emerging consensus, even though it is parents who select child care arrangements for their children. Thus, it is important to understand how parents view quality and what features of care they think are most indicative of quality.

It is also important to understand the extent to which different groups of mothers seek the same elements in a child care arrangement. It seems likely, for example, that mothers who seek relative care may differ from mothers who use family child care providers in their beliefs about the most important features of child care. Similarly, mothers who use regulated and nonregulated family child care providers might value different features of care. There is some evidence that African American and white mothers differ in responses to the Parent as Educator Interview (Schaefer & Edgerton, 1978) about what they believe is most important for young children to learn (Stoakley, 1994). For child care policy, it is important to understand whether the diversity of child care arrangements matches the diversity of values that parents hold for their children, or whether the distribution of children into different arrangements is more haphazard.

To enable us to study these aspects of child care, we asked mothers to rate 19 characteristics of child care arrangements according to "how important you feel each one is to *high quality care* for children (your child's) age." A majority of mothers rated each of the 19 items as "extremely important" or "very important" (1 or 2 on a 5-point scale). Comparisons of mean ratings are complicated by the fact that different groups of mothers used the response scale in somewhat different ways. Latino mothers, on average, rated 11.3 out of 19 items as "extremely important," compared to 10.5 out of 19 for African American mothers, and 9.3 out of 19 for white mothers, a highly significant difference, [$F_{(2, 788)} = 11.13$, $p < .001$]. Thus, we focus initially on within-group rank orders of items, based on importance ratings for different groups.

By Care Arrangement Selected

Table 8.1 lists the features of care in order of their overall ranking, based on mean ratings across all mothers. It also shows the rankings separately for mothers who reported using regulated and nonregulated family child care providers and those who reported using relative care. Finally, it shows rankings for the same items by the sample of child care providers. (Providers initially rated more items; the table shows only items common to both groups.)

TABLE 8.1. RELATIVE IMPORTANCE OF FEATURES OF CHILD CARE TO QUALITY ACCORDING TO ALL MOTHERS, TO SUBSETS OF MOTHERS USING REGULATED AND UNREGULATED FAMILY CHILD CARE PROVIDERS AND RELATIVE CARE, AND TO PROVIDERS

Feature of Child Care	All Mothers (n = 820)	Mothers, by Provider Group			Providers (n = 265)
		Regulated Providers (n = 288)	Nonregulated Providers (n = 267)	Relative Providers (n = 265)	
Attention to children's safety	1	1	1	1	1
Provider's communication with parents about their children	2	2	2	3	4
Cleanliness	3	5	5	2	6
Attention children receive	4	4	4	4	3
Provider's warmth toward children	5	3	3	5	2
Provider's style of discipline	6	8	6	7	11
Attention to nutrition	7.5	9	9	6	5
Provider's experience in taking care of children	7.5	7	7	8	10
The way the provider teaches children to get along with other children	9	6	11	9	6
Number of children for each adult	10	10	10	11	14
Provider's openness to parents' dropping in to see children during the day	11	12	8	10	8
Provider who shares parents' values	12	15	12	12	13
Number of children in the group	13	11	13	15	15
Provider's training in taking care of children	14	14	15	13	16
Care that is available day in and day out	15	13	16	14	12
More like home than school	16	16	14	17	9
Provider with a close relationship to a child's family*	17	18	17	16	19
Provider who is licensed or registered by the state	18	17	19	19	17
Teaching of cultural or religious values	19	19	18	18	18

*Providers had two items: provider who is a relative and provider who is a close friend. Both ranked below all other items, so are combined in last position here.

126

The picture that emerges from Table 8.1 is of overwhelming consensus across the different groups about what is important to high quality child care. The rankings by mothers who used the three types of providers were quite similar, with Spearman rank-order correlations between groups of mothers ranging from .93–.95, $p < .001$. Kendall's Tau b is another measure of the extent to which two groups agree on the relative ranking of all possible pairs of value items. For the three groups of mothers, Tau b ranged from .75–.84, indicating that different groups agreed about relative importance of pairs of items between 88% and 92% of the time. The greatest agreement was between mothers who used relatives and those who used nonregulated family child care providers. All groups of mothers put the same characteristics of care into the top five in importance to quality:

- Attention to children's safety
- Provider's communication with parents about their children
- Cleanliness
- Attention children receive
- Provider's warmth towards children

All felt that having a provider who had a close relationship to the child's family, a provider who was regulated by the state, and the teaching of cultural and religious values were relatively unimportant, although still between somewhat important and very important in mean rating. No item was ranked more than four places apart by any two groups of mothers.

Mothers and providers were also in close agreement about what constitutes quality care. The Spearman rank order correlation was .89, $p < .001$, and Tau b was .72, corresponding to agreement on 86% of relative ranks. Only two items were ranked five or more places apart by the two groups. Providers ranked "more like a home than a school" higher than did mothers; and mothers ranked "the provider's style of discipline" higher than did providers.

By Ethnicity

Table 8.2 presents the relative importance of different features of child care to mothers of white African American, and Latino ethnicity (mothers of other ethnicities are omitted). Again, high levels of agreement were evident across all three groups, but especially for mothers of color. Spearman's rank order correlation ranged from .85 (between whites and African Americans) to .91 (between African Americans and Latinos), $p < .001$ for all three. Kendall's Tau b ranged from .68 to .79, indicat-

TABLE 8.2. RELATIVE IMPORTANCE OF FEATURES OF CHILD CARE TO QUALITY ACCORDING TO MOTHERS OF DIFFERENT ETHNICITIES

Feature of Child Care	All Mothers (n = 791)	White (n = 347)	African American (n = 190)	Latino (n = 254)
Attention to children's safety	1	1	1	1
Provider's communication with parents about their children	2	2	3	4
Cleanliness	3	5	2	2
Attention children receive	4	4	4	3
Provider's warmth toward children	5	3	5	5
Provider's style of discipline	6	6	10	7
Attention to nutrition	7.5	11	6	6
Provider's experience in taking care of children	7.5	8	8	8
The way the provider teaches children to get along with other children	9	10	7	9
Number of children for each adult	10	7	14	11
Provider's openness to parents' dropping in to see children during the day	11	9	12	10
Provider who shares parents' values	12	14	13	13
Number of children in the group	13	12	15	15
Provider's training in taking care of children	14	16	11	12
Care that is available day in and day out	15	13	9	17
More like home than school	16	15	16	16
Provider with a close relationship to a child's family	17	17	17	14
Provider who is licensed or registered by the state	18	18	18	19
Teaching of cultural or religious values	19	19	19	18

Note: Mothers of other ethnicity omitted.

ing between 84% and 89% agreement on relative ordering of pairs of ranks. Again, there was complete agreement about the five most important features of care and the two least important, although not about their exact ordering.

Four items were five or more ranks apart for different groups: white mothers ranked the number of children for each adult as more important than did African American mothers, and both attention to nutrition and the provider's training in taking care of children as less important than did either group of mothers of color. African American mothers ranked care that is available day in and day out as more important than did the other two groups.

Although all groups of mothers showed considerable consensus in their beliefs about the relative importance of different features of care, there were a few differences in mean ratings that are worth highlighting. Because of the overall mean difference in rankings by mothers of different ethnicities, mean differences on individual items are reported only for items that both reached significance, with a Bonferroni correction for multiple tests (p criterion = .0026), and that showed at least twice the magnitude of the average intergroup difference (.40 between largest and smallest scores). Two of the five items that met this criterion are shown in Table 8.3. African American and Latino mothers valued training more than did white mothers, and as in the rank order differences, African American mothers valued care that is available day in and day out more than did the other two groups.

The last three features that were rated differently by the three ethnic groups also showed significant (Bonferroni-corrected) differences between mothers served by the three groups of providers. (No further criterion was used, because these groups of mothers had virtually iden-

TABLE 8.3. ETHNIC DIFFERENCES IN MOTHERS' MEAN IMPORTANCE RATINGS (FOR ITEMS THAT DID NOT DIFFER BY TYPE OF CARE)

	Mothers, by Ethnicity			
Feature of Child Care	White (W) (n = 190)	African American (A) (n = 190)	Latino (L) (n = 254)	F (2,786–787) (Scheffe)
Provider's training in taking care of children	4.03	4.42	4.46	30.34* (L,A > W)
Care that is available day in and day out	4.26	4.52	4.06	18.2W* (A > E > L)

*p < .0026
Note: 5 = extremely important to quality.

tical means across all items: 4.35–4.37.) These were "provider with a close relationship to a child's family," "teaching of cultural and religious values," and "provider who is licensed or registered by the state." In light of these differences, we examined the joint effects of ethnicity and type of care arrangement in predicting mothers' ratings of these characteristics.

Means for mothers' ratings of "provider with a close relationship with a child's family" by mother's ethnicity and type of care are shown in Table 8.4. Two-way analysis of variance showed that the importance mothers ascribed to this feature of care was related to both ethnicity, $[F (2, 781) = 42.26, p < .001]$, and type of care, $[F (2, 781) = 4.19, p < .01]$. Latino mothers valued a close relationship most highly, followed by African American mothers, and lastly white mothers (note that white mothers still rated it closer to "very important" than to "somewhat important," on average). Not surprisingly, mothers who used relative care endorsed this feature most strongly, and mothers who used regulated family child care providers found it least important. There were no interaction effects.

Mothers' ratings of "teaching of cultural and religious values" were also associated with their ethnicity and the type of care they used, as shown in Table 8.5. Latino mothers rated this characteristic of care far higher than did white mothers, with African American mothers intermediate between these groups, but closer to the Latinos $[F (2, 774) = 37.46, p < .001]$. Patterns were similar to those for a close relationship. Mothers served by relatives rated teaching of cultural and religious values as most important, and mothers served by regulated family child care providers rated it as least important, with mothers served by non-regulated providers in between, $[F (2, 774) = 5.97, p < .01]$. There was also a significant interaction between ethnicity and type of care, $[F (4,$

TABLE 8.4. MOTHERS' IMPORTANCE RATINGS FOR "PROVIDER WITH A CLOSE RELATIONSHIP TO A CHILD'S FAMILY" BY MOTHERS' ETHNICITY AND TYPE OF CARE

	Mothers, by Ethnicity		
Feature of Child Care	*White (n = 346)*	*African American (n = 190)*	*Latino (n = 254)*
Regulated care	3.50 (178)	3.94 (67)	4.00 (23)
Unregulated	3.66 (103)	3.95 (43)	4.39 (112)
Relative	4.03 (60)	3.96 (80)	4.34 (*n* = 119)

Note: 5 = extremely important to quality.

774) = 4.42, $p < .01$]. Examination of the means in the table suggests that the overall pattern of variation by type of provider did not hold for African American mothers. The effects of ethnicity were most evident for mothers using nonregulated providers.

Table 8.6 shows mothers' ratings of the importance of "a provider who is licensed or registered by the state" to quality of care. It is not surprising that mothers who used regulated care found licensing more important than did the other two groups; those who used nonregulated care rated this lowest in importance, [$F(2, 780) = 56.02$, $p < .001$]. What is, perhaps, surprising is that Latino and African American mothers, who were less likely to use regulated care, believed more strongly than did whites that licensing is important to quality [$F(2, 780) = 35.18$, $p < .001$]. This parallels the finding that mothers of color valued training more than did white mothers. There was also a significant interaction between ethnicity and type of care, such that Latino mothers varied less across types of care than did other groups in the importance ascribed to

TABLE 8.5. MOTHERS' IMPORTANCE RATINGS FOR "TEACHING OF CULTURAL OR RELIGIOUS VALUES" BY MOTHERS' ETHNICITY AND TYPE OF CARE

| Provider Group | Mothers, by Ethnicity | | |
	White (n = 342)	African American (n = 185)	Latino (n = 253)
Regulated care	2.74 (180)	3.71 (66)	3.35 (23)
Nonregulated	3.02 (103)	3.50 (42)	4.13 (112)
Relative	3.53 (59)	3.60 (80)	4.01 (118)

Note: 5 = extremely important to quality.

TABLE 8.6. MOTHERS' IMPORTANCE RATINGS FOR "A PROVIDER WHO IS LICENSED OR REGISTERED BY THE STATE" BY MOTHERS' ETHNICITY AND TYPE OF CARE

| Provider Group | Mothers, by Ethnicity | | |
	White (n = 346)	African American (n = 189)	Latino (n = 254)
Regulated care	3.86 (183)	4.42 (67)	4.04 (23)
Unregulated	2.59 (103)	3.07 (42)	3.81 (112)
Relative	3.18 (60)	3.55 (80)	3.78 (119)

Note: 5 = extremely important to quality.

licensing [F (4, 780 = 4.26, $p < .01$]. Indeed, Latino mothers using all types of care considered licensing to be as important as did white mothers who used regulated care.

Summary

Perhaps the most important finding to emerge from this examination of mothers' values is the substantial consensus among all groups of mothers about what constitutes quality of care. Mothers of all ethnicities and those who used all types of care agreed that children's safety, provider's communication with parents about children, cleanliness, and the warmth and attention the provider showed children were the features of care most important to high quality. Providers placed these five features in their top six, adding the feature of "attention to nutrition." Agreement on the value of these characteristics of care is supported by our findings that quality care involves warm, sensitive interactions between children and caregivers. Further agreement was expressed by all groups of mothers that having a regulated provider and teaching of cultural or religious values were relatively unimportant. Even Latino and African American mothers who saw these features of care as more important than did whites still rated them lower than the other seventeen features of care. Providers saw licensing as somewhat more important than did mothers, although it was still not high on their lists. Our observational data suggest, contrary to parents' perceptions, that regulation is related to quality of care.

Despite the substantial agreement among different groups of mothers about the *relative* importance of different features of care to quality, and the high rank order correlations, there were some notable differences in *mean* ratings. Mothers of color and mothers who used relative care saw both a close relationship between the provider and the child's family and the teaching of cultural or religious values as more important than did white mothers and mothers who used either regulated or nonregulated family child care. This emphasis on closeness to the family and on religion and culture may be one reason that African American and especially Latino families were more likely to use relative care for their children. White mothers who emphasized these values were also more likely to use relative care.

In light of the fact that African American and especially Latino mothers were *less* likely than were white mothers to use regulated providers, it was surprising that mothers of color saw licensing and training as *more* important to quality than did white mothers. This finding suggests that efforts to train and license both relative and nonrelative providers might be especially welcome in minority communities.

African American mothers also saw care that was available day in and day out as more important to quality than did white and Latino mothers. Because such care facilitates the mother's ability to work, this finding may reflect the substantial level and long history of labor-force participation by African American women.

LEARNING EXPERIENCES AND TRAINING

As another window into mothers' beliefs about quality of care, mothers were asked about two aspects of child care that experts associate with quality. We asked a random half of the mothers we interviewed what sort of learning experiences they thought most important and least important for children their child's age, while they are in child care. The other half of mothers were asked several questions about training for providers (importance, reasons, and type). These questions were open-ended.

Children's Learning in Child Care

A loglinear analysis showed an effect for ethnicity on what mothers believed was most important for their child to learn, [χ^2 (10) = 22.92 $p <$ .05], but not for type of care [χ^2 (10) = 11.53, n.s.]. Table 8.7 shows mothers' answers by ethnicity. Thus, results are reported by ethnic group.

Overall, a majority of mothers (54%) thought that social experiences were most important for children their child's age; this was slightly more true among white mothers (61%) compared with African American mothers (52%) and Latinos (48%). Latinos (22%) and African Americans (20%) were more likely than were whites (10%) to mention edu-

TABLE 8.7. WHAT MOTHERS THINK IS IMPORTANT FOR CHILDREN TO LEARN IN CHILD CARE, BY ETHNICITY

	Mothers, by Ethnicity			
Learning Experiences	All Mothers (n = 392)	White (n = 174)	African American (n = 95)	Latino (n = 106)
Social experiences, communication	54	61	52	4
Educational skills	16	10	20	22
Motor skills	11	13	8	10
Love and trust	7	9	3	7
Discipline	6	3	7	10
Other	6	4	9	3

cational skills. Overall, motor skills were mentioned next most frequently, followed by love and trust, discipline, and a variety of other
topics. Latinos (10%) and African Americans (7%) were more likely than
were whites (3%) to mention discipline.

About a third of the mothers we asked could not say what was
least important for their child to learn: they said they did not know,
that all learning was important, or that no learning was important for
children their child's age. Of the 245 who answered, 45% said academic skills, 13% said cultural or religious values, 7% said watching
TV, 7% mentioned one of a number of self-care skills, 6% said discipline or manners, 5% said schedules, and the remainder listed a great
many other alternatives, from sex education to creative play to bad
habits. When we reduced the codes to three—educational skills, cultural and religious values, and other—and combined relative and nonregulated family child care to increase cell sizes, a loglinear analysis
suggested a significant effect of ethnicity [χ^2 (4) = 18.28, $p < .01$] but
not of type of care [χ^2 (2) = 1.41, n.s.]. White mothers were more likely
to say that academic skills were least important (56%) than were either
African American (35%) or Latino mothers (34%). White and African
American mothers (15% and 14%) were more likely than were Latino
mothers (9%) to say that teaching of cultural and religious values was
least important.

Providers' Training

The random half of mothers who were not asked about learning experiences for their children were instead asked several questions about
training for providers. First, they were asked whether it was important
for the person who cared for their child to have special training. Overall, 71% of mothers agreed that it was, but a loglinear model showed
that this varied by both ethnicity [χ^2 (2) = 12.08, $p < .01$] and type of
care [χ^2 (2) = 11.33, $p < .01$]. There was no interaction. African American mothers were most likely to agree that training was important
(80%), followed by Latino mothers (73%) with white mothers (63%) last.
Mothers who used regulated care were more likely to agree that training was important (79%), followed by mothers who used relative care
(73%), and lastly mothers who used nonregulated care (61%).

Whatever their answers, mothers were asked why they felt that way.
Mothers' reasons for why providers should have training varied by eth-
nicity [χ^2 (8) = 19.26, $p < .05$] but not by type of care [χ^2(8) = 10.72, n.s.].
There was no interaction. These reasons are shown in Table 8.8.

The two most popular reasons mothers gave for why providers
should have special training were so that they could handle special

TABLE 8.8. Mothers' Reasons Providers Should Have Training, by Ethnicity

| | Mothers, by Ethnicity | | | |
| | All Mothers (n = 292) | White (n = 106) | African American (n = 74) | Latino (n = 103) |
Reason				
To handle special problems	32%	38%	20%	33%
For basic child care	30	21	34	38
To understand child development	16	20	23	8
Providers are not born with skills	10	8	11	11
Other	12	13	12	11

TABLE 8.9. Mothers' Reasons Providers Should Not Have Training, by Type of Care

| | Mothers, by Provider Group | | | |
| | All Mothers (n = 118) | Regulated (n = 27) | Non-regulated (n = 52) | Relative (n = 39) |
Reason				
Only common sense and patience needed	44%	57%	50%	25%
Provider is experienced	37	37	40	33
Provider is relative, trust	12	3	0	36
Other	7	3	10	6

problems and in order to learn about basic child care. African American mothers were least likely to endorse the first reason, and white mothers were least likely to endorse the second. The third reason, more popular among African Americans and whites than among Latinos, was to understand child development. About a tenth of the sample said that providers are not born with child care skills. Other reasons, offered by fewer respondents, included obtaining new ideas and support, helping mothers to feel more secure about leaving their children with the provider, and becoming more organized.

Mothers' reasons for why providers should not have training varied by type of care [χ^2 (6) = 28.35, $p < .001$] and by ethnicity [χ^2 (6) = 17.69, $p < .01$] with no interaction effect. Table 8.9 shows reasons by type of care.

Mothers who felt that providers did not need training most commonly felt that common sense and patience were all that was needed (44%) or that the provider's experience was enough (37%). Differences between the groups were due largely to a third of mothers who used relative care answering that the provider did not need training because she was a relative, and the mother trusted her. Mothers who used regulated and nonregulated providers did not offer this explanation. White mothers were most likely to explain that common sense and patience were enough (60%); African Americans and Latinos were more likely to offer the provider's experience (56% and 42%, respectively) as a reason she did not need training.

Whether or not mothers believed that training was important, we asked them what type of training providers should have. Because mothers' answers were highly related to whether or not they thought training was important [χ^2 (6) = 52.65, $p < .001$], we present their answers according to this variable in Table 8.10. Overall, the most popular choices were CPR (emergency resuscitation techniques) and safety, child development, basic child care needs, and experience with her own children. Mothers who did not believe training was important were less likely than were other mothers to offer the first three types of training, and more likely to say providers needed experience, love and patience, or no training at all.

Next we examined associations of ethnicity and type of care with the first four answers in Table 8.10, eliminating "other," "none," and "love and patience" as answers. A loglinear model suggested that type of care was not important [χ^2 (6) = 8.98, n.s.] but that ethnicity was [χ^2 (6) = 21.24, $p < .01$]. Answers by Latino mothers were very close to those of the sample as a whole. African Americans were more likely than were other groups to say that providers needed training in child development (33%). Whites were more likely to mention safety and CPR.

TABLE 8.10. TYPE OF TRAINING PROVIDERS SHOULD HAVE BY IMPORTANCE OF TRAINING TO MOTHERS

	Mothers, by Importance of Training		
Type of Training	All Mothers (n = 404)	Not Important (n = 117)	Is Important (n = 287)
CPR & safety	39%	34%	41%
Child development	20	9	24
Basic child care needs	15	13	16
Experience with own children	13	23	9
Love and patience	5	8	4
None	4	12	1
Other	3	2	4

Summary

Mothers' beliefs about what children should learn in child care, and about what training providers should have, offer another window into their views of quality care. Again, there was considerable, but not total, consensus across different groups of mothers. A majority of mothers felt that the social experience of being in child care was more important than particular skills, although a substantial minority of both Latino and African American mothers believed children should gain educational skills.

Nearly three quarters of mothers thought that providers should have training, and this was especially true for African American mothers and for those who used regulated care. The minority who disagreed felt that experience, or common sense and patience, were enough. Those who felt that providers should have training mentioned training in safety and CPR and training in basic child development as important. The first, which would enable the provider to handle special problems or emergencies, was more likely to be endorsed by white mothers. African American mothers were more likely to think the provider needed training in child development. The interest of African American, and, secondarily, Latino mothers in training mirrors their greater emphasis on training as a characteristic of care that was important to quality, and again suggests that training programs for family child care and relative care providers might be especially welcome in African American and Latino communities. Although mothers who used relative providers were less likely than were those who used regulated care to value training, they were more likely to endorse training than were those who used nonregulated care, and they did not differ in the types of training they thought valuable. This suggests that training programs for family child care providers should be open to relative providers as well.

SELECTING CHILD CARE

Now we turn to the process of seeking and settling on a child care arrangement. We explore how mothers found their provider and why they selected her. Parents may select child care on the basis of beliefs, such as those we have just explored, on the basis of quality of care, or on other bases, such as availability, cost, or convenience. Parents' values are most likely to be a factor if there are multiple child care options available for them to choose among, but this is not always the case. Thus, to explore the extent to which the process of selecting care reflected parental values, we also explored how difficult mothers found the search for child care, their reasons for selecting their provider, and whether they had more than one satisfactory arrangement from which to choose.

Ways of Learning About Providers

Obviously, mothers who chose relatives to care for their children knew the provider before placing a child with her. The way that other mothers first learned of their family child care provider varied according to whether or not she was regulated [χ^2 (5) = 104.81, $p < .001$]. As shown in Table 8.11, four fifths of mothers who used nonregulated providers either knew the provider personally or were referred to her by a friend, neighbor, or relative. Mothers who used regulated providers found them in more varied ways. A third were referred to the provider by someone they knew. Fifty-seven percent of mothers (approximately one fifth for each reason) already knew the provider, used advertisements, or used resource and referral assistance. Not surprisingly, a majority of providers located via resource and referral were regulated.

Difficulty in Finding Care

Reports of difficulty in finding care were bimodal, with 48% of mothers finding it "very easy" or "somewhat easy," but 45% finding it "very difficult" or "somewhat difficult." A two-way analysis of variance found

TABLE 8.11. How Mothers Who Used Regulated and Nonregulated Family Child Care Providers First Learned About Their Provider

	Mothers, by Provider Group		
Source of Information	Nonregulated (n = 265)	Regulated (n = 262)	Total (n = 527)
Knew provider already as friend, neighbor, or day care center staff member	52%	19%	36%
Referred by friends, neighbors, or relatives	30	31	31
Ads, bulletin boards, newspaper, yellow pages	10	18	14
Resource and referral service	2	20	11
Referred by another provider	3	8	5
Referred by other community organization	2	4	3

Note: Regulated relatives are omitted from this table. Mothers were not asked how they first learned about their relatives, regardless of regulatory status.

a main effect of type of care on ease of finding care [F (2, 782) = 31.97, $p < .001$] but no effect of ethnicity [F (2, 782) = .10, n.s.]. There was a significant interaction between ethnicity and type of care [F (4, 782) = 3.20, $p < .05$]. Mothers who used relative providers found it substantially easier to find care (mean of 3.8 on a 5-point scale, where 5 is "very easy") than did mothers who used either regulated or nonregulated family child care providers (means of 2.9 and 2.8, respectively). White mothers who used regulated care and African American and Latino mothers who used nonregulated care reported particular difficulty in finding care. Among mothers who used nonrelative providers, there were few differences in ease of finding care between those who knew the provider previously (2.9), those who were referred by friends (2.8), and those who used other sources (2.6) [F (2, 524) = 1.61, n.s.].

Another measure of difficulty in finding care is the length of the search process. Overall, mothers spent a median of two weeks between the time they started looking for care and the time they made final plans for their child to stay with the provider. A substantial number spent much longer, however. A quarter of mothers spent six weeks or more, and 10% spent four months or more looking for care. Mothers who used relative providers found care much faster, with a median of just 2 days between the time they started looking for care and the time they made final plans. This time was highly variable: the middle half of the distribution spent between 0 days and 1 month. For mothers who knew the provider previously, the median time was 2 weeks, with the middle half of the distribution between 2 days and 2 months. Mothers who were referred by a friend spent longest—a median of 4 weeks—with the middle half of the distribution between 1 week and 2 months. Mothers who answered ads or got referrals from friend or neighbor resources, or from referral services or other organizations, spent a median of 3 weeks looking, with the middle half between 1 week and 1 month.

A two-way analysis of variance (on log-transformed data, to reduce skewness) showed effects of both type of care F (2, 774) = 11.13, $p < .001$] and ethnicity [F (2, 774) = 8.78, $p < .001$] on the time it took mothers to find care. Mothers who used relatives, and Latino mothers, found care faster than did other groups. There were no interaction effects. Not surprisingly, time spent looking for care (log transformed) was correlated with perceived difficulty of finding care for all mothers (r *(810) = .38, p < .001)*.

Reasons for Selecting a Provider

We asked mothers to indicate up to two reasons why they selected the provider they did and coded their responses. These reasons, shown in Table 8.12, were quite different for mothers who used different types of

TABLE 8.12. MOTHERS' REASONS FOR SELECTING CHILD CARE ARRANGEMENT BY TYPE OF CARE

| | Mothers, by Provider Group | | | | | |
| | Reason 1 | | | Reason 2 | | |
Reason	Relative (n = 265)	Nonregulated (n = 266)	Regulated (n = 288)	Relative (n = 262)	Nonregulated (n = 267)	Regulated (n = 287)
Prefers family	55%	1%	5%	12%	1%	2%
Provider's personality, experience	5	16	18	7	9	11
Trust, reliability	14	13	11	17	8	10
Knew provider previously	1	21	12	1	4	3
Children's interactions with provider, one another	4	11	15	8	10	8
Convenience (hours, location)	4	8	8	21	23	24
Cleanliness, safety, nutrition	3	7	7	8	13	12
Cost	7	4	4	12	13	10
Home environment	2	2	8	1	2	4
Cultural or religious values	1	5	3	2	5	1
Quality (unspecified)	2	4	3	6	3	2
Group size or ratio	0	4	4	1	3	5
Availability, no choice	3	3	1	3	3	2
Other	0	1	2	0	1	4

care [χ^2 (26) = 414.91 for the first reason; and χ^2 (26) = 94.4 for the second— $p < .001$ for both].

Mothers who used relative care gave a preference for family as the primary reason they chose their care arrangements in over half of all cases. Trust in the provider, or the sense that she was reliable, was the second most popular choice. Mothers who used family child care providers also made selections on the basis of their knowledge of or faith in the provider: Among those using both regulated and nonregulated providers, knowing the provider previously, her personality or experience, and trust in her were among the most popular answers. Altogether, 84% of mothers using relative care, 64% of mothers using nonregulated family child care providers, and 61% of mothers using regulated providers mentioned at least one of these four reasons for selecting care; 27% of mothers who used relatives, 11% of those using nonregulated providers, and 12% of those using regulated care mentioned two of these reasons [χ^2 (4) for 0, 1 or 2 mentions by type of care = 58.33, $p < .001$].

Formal credentials did not figure among mothers' primary reasons for selecting care: Altogether, only 3 mothers out of 820 mentioned the provider's education and 4 mentioned her regulatory status (in all but one case, as a secondary reason for selecting care). Although these were not salient issues to mothers, we wondered whether providers whom the mother believed to be regulated were more likely to elicit their trust. This turned out not to be the case. Citing trust and reliability or the provider's personality and experience as either of the two reasons for selecting a provider was not associated with mothers' beliefs that the provider was regulated [χ^2 (1) = 0.7, n.s. (analysis omitted mothers who used relative providers)].

Cost and/or convenience were mentioned either first or second by 41% of mothers, most typically as their second reason for selecting care; 4% of mothers mentioned both these reasons. There were no differences in whether these were mentioned by type of care [χ^2 (2) = 0.52, n.s.]. The child's interactions with the provider or with other children were mentioned more frequently by mothers using family child care (20% for nonregulated providers, 22% for regulated ones) than by mothers using relative care (12%) [χ^2 (2) = 11.07, $p < .001$], as was cleanliness, safety, and nutrition (19% each for mothers using nonregulated and regulated providers versus 11% for mothers served by relatives [χ^2 (2) = 9.58, $p < .01$]. Other characteristics of care—including a home-like environment, teaching of cultural or religious values, group size or ratio, and unspecified aspects of quality—were mentioned by only small proportions of mothers.

Care Options Considered

We asked mothers whether they "seriously consider(ed) using other providers or types of providers, such as a daycare center, nursery school, care in someone else's home, care in your own home, or staying home yourself" before they chose their current child care provider. Overall, 62% of mothers seriously considered other options, but this percentage was much higher among mothers who used regulated family child care (73%) than it was among mothers who used relative care (49%), with mothers who used nonregulated family child care in-between (65%) [χ^2 (2) = 34.49, $p < .001$].

Whether mothers who used nonrelative care seriously considered other providers or other options for care was associated with how they located care [χ^2 (5) = 13.78, $p < .05$]. Of mothers who knew the provider themselves, 61% considered other options. Of those who were referred by friends, other providers, or resource and referral services, 70%–75% considered other options. Finally, of those who answered ads or used other referral sources, 80%–88% considered other options. In other words, the more impersonal the search process, the more likely it was that mothers considered other options. Almost all mothers reported that they visited the provider's home to see how their child would be cared for, including 93% of mothers who had a personal contact with the provider and 99% of those who did not [χ^2 (1) = 11.2, $p < .001$].

Of all mothers who seriously considered other options, nearly two thirds (63%) were unable to find a single other choice they considered "satisfactory." Of those who succeeded in locating other satisfactory care, 57% found one alternative to the provider they chose, 33% found two, and 10% found three or more. A two-way analysis of variance revealed that there were no effects of type of care actually used or of mother's ethnicity on the number of satisfactory choices found [F (2, 480) = 0.61, n.s. for type of care and 2.30 for ethnicity, n.s.].

Preference for Other Child Care Arrangement

Twenty-eight percent of mothers said that they would have preferred some other child care arrangement rather than the provider they used. A loglinear analysis showed independent, additive effects both for types of care [χ^2 (2) = 19.95, $p < .001$] and for ethnicity [χ^2 (2) = 15.51, $p < .001$]. The percentage of mothers who would have preferred some other arrangement was highest for mothers using nonregulated family child care providers (34%), followed by those using regulated family child care providers (29%), and lowest for mothers served by relatives (2%).

African Americans were more likely to prefer another form of care (37%) than were Latinos (27%) and whites (24%).

Among the 227 mothers who would rather have had some different form of care, 39% preferred a center, school, or Head Start program and 19% preferred to care for their child themselves. These alternatives were followed by family child care (by a different provider, in the case of those who already used this arrangement) (14%); in-home care (13%); relative care (or care by a different relative) (13%); and assorted other arrangements. Because patterns for African American and Latino mothers were quite similar, these groups were collapsed, as were relative and nonregulated providers, post hoc, in a loglinear analysis, which showed a significant difference between white mothers and mothers of color in preferred alternative arrangement [χ^2 (4) = 13.84, $p < .01$]: A significant effect of present care arrangements [χ^2 (4) = 12.72, $p < .05$] but no interaction. White mothers were more likely than were the combined group of African Americans and Latinos to want in-home care (22% vs. 8%) or to stay home to care for the child (28% vs. 14%); mothers of color were more apt to prefer center-based care (48% vs. 27%). Similarly, mothers currently using nonregulated or relative care were more apt than those using regulated care to prefer centers (52% versus 21%).

Summary

Neither cost nor convenience nor quality of the child's experience in care were the primary reasons that mothers selected child care. Rather, mothers wanted to feel comfortable with the provider, because she was "family," because they knew her previously, because of her personality or experience, or simply because they trusted her. These reasons correspond to two of those at the top of parents' list of what constitutes quality care—namely safety and the provider's communication with parents about their children—but are at odds with the much lower placement of "provider with a close relationship to a child's family" in mothers' hierarchy of features important to quality care. Comfort with the provider was especially important for mothers who selected relative care, who also saw a close relationship as somewhat more important to quality.

Mothers' fifth most popular reason for selecting care, children's interactions with the provider and with one another, corresponds more closely to their beliefs that the provider's warmth and her attention to children are important to quality. Perhaps a family member, someone the mother knows or trusts, or someone with a good personality or experience may be presumed to be warm and attentive to the child as well, but this is not obvious.

Cost and convenience figured prominently as secondary reasons for choosing child care arrangements for all three groups of mothers. Other characteristics of care, as they would affect children, were not high on anyone's list, but were mentioned more often by mothers who chose regulated or nonregulated provider arrangements.

Although mothers frequently mentioned trust in the provider, or her personality and experience as a reason for selecting her, they almost never mentioned formal credentials, such as education and regulatory status. Nor was regulatory status related to these aspects of comfort with nonrelative providers. Although regulatory status did not appear to influence mothers' selection of care, it might directly or indirectly influence their satisfaction with care. We examine predictors of satisfaction, and other maternal outcomes, later in this chapter.

Mothers' reasons for selecting care fit with their patterns of seeking it: Half of those who used regulated family child care providers, four fifths of those who used nonregulated providers, and presumably all of those who used relatives selected someone with whom they had a previous relationship or who was recommended by a friend, neighbor, or relative. The more personal the contact, the less likely the mother was to seek other options. Mothers who used relative care also reported that care was easier to find and spent less time looking than did mothers who used other forms of care.

Although many mothers, especially those who chose relative providers, found care quickly and easily, nearly half of the mothers surveyed said that finding care had been somewhat difficult or very difficult, and 10% spent four months or more looking. Of the three fifths who seriously considered other options, nearly two thirds were unable to find a single satisfactory alternative to the provider they chose. Perhaps parents stopped looking once they had found a satisfactory arrangement. This would correspond to Simon's (Simon, 1956) notion that consumers often "satisfice" rather than optimize in making choices. A more pessimistic view is that parents may have been discouraged from seeking alternative care arrangements by the fact that few were available, much as discouraged workers leave the labor force. In support of this view is the finding that over a quarter of mothers—and over a third of African American mothers—settled for an arrangement other than the one they would have preferred at the time they selected their provider Parents may have difficulty assuring that their children have high quality care if there are no alternative arrangements from which to choose.

In addition to having options, parents must have an accurate view of different child care arrangements if they are to make choices that reflect their values. The next section explores the extent to which parents have the information they need to make informed choices.

MOTHERS' PERCEPTIONS OF REGULATABLE ASPECTS OF CARE

Mothers who select family child care and relative care are often in a good position to know a great deal about the provider. In our sample, 36% of mothers who were not related to their providers knew them previously as friends or neighbors, or as daycare center staff members, and three quarters of mothers (76%) reported they had dropped in during the day to see how things were going in the past three months. This proportion did not differ by type of care [χ^2 (2) = 2.43, n.s.]. Parents are also likely to see the care arrangements at drop-off and pick-up times, although these may not be representative times as far as group size and ratio are concerned.

To determine how accurate mothers' perceptions of care are, we turn to the subsample of matched mothers and providers who are the subject of the rest of this book. Because of problems in communications among research sites, there were a few cases in which we were not certain of the correct match between a mother and a provider. Thus, analyses are confined to the 218 pairs for which we could verify a correct match.

Questions with which we could compare mothers and providers were largely confined to regulatable aspects of care. On the mothers' side, all data are derived from self-report interviews. For providers, data may come from either the provider herself or from the observers who visited providers in their homes, or, in the case of regulatory status, from government records.

We checked the accuracy of mothers' reports against state licensing lists for the subset of 218 mothers for whom we also had provider data, and hence access to the state information (the cases include providers who were relatives, but overrepresented regulated providers, since we had matches for all providers from the reverse sample but not for all mothers selected from the community sample.). This comparison suggested that mothers were reasonably accurate. In 89 of the cases, mothers reported that the provider was not regulated; in 86 of these cases she was correct (97% accurate). In 125 cases the mother reported the provider was regulated, and in 106 of these she was correct (85% accurate). We believe that some of the divergent cases were ones in which the provider's license or registration had expired, unbeknown to the mother and, in some cases, unbeknown to the provider as well. Thus, overall, mothers were accurate in 192 of the 214 cases in which they believed that they knew the provider's licensing status, or 90% of the time.

In spite of this high accuracy rate for mothers' knowledge of regulatory status, we should not expect perfect agreement among these sources for other regulatable aspects of care. A single person, asked the same question at two points a month apart, will often not give the same answer. Answers are more likely to be the same for factual information than for opinions, but factual situations, such as the number of children in a group, can change over time, and providers and mothers were typically interviewed from 10 days to a month apart. Also, even apparently factual situations may be subject to interpretation. Does the number of children in care include the child who comes after school on two days a week or only children who are there all day every day? Observers see only what is happening on the day that they visit. Although they have the advantage of bringing a common frame of reference to a variety of family child care and relative care situations, they sample only a single day. To the extent that some features of care, such as the number of children or number of providers present, varies across days (for example, because a child is sick or a new child enrolls in care) this will also reduce the correspondence between mothers' and observers' ratings.

Table 8.13 shows correlations between mothers and observers for number of children in care, number of adults providing care, and the ratio of children to caregivers. It also shows correlation among mothers' and providers' reports regarding the provider's training and experience. The table shows correlations between mothers and either observers' or providers' reports for the full sample and for different types of care.

In the full sample, mothers' reports were reasonably but variably accurate, sharing between 8% and 58% of the variance with observers' and providers' reports. Correlations tended to be highest in this sample, where there was the most variability, but in general, type of care did not appear to be consistently related to the size of correlations.

Mothers were more accurate with respect to observable aspects of care—such as number of adults, number of children, and ratio—than with respect to the provider's training and experience. Mothers also reported on the number of children in each of four age groups, with reasonable accuracy for the three youngest age groups under 6 (r (188-196) ranged from .55–.67]. Their accuracy dropped somewhat for children over 6 (r (180) = .34) where children were probably not in care for full days.

Mothers' reports of whether the provider had training in child care were correlated more highly with providers' reports of their general level of formal education (r (178) = .44) than with providers' reports of whether they had in fact had family child care training (r (180) = .28). The difference between the correlations was significant (t (177) = 2.27,

TABLE 8.13. CORRELATIONS BETWEEN MOTHERS' PERCEPTIONS AND OBSERVERS' OR PROVIDERS' REPORTS OF CHARACTERISTICS OF CARE ARRANGEMENTS BY TYPE OF CARE

Characteristics of Care Source of Data Correlated With Mother's Report	Mothers, by Provider Group			
	All Mothers (n = 180–216)	Regulated (n = 92–108)	Nonregulated (n = 40–56)	Relative (n = 47–52)
Number of children (observer)	.76***	.60***	.73***	.59***
Number of adults caring for children (observer)	.54*** .01	.69***	.16	
Ratio of children to adults (observer)	.61*** .50***	.36***	.50***	
Training in child care (provider)	.28*** -.02	.11	.11	
Child care training (mother's report) with level of education (provider's report)	.44***	.27**	.34*	.35*
Years of experience (mother categorized, provider continuous)	.29***	.32***	.33*	.26

*p < .05; **p < .01; ***p < .001

$p < .05$) and the same pattern appeared in each subgroup. Mothers' reports of the providers' experience were only modestly correlated with the providers' own reports.

Summary

Overall, mothers seemed to have a fairly accurate understanding of the regulatable aspects of their child care arrangements, including whether the provider was regulated, how many children there were in what age groups, and how many adults cared for them. They knew less, but still a reasonable amount, about the provider's training and experience. Where mothers made errors, they were frequently understandable, for example, taking overall level of education to stand for training in child care.

RELATIONSHIP BETWEEN QUALITY OF CARE AND MOTHERS' SATISFACTION AND WELL BEING

Little is known about how global quality and specific characteristics of care affect parents, mothers in particular. A number of studies have documented parental satisfaction with their family child care arrangements (reviewed in Kontos, 1992) but that satisfaction with care is uncorrelated with quality (Kontos, 1994). There is growing evidence, however, that parental perceptions of child care (e.g., satisfaction, supportiveness) are related to maternal well being (Buchanan, 1993). It is to these issues that we now turn in the following sections.

Effect of Quality of Care

First we examine mothers' evaluations of global and process quality. As our measures of quality, we took FDCRS scores and ratings of detachment, sensitivity, and restrictiveness on the Arnett measure, as described in Chapter 4. Mother's global satisfaction with child care was a three-item index (alpha = .73) assessing overall satisfaction, whether or not the respondent would send her child to the provider if she "had to decide all over again," and whether or not the respondent would recommend the provider to a friend. Items were z-scored because the response scales were not comparable.

In addition to satisfaction, we considered three other aspects of mothers' well being that might be related to their child care arrangements. The first two of these were derived from Hock's (Hock et al., 1983) measure of Maternal Separation Anxiety. We took the highest loading items from two of the three subscales of the original measure, including all seven items on the child benefits subscale and the 11 highest-loading items of the separation anxiety subscale. One item was later deleted from the original seven items of the child benefits subscale because it failed to load on either subscale in a two-factor solution and reduced the alpha. The remaining six-item child benefit subscale had an alpha of .65; a sample item is "Exposure to many different people is good for my child." The 11-item maternal separation subscale had an alpha of .83; a sample item is "When I am away from my child, I feel lonely and miss (him/her) a great deal." The two subscales were uncorrelated ($r(818) = .02$), and each was retained separately for analyses. Mothers responded on a 5-point Likert scale ranging from "strongly agree" to "strongly disagree." An average item score for each subscale was created, for which a higher number indicated more separation anxiety or more perceived benefits to maternal separation from the child. We anticipated that mothers using high quality family child care or relative care would be more satisfied with it, that they would be more likely to believe that their child benefits from being in care, and that they would experience less separation anxiety.

Because child care arrangements may contribute to stress as well as to satisfaction, we also assessed the relationship between high quality care and a measure of maternal stress. This was a six-item index (alpha = .74) assessing how often, in the past 3 months, the respondent felt overwhelmed or unable to cope. A sample item is "That you could not cope with all the things that you had to do." Items were measured on a 5-point frequency scale from "very often" to "never," and summed to create a total score. A higher score indicates more stress.

Table 8.14 shows correlations between the four measures of global quality based on observer ratings and the four measures of maternal well being. Evidence of a relationship between maternal well being and quality of care is exceedingly modest. Four of the sixteen correlations were significant at the .05 level, and none exceeded .3 in magnitude. There is some suggestion from the table that overall quality, as measured by the FDCRS, was mildly related to global satisfaction and negatively related to separation anxiety. Detachment was positively, and sensitivity negatively, related to separation anxiety. No aspect of quality was even marginally related to maternal stress or to the mothers' perception that the child benefits from being in care. There was no evidence of stronger effects in the subgroups based on type of care.

When partial correlations were calculated controlling for mother's education, ethnicity, family income, and the child's age, all the previously significant correlation coefficients became nonsignificant. One new correlation (out of 16) emerged, but in the opposite direction to that predicted: The provider's rated sensitivity was negatively related to the mother's perception that the child benefited from being in care.

TABLE 8.14. CORRELATIONS BETWEEN OBSERVATIONAL MEASURES OF QUALITY AND MATERNAL SATISFACTION AND WELL BEING (*N* = 209-217)

	FDCERS	Detachment	Sensitivity	Restrictiveness
Global satisfaction	.14*	-.10	.08	-.00
Stress	-.04	.07	-.04	.00
Child benefits	.00	-.01	-.08	.04
Separation anxiety	-.29**	.16*	-.23**	-.04

*p < .05; **p < .001
Only correlations marked *** are significant with a Bonferroni correction for 16 tests (new *p* criterion = .003).
Note: all significant correlations become non-significant when demographic variables are partialled.

Effect of Particular Aspects of Care

This last section of the chapter describes associations between mothers' satisfaction with particular aspects of care and maternal well being (mothers' global satisfaction with care, their belief that their child benefits from being in care, their separation anxiety, and their levels of stress). Using multiple regression analysis, we attempted to predict maternal well being with three clusters of predictor variables: characteristics of care, satisfaction with particular facets of care, and job characteristics. Demographic characteristics (mother's age, education, and ethnicity, as well as age of the child) were controlled.

Job characteristics (job autonomy and job demands) were included because of their possible relevance to stress and anxiety. Job autonomy is a four-item index (alpha = .66). A sample item is, "I have a lot of say about what happens on my job." Job demands is a five-item index (alpha = .73). A sample item is, "My job requires working very hard." Both were measured on 5-point Likert response scales, from "strongly agree" to "strongly disagree."

Nine characteristics of care as described by mothers (e.g., ratio, hours per week, whether the provider was regulated or a relative) were chosen to represent a larger set of features of care. Where potential predictors were highly correlated (e.g., group size and adult–child ratio; regulatory status and training), characteristics were chosen to represent the larger set, based on conceptual importance, accuracy of perceptions in the subsample in which we had observational data, and low amounts of missing data. We subjected these nine perceived characteristics of care to a principal components analysis to reduce the number of variables further (see Appendix B for details). Three factors emerged that explained 52% of the variance in the set of nine variables (see Table B.1 in Appendix B). The three factors are: professional provider, friendly communication, and availability.

The measure of facet satisfaction with child care involved mothers rating their satisfaction with 23 aspects of care on 5-point Likert-style scales. An initial factor analysis produced a 5-factor solution: satisfaction with size, satisfaction with parental needs, satisfaction with the provider, satisfaction with warmth, and satisfaction with shared values. One item—satisfaction with the location—failed to load on any factor. Because the five satisfaction indices were highly correlated, we subjected them to a secondary principal components analysis, which suggested that all loaded on a single-facet satisfaction index. Details regarding the factor analysis of facet satisfaction are presented in Appendix B.

Analysis Plan

Four separate hierarchical regression analyses were conducted predicting mothers' global satisfaction with care, their belief that their child benefits from being in care, their separation anxiety, and their levels of stress. These outcomes had little variance in common: The maximum correlation among them was $r(818) = .21$, $p < .001$, between separation anxiety and stress.

At the first step, child's age, mother's education, family income, and two dummy variables describing mother's ethnicity (to indicate African American versus Latino versus white) were entered as control variables. At the second step, the three factors describing characteristics of care, as perceived by mothers, were entered. These were entered before satisfaction, because they represented mother's perceptions of factual situations (e.g., Is the provider a relative?) rather than her more global evaluation of these characteristics. At the third step, the single factor representing mothers' satisfaction with all facets of care was entered. Finally, because overall stress levels and attitudes of employed mothers may depend on their job situations as well as on their child care situations, two job variables—autonomy and demands—were entered. Table 8.15 shows the relative importance of each set of variables to each outcome, as determined by the percentage of variance explained. Table B.2 in Appendix B presents Beta weights showing the relative contribution of each potential explanatory variable to the out-

TABLE 8.15. Relative Importance of (Percentage of Variance Explained by) Predictors of Mothers' Outcomes

Predictor Set	Global Satisfaction	Benefits to Child	Separation Anxiety	Stress
Demographics (5 variables)	.02*	.01	.23***	.01
Characteristics of care (3 variables)	.13***	.02**	.01*	.04***
Facet satisfaction (1 variable)	.32***	.00	.02***	.03***
Job characteristics (2 variables)	.00	.01	.02***	.09***
Total (may not add due to rounding)	.46***	.04**	.27***	.17***
$F(11,757)$	59.19	2.87	26.24	13.93

*$p < .05$; **$p < .01$; ***$p < .001$

comes. We describe these results below. Where it is useful to understand what particular features of care or elements of satisfaction contributed to results, we refer to the second set of analyses (not tabled),
which included the individual child care characteristics and five satisfaction indices rather than the global indices.

Global Satisfaction. Global satisfaction was modestly associated
with the family's demographic characteristics. In particular, family
income was positively associated with satisfaction [Beta = .11, $p < .05$].
However, the association disappeared after characteristics of care,
including the cost of care, were included in the equation. Not surprisingly, characteristics of child care, as perceived by mothers, were highly
related to maternal satisfaction, explaining 13% of the variance. The
most important predictor was friendly communication [Beta = .34, $p <
.001$], followed by availability [Beta = .09, $p < .01$]. All three aspects of
friendly communication—perceiving the provider as a friend, feeling
encouraged to drop in, and talking with the provider about the child—
made an independent contribution when individual characteristics
were entered into the equation. Of the two variables that make up availability of care, only "not having to make special arrangements because
the provider was unavailable" contributed to satisfaction. Professional
care was not initially important, but made a significant contribution
after all other variables were entered into the equation [Beta = .11, $p <
.01$]. In particular, mothers were more satisfied with more expensive
care. Friendly communication dropped to marginal significance after
facet satisfaction was entered, and availability dropped out altogether.

Satisfaction with the various facets of child care was strongly associated with global satisfaction [Beta = .65, $p < .001$]. This finding is not especially interesting, because one would expect global satisfaction to be
related to facet satisfaction. When individual satisfaction indices were
included in the equation rather than the combined index of facet satisfaction, 4 of the 5 indices made separate contributions. Only satisfaction
with size was unimportant. Most important, by far, were satisfaction with
shared values and with the provider's warmth. Satisfaction with the extent
to which the provider met the parent's needs and with the provider's qual-
ifications were of secondary importance, although still highly significant.

Job characteristics did not contribute to global satisfaction with
child care. This remained true even when satisfaction with facets of
care was removed from the equation, leaving more variance to be
explained by the job variables.

Benefits to Child. Only characteristics of child care arrangements
predicted the mother's perception that her child benefited from child

care. Neither the family's demographic characteristics, the mother's satisfaction with care, nor characteristics of the mother's job explained a significant proportion of variance. In particular, having a more professional provider was positively associated with the mother's belief that her child benefited from being in care [Beta = .17, $p < .001$]. When variables from this set were entered into the analysis separately, having a relative as a provider was negatively associated with the perception that the child benefited, and having a higher ratio of children to caregivers was positively associated with the perception that the child benefited. After the facet satisfaction subscales were entered into the equation, friendly communication emerged as a marginally positive predictor of child benefits, but no individual characteristic of care emerged to explain this further.

Maternal Separation Anxiety. Demographic factors were by far the most important predictors of maternal separation anxiety. Higher levels of household income and maternal education were associated with lower levels of separation anxiety [Beta = $-.24$, $p < .001$ and $-.11$, $p < .01$, respectively]. Latino and other ethnicity, as compared to African American and white ethnicity, was also associated with substantially higher levels of separation anxiety [Beta = .27, $p < .001$]. Interestingly, age of child did not contribute to separation anxiety. All of these factors retained their significance, and very nearly their size, in the final equation.

The set of characteristics of care explained a modest 1% of variance in separation anxiety, but none of the individual predictors reached significance. Friendly communication and availability were both marginally associated with lower levels of separation anxiety when initially entered into the equation. These factors dropped out when other predictors were entered, but having a professional provider was marginally associated with lower levels of separation anxiety in the final equation.

Satisfaction with care was associated with lower levels of separation anxiety and explained 2% of the variance [Beta = $-.16$, $p < .001$]. Job characteristics also explained 2% of the variance, with job demands associated with higher levels of anxiety [Beta = .14, $p < .001$].

Maternal Stress. Although maternal stress was modestly correlated with separation anxiety, their predictors were quite different. Demographic factors did not make a significant contribution to explaining stress. Child care characteristics explained 4% of the variance, with a professional provider associated with *increased* stress [Beta = .13, $p < .01$], and friendly communication associated with reduced stress [Beta = $-.13$, $p < .001$]. Only professional providers retained a marginally significant level of predictive power in the final equation. At the level of individual characteristics of care, having a provider whom the mother considered to be a friend was associated with lower stress. A larger ratio, and "having to make special arrangements because the provider was unavailable," were associated with increased stress.

Satisfaction with care was associated with reduced stress [Beta = −.21, $p < .001$], explaining 3% of the variance. Job characteristics contributed most, explaining 9% of the variance. Job demands were associated with increased levels of stress [Beta = .27, $p < .001$] and job autonomy was associated with reduced levels [Beta = −.13, $p < .002$]. After job demands were entered, only satisfaction with care retained any independent predictive power. At the level of specific facets of satisfaction, only satisfaction with parental needs and shared values were important.

Summary

Although mothers were reasonably knowledgeable about the regulatable aspects of their child care arrangements, consistent with past research (Kontos, 1994; Shinn et al., 1990) they were not more satisfied with care rated by observers as being of high quality. Observed quality of care was unrelated to maternal stress or to perceptions that the child benefits from care, and was only modestly related, in the expected directions, to separation anxiety. However, even this relationship disappeared after controlling for mothers' demographic characteristics. If mothers do not recognize those aspects of quality of care that observers rate, there is no reason to expect that they will seek out these aspects of quality for their children.

The four maternal outcomes had entirely different patterns of predictors. Separation anxiety was explained largely by characteristics of the mothers themselves, and only secondarily by characteristics of the child care arrangements and of the job. Indeed, the patterns of association suggest that causality may be reversed: Mothers who are more anxious may be somewhat less satisfied with child care and perceive their jobs as somewhat more demanding and stressful.

Stress, or feeling overwhelmed and out of control of one's life, was primarily associated with characteristics of the job. Satisfaction with child care, particularly aspects of child care that eased parents' lives and with shared values, also contributed to lower levels of stress. Satisfaction with parent needs, such as schedule flexibility and continued availability of care, may have facilitated parents' ability to work. Satisfaction with shared values may have reduced anxiety associated with children's safety and appropriate care. Aspects of care that affected children's psychological well being, such as warmth and attention, were unrelated to maternal stress.

Global satisfaction with care and the perception that the child benefits from being in care were both predicted by characteristics of the care arrangements, the first strongly, and the second modestly. Appropriately, job characteristics made no contribution. Mothers were more satisfied with care that met both their children's needs and their own. Friendly communication with the provider and care that was regularly available were especially important. Mothers were also more satisfied with more professional care, especially higher priced care, but only after all other variables were in the equation.

Professional care was the primary predictor of the perception that the child benefits from care. The negative association between having a relative as a provider and the perception that the child benefits from care corresponds to the earlier finding that mothers perceived care by a provider with a close relationship to the family as relatively unimportant to high quality care. Friendly communication with the provider was marginally important.

Focusing on predictors, rather than outcomes, we see that demographic factors were important only to separation anxiety, which was negatively related to mothers' socioeconomic status and positively related to Latino ethnicity. Having a relative as a provider was negatively associated with separation anxiety, but also negatively associated with the perception that the child benefited from care. Having a regulated provider also reduced separation anxiety. More generally, the professional care factor was associated with global satisfaction and the perception that the child benefited from care, but also with marginally higher levels of separation anxiety and stress.

Friendly communication between parent and provider was always at least marginally beneficial to maternal well being, being particularly important to global satisfaction (before facet satisfaction was entered) and to reduced stress. Availability also increased satisfaction and marginally reduced separation anxiety and stress. Facet satisfactions were obviously associated with global satisfaction and also with reduced separation anxiety and stress, but not with the perception that the child benefited from care. Different facets of satisfaction mattered for different outcomes. Satisfaction with parental needs was associated with lower levels of both separation anxiety and stress; satisfaction with size was associated with lower separation anxiety, and satisfaction with shared values with reduced stress. All facets of satisfaction except size were associated with global satisfaction, but especially shared values and attention.

Job characteristics were not associated with global satisfaction with child care or with the perception that the child benefited from care, but were associated in the predicted direction with stress and, to a lessor extent, with separation anxiety.

CONCLUSIONS

It is noteworthy that mothers, regardless of income or ethnicity, agree on the essential components of quality and that these essential components concur with those given priority by providers. Although this consensus is useful for the field, it is a matter of concern that neither mothers nor providers perceived regulation or training as important to quality. Because our data show that these aspects of quality are crucial, this will be a priority for child care consumer education.

Mothers' criteria for selection of family child care or relative care arrangement (comfort and trust as opposed to "credentials") are consistent with their definition of quality. The results suggest, contrary to popular opinion, that cost and convenience are not the primary selection criteria. Should mothers learn to associate comfort and trust with regulation and training rather than with familiarity, the chances of their selecting quality child care might be increased.

The selection process, as described by mothers, may be better described as a "search" process in light of the fact that two thirds of mothers say they had no other choice than the one they are now using. It is clear from the perspective of family child care and relative care users that the principle of family choice underlying some funding policies has not become a reality for many parents.

These data suggest that parents are knowledgeable about the regulatable aspects of their child's family child care or relative care arrangement but appear to be less sensitive to process aspects of quality, if satisfaction with care is a reliable indicator. Because parents seem capable of observing some aspects of quality, it is reasonable to assume that, with additional assistance, they could learn to observe other aspects as well, such as provider sensitivity.

Although global satisfaction with care was not related to quality, the results of the regression analyses indicated that maternal well being (including global satisfaction) was affected by friendly communication with the provider, more professional and regularly available care, and care that met the child's and mother's needs. Thus, mothers cannot be portrayed as being insensitive to variations in the characteristics of care.

9

The Impact of Quality of Care on Children

E ach family whose provider participated in our study was represented by a child in family child care and relative care referred
to throughout as a "target" child. In this chapter, we describe
the development of these children. There is a rich literature describing the development of children in child care, the majority of it concerned with child care centers (for a review, see Howes & Hamilton,
1993). Although children enter child care influenced by experiences
within their families, the development of children who attend child care,
particularly when assessed in child care settings, is still partially a
product of the child care environment (Howes & Hamilton, 1993). In
this chapter we first describe the development and behavior of the target children in the three provider groups (regulated, nonregulated, and
relative) and their daily activities. We then discuss how variations
within the providers' homes in our study are related to the behavior
and development of the target children.

The target children averaged 26.3 months of age ($SD = 11.87$, range
= 10–65). Forty-three percent of the children were girls. There were
no differences among provider groups in age or sex of children.
Because preliminary analyses revealed that quality of the child care
setting was similarly associated with children's development across
the three primary ethnic groups (white, African American, and Latino),
the analyses were conducted on all the children together, controlling
for family socioeconomic status and ethnicity.

COMPARISONS OF DEVELOPMENT AND BEHAVIOR IN THE THREE TYPES OF CARE

We examined four aspects of children's development: social, emotional, cognitive, and language. The measures of these four developmental domains were selected based on their theoretical and practical relevance to children's development in child care and on their successful prior use in child care research. Children's social development was measured through observations of children's peer play. Emotional development was assessed via an observation of attachment security and a provider rating of child behavior problems. Cognitive development was measured through observations of children's object play. Language development was assessed via a provider rating of children's use of language in child care. The provider ratings were appropriate only for children 30 months of age or older.

Cognitive and Social Development

During the 2-hour observation of the target child and provider, the observer coded four 5-minute time samples of the social behavior and activities of the child. The time samples were spaced evenly throughout the observation period. Each 5-minute time sample was broken into fifteen 20-second intervals.

Interobserver reliability on these measures was established to an 82% agreement (agreements/agreements+disagreements) for all behaviors in an interval prior to data collection. Interobserver reliability was reestablished at the midpoint of data collection. Median reliability scores from these reliability checks ranged from kappa = .80 to kappa = .93 (median = .87).

Play with Peers. Children's play with peers was coded using a revised version of the Howes Peer Play Scale (Howes, 1980; Howes & Matheson, 1992). The Peer Play Scale has acceptable stability over time and can be used as a marker of social competence with peers (Howes, 1988; Howes & Matheson, 1992). There are six scale points, ranging from parallel play with no mutual awareness to pretend play with meta-communication. Low-level peer play includes the bottom three levels: parallel play with and without mutual regard and simple turn-taking. High level peer play includes the top three levels: complementary and reciprocal games (e.g., run-chase); cooperative social pretend; in which the actions of one child reflect an understanding of the actions of the other (e.g., tea party); or complex social pretend play, in which roles are named and the play script is discussed.

Seventy-six percent of the target children had similar-aged peers available for play. Regulated (95%) and nonregulated (74%) providers were more likely than were relative (39%) providers to have available peers [χ^2 (2) = 62.03, p < .0001]. When there were peers available, children spent on average 54% (*SD* = .27, range = 0–.98 percent) of the observation period engaged in parallel peer play, the lowest level involving a peer. Twenty-seven percent of the children engaged in some form of high-level play with peers.

There were significant multivariate differences among provider groups in play with peers [(*F* (6, 430) = 15.73, p < .001]; see Table 9.1. Because older children play in more complex ways than younger children do, the low- and high-level play scores are standard scores with the variance attributable to age removed. Children with regulated providers spent more time with peers but more of their play was low level. Children in relative care spent less time with peers, but their play was more complex. This finding may not be generalizable because a very low percentage (17%) of the children in relative care engaged in high-level play.

Object Play. Object play reflects the cognitive development of the children. The complexity of the children's object play was assessed with an adaptation of Smilansky's (1968) (Howes & Stewart, 1987) cognitive

TABLE 9.1. COMPARISONS OF TARGET CHILDREN'S PLAY WITH PEERS, BY PROVIDER GROUPS

	Children, by Provider Group			
	Regulated (n = 112)	*Nonregulated* (n = 60)	*Relative* (n = 54)	*F-tests/ Scheffe/χ^2*
Percentage of time spent with peers	61%	46%	34%	12.90* Reg > Nonr, Rel
Low-level play	.66	.04	-.89	11.61* Reg > Nonr, Rel
Percentage of children who engaged in high level play	36%	25%	17%	2.99
High-level play	-.06	-.15	1.28	4.93* Rel > Reg, Nonr

*p < .01

play scale. Frequency of children's play was coded into one of six categories: no cognitive play (e.g., talking to a peer), functional play without objects, functional play with passive use of objects, functional play with active use of objects, constructive play, and dramatic play. Constructive and dramatic play are considered to be high level; the other four categories are considered low level.

Children spent most ($M = 72\%$, $SD = .23$, range $0 = 1.0$) of the observation period playing with toys or other objects. Forty percent of the children engaged in high-level object play.

There was a significant multivariate difference among provider groups in play with objects [$F (6, 430) = 2.72$, $p < .01$]; see Table 9.2. Because older children play in more complex ways than younger children do, the low- and high-level play scores are standard scores with the variance attributable to age removed. Children with regulated providers engaged in more frequent high-level play than did children with relative providers. In addition, a chi-square analysis revealed that more children in regulated and nonregulated care engaged in high-level play than in relative care.

Emotional Development

There were two measures of emotional development, one observational and the other a provider rating.

Attachment Relationship with the Provider. The child's attachment relationship with the provider refers to the child's emotional security

TABLE 9.2. COMPARISONS OF TARGET CHILDREN'S PLAY WITH OBJECTS, BY PROVIDER GROUPS

	Children, by Provider Group			
	Regulated ($n = 112$)	Nonregulated ($n = 60$)	Relative ($n = 54$)	F-tests/ Scheffe/χ^2
Percentage of time spent with objects	75%	69%	68%	1.90
Low-level play	-.11	-.27	.11	.97
Percentage of children engaging in high level play	33%	26%	14%	11.59*
High-level play	.26	-.01	-.62	7.03* Reg > Rel

*$p < .01$

with the provider. Children who are more emotionally secure with their providers in child care are better able to use the materials and resources available in the child care setting and to form competent and trusting relationships with peers when they are older (Howes, Matheson & Hamilton, 1994; Howes & Smith, 1994).

In order to assess the children's attachment relationships, we observed each child with the provider for a minimum of two hours during the scheduled visit described in Chapter 2. Following the observation, the observer completed the 90-item Attachment Q-Set (AQS) (Waters & Deane, 1985) by sorting each item into one of nine piles according to how typical it was of the child. If an item was not seen, it was placed in the middle pile. For no item was the modal score 5, which would have indicated that the item was usually placed in the middle pile.

Observers were trained to an 85% exact agreement criterion on each item prior to data collection. Interobserver reliability checks were conducted throughout data collection. Median interobserver reliability was Kappa = .85.

Each child was classified into one of three attachment behavioral profiles based on a profile analysis of AQS subscales completed on this sample plus a center-based child care sample (Howes & Smith, in press). In this classification scheme, the "difficult" profile is characterized by low avoidance, high difficult negotiation and low positive negotiation behaviors. The "avoiding" profile is characterized by high avoidance, low secure base and low comfort-seeking behaviors. The "secure" profile is characterized by low avoidance, high secure base and high comfort-seeking behaviors.

In secure attachment relationships, children exhibit behaviors indicating that they feel trusting and secure with the provider. For example, if children fall down, they look to the provider to give comfort. In anxious/difficult relationships, children are not able to be comforted by the provider. Such children may initially look to the provider for comfort, but if the provider picks them up, the children are apt to bite, arch their back, scream, and otherwise resist the provider's comforting. In anxious/avoidant relationships, children will actively avoid the provider or behave as if the provider does not exist. If these children fell down, they would not look to the provider for comfort and would refuse to acknowledge the provider if she approached.

In addition to a security classification, each child received a security score from the AQS. To obtain security scores, the raw scores from the AQS were correlated with the criterion scores provided for security by Waters & Deane (1985). The correlation coefficients are the children's security scores. A higher score indicates greater security.

Target children's security scores averaged .33 (*SD* = .24 range = −.48 to .75). There were no differences among security scores in provider groups. Fifty percent of the children were classified in the secure, 34% in the avoiding, and 16% in the difficult attachment behavior profile. In low-to-moderate quality child care centers, approximately 50% of the children are securely attached (Howes et al., 1992). In contrast, approximately two thirds of the children are secure when observed in good quality centers (Howes & Hamilton, 1993) or with their mothers (Ainsworth, Behar, Waters, & Wall, 1978). In our study, children were no more likely to be attached to relative providers than to nonrelative providers.

Behavior Problems. Providers completed the Behar Preschool Behavior Questionnaire (PBQ) (Behar & Stringfield, 1975) for all target children who were at least 30 months of age. This instrument is specifically designed to screen preschool-aged children in group care settings for aggression, anxiety, and hyperactivity. It has been used successfully in the past in child care research (Kontos, 1991; Phillips, Scarr, & McCartney, 1987). Behar (1977) reports test-retest reliability of .93 (aggression), .60 (anxiety), and .94 (hyperactivity) and inter-rater reliability of .84. The scale differentiates between children attending a therapeutic nursery and a normative sample (Behar, 1977). The scale ranges from 1–3. A higher score indicates more behavior problems. Because of relatively few items on the subscales and the low reliability for the anxiety subscore, an average item score across the three subscales was used for this analysis. Internal consistency for the total score was .86 (Cronbach's alpha). The average item score was 1.35 (*SD* = .25, range 1 to 2.43). This means that the average provider reported that the target child had very few behavior problems. There were no differences in reported target child behavior problems among provider groups.

Language Development

Providers completed the Adaptive Language Inventory (ALI) (Feagans & Farran, 1979) for all children at least 30 months of age. The ALI was developed for adults to rate children's use of language related to comprehension, production, rephrasing, spontaneity, listening, and fluency. Like the PBQ, it has also been used successfully as a caregiver rating in child care research (Kontos, 1991; Phillips et al., 1987). Preschool ALI scores predict second-grade reading achievement (Feagans, Fendt & Farran, 1991). The ALI consists of 18 items, each rated on a 5-point scale. A higher score indicates higher communicative competence. Intraclass correlations for the subscales range from .76 to .93

(D. Farran, personal communication, 1984). Internal consistency of the total scale for this sample was .94 (Cronbach's alpha). The average score for target children in our study was 3.32 (*SD* = .52, range = 2.5–3.78). This means that, on average, providers reported that target children were using language appropriate for their age. There were no differences between provider groups in adaptive language scores.

Summary

The developmental assessments of the target children present a mixed picture. Although providers report that target children 30 months of age and above had few behavior problems and exhibited age appropriate use of language, only half of the children were considered to be securely attached, that is, to be emotionally secure with their provider. This is surprising because the smaller, more intimate character of family child care and relative care might be expected to produce greater emotional security. This is also a cause for concern because emotional security is a basic requirement for concurrent and future adaptive development

Only about one quarter of the target children engaged in high-level peer play and only 40% of the target children in high-level object play, taking into account their age. This is less than would be expected according to developmental norms and suggests that children in family-based care are not experiencing caregiving environments likely to promote optimal development. It is important to note that the provider reports of children's development (behavior problems and adaptive language) are more optimistic and reassuring about children's development in care than were our observers' assessments, based on the behaviors they saw in the child care environments. The inconsistency may result from the fact that providers rated different aspects of children's development than observers assessed, or that providers have had much more exposure to the children's behavior than observers have had. Also, observers use a standardized system of observation, whereas providers have no standard point of comparison. Nonetheless, these data suggest that researchers must assess the validity of provider reports of children's development, particularly when providers vary widely in educational level and have relatively low levels of training in child development.

DAILY ACTIVITIES IN CHILD CARE

In order to understand the activities of children and providers during the day in family child care and relative care, we interviewed providers about how they organized their day and we observed the activities of the target children. Because family child care and relative care has been a private, informal child care arrangement, relatively little is known about the daily activities (Kontos, 1992). In selecting our interview questions and observational categories, we were cognizant of debates within the family child care community over the relative importance of every-day, home-like activities (e.g., matching socks as they come out of the dryer; setting the table for lunch) and more traditional learning experiences (playing with leggos or puzzles; art projects). Our intent was to sample both of these activity categories.

We found that children and their providers spent their days in a variety of activities. The activities of the target children are depicted in Table 9.3. We calculated the hours per weekday mornings, assuming that this accounted for 14.5 hours per week. Using this formula, stimulating activities are probably overreported because target children and providers are observed in the mornings, when planned activities are most likely to occur, as opposed to meals, nap time, or late afternoon, when such activities are less frequent.

Children spent most of the observation time with manipulatives (puzzles, leggos) and in gross motor activities (running around) and the least amount of our observation time playing with blocks and taking care of younger children. These activities differed by provider groups [multivariate F (32, 404) = 1.99, $p < .001$]. Children with regulated providers spent more time listening to stories. Children with nonregulated providers spent more time with adult commercial TV, and children with relatives spent more time in indoor, gross-motor play (e.g., roughhousing on the sofa).

Summary

Recall that most of the providers in our sample typically perceived family child care and relative care as a home-like, informal, unstructured child care arrangement. This is consistent with the relatively high frequencies of gross-motor indoor and outdoor play, unoccupied and onlooker behavior, and TV watching we observed. However, we also observed substantial amounts of more typical preschool activities: manipulative play, fantasy play, art, and stories. Although some believe that family child care and relative care is an ideal environment for learning through everyday activities, we saw very little of this type of activity. It is, of course, possible that these occur earlier in the morning or later in the afternoons (or when observers were not present).

TABLE 9.3. PERCENTAGE OF OBSERVATION PERIOD AND EQUIVALENT HOURS PER WEEK THAT TARGET CHILDREN SPENT IN VARIOUS ACTIVITIES

| Activities | Percentage of 2-hour Observation Period, by Provider Group | | | | Conversion to h/wk |
	Regulated (n = 112)	Non-regulated (n = 60)	Relative (n = 54)	F-tests/ Scheffe	All Provider (n = 226)
Unoccupied	.04	.05	.05	.51	.6 h
Onlooker	.06	.08	.06	1.45	.9 h
TV					
Children's noncommercial	.03	.05	.08	2.36	.6 h
Children's commercial	.02	.03	.04	1.22	.5 h
Adult commercial	.002	.05	.02	3.79* N > R	.3 h
Art					
Open-ended	.07	.06	.03	1.49	.9 h
Product-oriented	.03	.02	.002	2.49	.3 h
Manipulatives	.25	.19	.20	1.75	3.3 h
Blocks	.01	.01	.01	.29	.2 h
Fantasy play	.07	.12	.07	.96	1.2 h
Stories	.08	.05	.02	5.52** R > Rel	.9 h
Music	.04	.03	.02	.96	1.5 h
Gross motor					
Indoors	.10	.15	.19	5.53** Rel > R	2 h
Outdoors	.15	.09	.10	1.71	1.8 h
Everyday activities (e.g. folding clothes)	.03	.04	.04	.05	.5 h
Taking care of younger children	.005	.002	.000	.58	.1 h

$*p < .05; **p < .01$

RELATIONSHIP OF QUALITY OF CARE, DAILY ACTIVITIES, AND FAMILY CHARACTERISTICS TO CHILDREN'S DEVELOPMENT

Our next task was to determine how children's development is affected by their daily activities in family child care and relative care and by the quality of care they are receiving, taking into account family characteristics that are likely also to be a factor. Previous research on quality in family child care reported in Chapter 1 supported our hypothesis of a positive relationship between quality and children's development. More specifically, we expected provider sensitivity and responsivity to be associated with attachment security in the child. We also expected more peer play to occur in homes with more children and more high-level object play in homes with higher global quality scores (because global quality captures both the quality of play materials and adult interaction with children). We also expected more behavior problems and less advanced use of language for children in low-quality child care.

Quality and Children's Development

What difference does quality of the child care home make to children's development? To investigate this question, the peer play, object play, and attachment security measures (the child development variables available for all target children) were correlated with structural, process, and global quality. Results are presented in Table 9.4. Of the structural quality measures, only group size and ratio were related to children's play or attachment. Larger groups and more children per adult positively predicted amount of peer and object play. When providers exhibited more low-level involvement, children engaged in less object play and in less high-level object play. When providers exhibited more responsive involvement, children engaged in more object play and in more high-level object play, and were rated as more securely attached to the provider. Limit setting was not related to children's play or attachment security. When providers were rated as more sensitive, target children were more likely to be engaged in object play and in high-level object play, and were more likely to be securely attached. Providers' self-ratings of nurturance positively predicted amount of high-level peer and object play. Providers' self-ratings of restrictiveness positively predicted amount of object play, high-level object play, and attachment security. Global quality positively predicted children's object play, high-level object play, and attachment security.

Another way to examine the effect of quality on children's development was to test for differences as a function of the level of quality offered by their provider (inadequate, adequate/custodial, good). We used analysis of covariance to examine differences in children's attachment security to providers, peer play, object play, language (score on the Adaptive Language Inventory), and behavior problems (scores on the Preschool Behavior Questionnaire) when global quality was inadequate, adequate/custodial, or good. We controlled for race, family income, and maternal education of the child. Children in family child care and relative care homes with good or adequate/custodial global quality scores

TABLE 9.4. CORRELATIONS OF CHILDREN'S OBJECT AND PEER PLAY AND ATTACHMENT SECURITY WITH STRUCTURAL, PROCESS, AND GLOBAL QUALITY

Quality	Peer Play	High Peer Play	Object Play	Low Object Play	High Object Play	Attachment Security
Structural						
Group size	.21**	.09	.16*	-.07	.11	-.01
Ratio	.22**	.05	.15*	-.12	.10	-.01
Formal training	.06	.09	-.02	-.09	.05	.01
Informal training	.13	-.06	.12	-.11	.09	.08
Process						
Observations						
Low Involvement	-.05	-.02	-.25**	.04	-.23**	-.37**
Responsive involvement	-.03	-.08	.30**	.07	.30**	.38**
Limit-setting	-.07	-.06	-.07	.12	-.07	-.09
Ratings						
Sensitivity	.09	.01	.20**	.09	.20*	.39**
Restrictiveness	.13	.12	-.10	-.12	-.04	-.12
Detachment	.11	.06	-.07	-.10	-.13	-.28**
Self-ratings						
Nurturance	.08	.14*	.09	-.07	.14*	-.07
Restrictiveness	.03	-.11	.18*	.01	.20**	.14*
Global						
FDCRS	.05	-.15*	.23**	.07	.22**	.18**

$*p < .05; **p < .01$

167

had higher security scores than did children in family child care and relative care homes with unacceptable global quality scores [F (2, 209) = 3.37, p = .04, Scheffe = .05]. There was a multivariate main effect for level of global quality on peer play [F (6, 312) = 3.12, p = .006]. Children in family child care and relative care homes with adequate global quality scores had more low-level peer play than did children in homes with either inadequate or good global quality scores [F (2, 157) = 8.49, p = .001]. There were no differences in total peer play or high-level peer play. Comparable analyses for object play, language, and behavior problems revealed no differences as a function of level of quality.

Daily Activities and Children's Development

To learn about how children's development relates to their involvement in daily activities in child care, the measures of children's development were correlated with the frequency of children's involvement in fantasy play, stories, blocks and manipulatives, adult commercial TV, children's commercial TV, gross motor play, music, everyday tasks, being unoccupied, and onlooking.

Attachment Security. Children's score for attachment security to providers was correlated with their involvement in daily activities. Children who engaged in less onlooking [r = −.16, p < .02] and more everyday tasks [r = .16, p < .02] were more securely attached. There were no other significant associations with daily activities.

Peer Interaction. Children's peer interaction variables were correlated with their involvement in daily activities. Results of these correlations are reported in Table 9.5. Children engaged in more peer interaction when they were involved in more fantasy play and in less blocks/manipulative activities. Amount of children's high-level peer interaction was positively correlated with involvement in fantasy play.

Object Play. Overall amount of object play, amount of low-level object play, and amount of high-level object play were correlated with the frequency of involvement in various daily activities in the family child care home. Results of these correlations are presented in Table 9.6. Children exhibited more object play when they were involved in more fantasy play, more blocks and manipulatives, and less adult commercial TV, unoccupied and onlooking. Children engaged in more low-level object play when they were involved in more gross motor, music, and everyday activities and less unoccupied and onlooking. Children engaged in more high-level object play when they were involved in more fantasy play, watched less adult commercial TV, and did less onlooking.

TABLE 9.5. CORRELATIONS OF CHILDREN'S PEER INTERACTION WITH DAILY ACTIVITIES

Activities	Peer Interaction	High-Level Peer Interaction
Fantasy	.37*	.43*
Stories	.05	-.09
Blocks/mManips.	-.15*	-.10
Adult comm. TV	-.05	-.03
Child comm. TV	-.02	-.03
Gross motor	.03	.09
Music	-.10	-.08
Everyday	.008	-.02
Unoccupied	-.01	.01
Onlooking	.12	-.03

*$p < .01$

TABLE 9.6. CORRELATIONS OF CHILDREN'S OBJECT PLAY WITH DAILY ACTIVITIES

Activities	Object Play	Low-Level Object Play	High-Level Object Play
Fantasy	.25**	-.01	.38**
Stories	.07	.07	.05
Blocks/Manips.	-.09	.14*	-.04
Adult Comm. TV	-.15*	.003	-.13*
Child Comm. TV	.11	-.04	.06
Gross motor	.05	.23**	-.03
Music	.08	.19**	.10
Everyday	-.02	.17**	-.02
Unoccupied	-.13*	-.15*	-.09
Onlooking	-.21**	-.20**	-.24**

*$p < .05$; **$p < .01$

Language and Behavior Problems. There were no significant associations between children's scores on these measures and their involvement in the daily activities of the family child care or relative care home.

Summary

Results of these analyses indicate that process and global quality are important predictors of children's object play and attachment security with providers. For structural quality, only group size and adult–child ratio were predictors of children's development, specifically the amount of peer and object play. Engaging in more fantasy play and more blocks/manipulative activities appeared to be associated with more

high-level peer and object play. Frequently being unoccupied or onlooking was associated with less desirable child outcomes. Children's language and behavior problems were not related, either to quality or to
daily activities.

FAMILY CHARACTERISTICS AND
MATERNAL WORKING CONDITIONS

As indicated in Chapter 8, understanding the development of children
in child care requires paying attention to the context of both home and
child care. In this chapter, we address how family characteristics and
maternal working conditions are related to children's development.
Maternal age and education, family income, maternal marital status
(dichotomously coded "single" versus "partnered"), maternal stress
(Cohen et al., 1983), and maternal separation anxiety (Hock, et al., 1983)
were correlated with attachment security, children's object play (amount
and amount of high level), children's peer play (amount and high level),
language development (based on scores from the Adaptive Language
Inventory), and behavior problems (based on the total score from the
Preschool Behavior Questionnaire). The latter two measures were
administered only for children 30 months of age or older. Results of
these correlations revealed that significant associations were relatively
few in number and small in size. Children's attachment security was
negatively correlated with maternal stress [$r = -.14$, $p < .05$]. Amount of
children's object play was correlated with maternal age [$r = .17$, $p < .05$],
maternal education [$r = .19$, $p < .19$], family income [$r = .16$, $p < .05$],
and maternal separation anxiety [$r = -.20$, $p < .01$]. Amount of children's
high level object play was correlated with maternal education [$r = .23$,
$p < .01$], family income [$r = .17$, $p < .05$], and maternal separation anxiety [$r = -.16$, $p < .05$]. Attachment security, play with peers, language
development, and behavior problems were not correlated with family
characteristics. Maternal marital status and stress were not correlated
with peer play, object play, language development, or behavior problems.

  These data indicate that children's object play is more frequent and
more likely to be high level when their family is on a higher socioeconomic level and when their mother has less separation anxiety. In this
sample, separation anxiety was significantly negatively correlated with
the family socioeconomic characteristics [r's $= -.41$ to $-.22$, p's $< .01$].
Thus, it may be that the association of object play with maternal separation anxiety is mediated by family socioeconomic status.

  Mothers' reports of hours worked weekly, job autonomy, and job demands were correlated with children's attachment security, peer play, object play, language development, and social adjustment. There were no significant associations.

Process and Structural Quality

We know from analyses reported above how providers' global quality category was related to children's development. Surprisingly, global quality category was only related to attachment security and to low-level peer play. It was important to go a step further, however, and learn if the children's interactions with the providers (process quality) and regulatable characteristics of the child care settings (structural quality, e.g. adult–child ratio, group size) contribute substantially to children's development after controlling for the child's family socioeconomic status (SES—maternal education and family income) and child care history (length of time with current provider). It was unnecessary to include child age in the analyses because the measures of levels of peer and object play already have the variance due to age removed.

Hierarchical multiple regression analysis was conducted for attachment security with provider to determine if structural (ratio and group size) and process quality (sensitivity and responsive provider interactions) predicted them after family SES and child care history were taken

TABLE 9.7. HIERARCHICAL MULTIPLE REGRESSION OF ATTACHMENT SECURITY ON FAMILY SOCIOECONOMIC STATUS, CHILD CARE HISTORY, STRUCTURAL QUALITY, AND PROCESS QUALITY (BETAS FOR EACH VARIABLE AT EACH STEP REPORTED)

Predictor	Step 1	Step 2	Step 3	Step 4
Family income	.10	.10	.12	.04
Maternal education	.11	.11	.11	.17
Number of months in care with provider		-.03	-.03	-.05
Ratio			.06	.05
Group size			-.12	-.14
Responsive				.28*
Sensitive caregiving				.40*
R-square (model)	.01	.01	.02	.31
F (model)	.67	.48	.42	6.05**
R-square (change)			.01	.29
F (change)				21.83
				$p < .001$

$n = 189$
$*p < .01; **p < .001$

into account (see Table 9.7). Responsive caregiving and sensitivity were the only predictors of attachment security, accounting for 29% of the variance over and above the other variables. Children who have more sensitive and responsive providers are more likely to be securely attached.

Hierarchical multiple regression analyses were conducted for amount of peer play and high-level peer play using an identical model of predictors and control variables as described above. Structural quality was a significant predictor of total amount of peer play, accounting for six percent of the variance. Children in family child care and relative care with more children, and more children per adult, engaged in more peer play (see Table 9.8). There were no predictors for high-level peer play.

Identical hierarchical multiple regression analyses were conducted for amount of object play and amount of high-level object play (see Tables 9.9 and 9.10). Family SES, child care history, structural quality and process quality each made a significant contribution to the variance in the amount of children's object play. Children who engage in more object play are those whose mothers are more educated, have spent more time with their provider, are in homes with more children

TABLE 9.8. HIERARCHICAL MULTIPLE REGRESSION OF AMOUNT OF PEER PLAY ON FAMILY SOCIOECONOMIC STATUS, CHILD CARE HISTORY, STRUCTURAL QUALITY, AND PROCESS QUALITY (BETAS FOR EACH VARIABLE AT EACH STEP REPORTED)

Predictor	Step 1	Step 2	Step 3	Step 4
Family income	.15	.15	.10	.09
Maternal education	-.18*	-.18*	-.19*	-.19*
Number of months in care with provider		.07	.08	.07
Ratio			.16	.16
Group size			.11	.10
Responsive				-.05
Sensitive caregiving				.07
R-square (model)	.025	.029	.091	.097
F (model)	2.44	1.92	3.71**	2.74**
R-square (change)		.004	.06	.005
F (change)		NS	6.23	.55
			$p < .01$	NS
df	2,187	3,186	5,184	7,182

$n = 189$
$*p < .05; **p < .01$

TABLE 9.9. HIERARCHICAL MULTIPLE REGRESSION OF FREQUENCY OF OBJECT PLAY ON FAMILY SOCIOECONOMIC STATUS, CHILD CARE HISTORY, STRUCTURAL QUALITY, AND PROCESS QUALITY (BETAS FOR EACH VARIABLE AT EACH STEP REPORTED)

Predictor	Step 1	Step 2	Step 3	Step 4
Family income	.10	.09	.07	.03
Maternal education	.15	.15	.14	.11
Number of months in care with provider		.22**	.23**	.27***
Ratio			.20	.24*
Group size			-.007	-.06
Responsive				.26***
Sensitive caregiving				.04
R-square (model)	.047	.093	.13	.20
F (model)	4.63	6.39	5.55	6.51
	$p < .05$	$p < .001$	$p < .001$	$p < .001$
R-square (change)		.046	.038	.07
F (change)		9.50	3.97	7.89
		$p < .01$	$p < .05$	$p < .001$
df	2,187	3,186	5,184	7,182

$n = 189$
*$p < .05$; **$p < .01$; ***$p < .001$

TABLE 9.10. HIERARCHICAL MULTIPLE REGRESSION OF COMPLEXITY OF HIGH-LEVEL OBJECT PLAY ON FAMILY SOCIOECONOMIC STATUS, CHILD CARE HISTORY, STRUCTURAL QUALITY, AND PROCESS QUALITY (BETAS FOR EACH VARIABLE AT EACH STEP REPORTED)

Predictor	Step 1	Step 2	Step 3	Step 4
Family income	.09	.09	.08	.05
Maternal education	.18*	.18*	.17*	.15*
Number of months in care with provider		.02	.03	.07
Ratio			.13	.16
Group size			-.03	-.07
Responsive				.23**
Sensitive caregiving				.04
R-square (model)	.06	.06	.07	.12
F (model)	5.83	3.91	2.483	3.71
	$p < .01$	$p < .01$	$p < .05$	$p < .01$
R-square (change)		0	.01	.05
F (change)		NS	NS	5.55
				$p < .01$
df	2,187	3,186	5,184	7,182

$n = 189$
*$p < .05$; **$p < .01$

per adult, and have providers who engage in more responsive interactions with them. Children who engaged in more high-level object play were those whose mothers were more educated and whose providers engaged in more responsive interactions with them.

▬▬▬▬▬▬▬
Summary

These data indicate that children's cognitive development, as reflected in their object play, is related to family characteristics (socioeconomic status), activities in family child care and relative care, as well as structural and process quality of the family child care and relative care. Maternal education and responsive provider interactions were the two most important predictors of children's object play. Family characteristics were unrelated to attachment security or peer play. The most important predictors of attachment security were sensitive and responsive provider interactions, whereas the most important predictor of peer play was structural quality. These results are consistent with previous research revealing that children's cognitive and social development is enhanced by responsive provider interactions (Howes & Hamilton, 1993; Howes et al., 1992; Kontos et al., in press) after family SES is controlled. Children engaged in more but not higher quality peer and object play when there were more children in the home.

Contrary to expectation, neither children's language development nor social adjustment were predicted by any aspect of family or child care characteristics. Both of these were measured by questionnaires completed by the providers themselves. Although child care providers have been shown in previous studies to be reliable raters of children's behavior (e.g., Kontos, 1994; McCartney, 1983), that may not have been the case in the present study, where the diversity of the sample was so great.

Maternal working conditions and number of hours worked were surprisingly unrelated to children's development. These results are *inconsistent* with the results of the National Child Care Staffing Study Family Study (Howes et al., in press) and were unexpected based on the diversity of the sample.

CONCLUSIONS

The overall picture presented for children's development and activities in child care is consistent with the picture of typical quality in family child care and relative care. On average, children are not exhibiting optimal behavior and development in environments that typically are not developmentally enhancing. In light of this consistency, the number and size of relationships between children's development and child care quality were less than expected. Attachment security and object play were the most strongly related to global and process quality. Peer play was associated with structural quality—adult–child ratio and group size. Language and behavior problems were not related to any aspect of quality. One reason for these findings may be that, for the observational measures of children's development, the means were low and the ranges were restricted, thus restricting the size of the associations. Moreover, we indicated earlier that we had concerns about the potential for inflated means with the provider ratings of language and behavior problems and about the advisability of relying on provider ratings when the provider group is so heterogeneous in terms of educational background. Thus, the results may be a reflection of measurement issues.

Our results for peer play suggest that having more peers with which to interact is more important to high-level peer interactions than anything the providers may do or say. In contrast, object play appears to be more sensitive to the provider's behavior and to the overall quality of the family child care or relative care home. These results reveal that when providers do not offer child-centered activities, and when there is little joint involvement in activities between children and adults, we see low levels of object play. Does this mean that object play is simply a reflection of how well equipped the child care setting is? Perhaps this is partially true. We submit, however, that opportunities to engage in higher levels of object play are developmentally enhancing, and that children who have more opportunities to engage in them will be more cognitively advanced as a result. In other words, a developmentally enhancing environment encourages or subtly "pushes" children to higher levels of development and makes learning exciting for them. Observing children engaging in low-level object play in family child care or relative care suggests that they are being deprived of the developmental benefits of higher level play because of the custodial quality of the setting. Thus, children's object play may be a reflection of the quality of the environment, as well as a reflection of the extent to which the environment has "pushed" the child's cognitive development.

The overall lack of associations between children's development and family characteristics and maternal working conditions suggests that our child outcomes were not sensitive to these factors, particularly to working conditions. We might have been better able to describe the correlates of maternal working conditions if we had observed children's play at home (in addition to child care) and attachment security to mothers (in addition to providers).

10

Effects of Regulation on Quality

U
nanimity does not exist on the purpose and effect of regulation on family child care. Some have assumed that, like center-based child care, regulation serves as the states' mechanism to safeguard the health and safety of the children in care, and that more stringent regulations result in higher quality care (Phillips, Lande, & Goldberg, 1990). Others believe that stringent regulations may actually reduce the number of providers willing to become regulated, thus negating the intended effect (Children's Foundation, 1989). Still others believe that stringent regulation without monitoring results in high rates of noncompliance but a false sense of security regarding quality and the protection children are receiving (Class, 1980; Morgan, 1980). Thus, even though no one seems to advocate doing away with family child care regulation, there appears to be a growing consensus that the present approach does not work (Kontos, 1992) and that alternative approaches need to be found, particularly if the goal is universal compliance with regulations (Adams, 1990; Morgan, 1980).

A major limitation to current debates on family child care regulation has been the lack of research on nonregulated providers. What little there is (e.g., Nelson, 1991b; Pence & Goelman, 1991; Willer et al., 1991), suggests that nonregulated providers care for fewer children and provide lower quality care than do regulated providers, and are misinformed about the nature and process of regulation. These data are useful but insufficient in amount or scope to inform a public policy debate. Thus, a major purpose of the present study was to answer the following questions, which we address in this chapter:

- Does regulatory context matter for quality care?
- Is there a relationship between regulatory context and the likelihood of regulated providers being in compliance and exempt providers being in conformance with regulations?
- Do regulated, nonregulated, and relative providers vary in their tendency to follow state and optimal guidelines for structural quality?
- How is compliance related to quality?

Before considering these questions, let us review the regulatory context in the three states—California, North Carolina, and Texas—sampled for this study. Differences in regulatory climate were determined via three criteria: group size, number of infants, and training requirements. Table 2.8 shows how the three states compare on these three criteria. Group size was similar across states. North Carolina is the only state of the three without limits to the number of infants served, as long as the number does not exceed the group size regulation. Texas is the only state with a training requirement, but it is relatively new (data collection began just over one year after the requirement took effect). All three cities in each state from which providers were sampled had active child care resource and referral (CCR&R) agencies, although the California R&R system is larger and more established than are the other two. All three cities had been selected to receive Family-to-Family child care training projects from Dayton–Hudson Corporation, and thus probably had more and better training available to them than did most typical cities in the United States. Clearly, although there were differences in the regulatory and training climates in these three sites, the differences were not dramatic. In examining the impact of the regulatory climate on the quality of care, we once again temporarily ignore the three provider groupings (regulated, nonregulated, relative).

DIFFERENCES IN QUALITY OF CARE BETWEEN STATES

Does quality of care differ across the three regulatory climates? To answer this question, we looked for differences in quality of care across the three states' regulatory climates by comparing process, global and structural quality, as well as adult working conditions and provider perceptions of quality. Because states vary in their demographics in ways that could influence quality independently of regulatory climate, there was a danger of making unfair comparisons among the three states. To avoid this danger, several family and provider characteristics were compared across states to determine whether to control for them in the analyses. Means for sample demographic characteristics by state are presented in Table 10.1. Results of these comparisons revealed that average family income (unadjusted for cost of living) varied across states. Families of target children in California reported higher incomes than did families in North Carolina and Texas. Maternal education also differed by state. Mothers in California had more formal education than did mothers in Texas. Finally, average household income of family child care providers varied across states. California providers had higher household incomes than did Texas providers. Although these results suggest that the California families and providers were relatively better off, and that the Texas families and providers were relatively worse off financially among the families and providers in the three states, the average cost of living index for the four quarters when data were being collected reveal that the cost of living in the Los Angeles area was approximately 30% higher (Index = 132.275) than in either North Carolina (Index = 100.05) or Texas (Index = 102.6). Thus, in spite of their higher incomes, California families and providers may have had less purchasing power than did those in the other two states. As a result of these comparisons, state quality comparisons were also calculated with family income, maternal education, and provider household income controlled.

Process Quality

There was a significant multivariate effect of state on process quality (see Table 10.2). There were no state differences in ratings of provider detachment and restrictiveness, and in self-reports of nurturant child-rearing attitudes. Providers did vary across states, however, on amount

TABLE 10.1. COMPARISON OF STATES ON DEMOGRAPHIC VARIABLES

Demographic Variable	California (n = 76)	North Carolina (n = 75)	Texas (n = 76)	F-test/ Scheffe
Family income	10.26	8.98	9.01	4.75** CA > NC, TX
Maternal education	4.76	4.44	4.00	3.87* CA > TX
Provider household income	3.78	3.19	2.94	4.89** CA > TX

Note: Education: 1 = little high school; 2 = some high school; 3 = high school graduate; 4 = some college or AA; 5 = 4-year degree; 6 = some graduate school; 7 = graduate degree
Income: 1 = under $5,000; 5 = $12,500–$14,999; 10 = $40,000–$49,999; 16 = $150,000
*p < .05; **p < .01

of responsive and low involvement, sensitivity ratings, limit setting, and restrictive child-rearing attitudes.

There was considerable variation in providers' involvement with children by state. California providers exhibited less low-level involvement than did providers in either North Carolina or Texas. Providers in all three states were significantly different in amount of responsive involvement they displayed. California providers exhibited more responsive involvement than did providers in North Carolina and Texas; North Carolina providers exhibited more responsive involvement than did those in Texas.

Provider sensitivity scores varied by state. Providers in North Carolina were rated as less sensitive in their caregiving than were providers in California and Texas. The differences in sensitivity were mirrored by differences in the amount of limit setting engaged in by providers. Providers in North Carolina engaged in more limit setting than did providers in California and Texas. North Carolina providers set nearly twice as many limits as did Texas providers and six times more than did California providers. California providers, the most infrequent limit setters, also reported the least restrictive child-rearing attitudes.

TABLE 10.2. PROCESS QUALITY BY STATE

	California (n = 76)	North Carolina (n = 75)	Texas (n = 76)	F-test/ Scheffe
Process Quality				11.11*
Ratings				
Sensitivity	3.05	2.64	2.87	8.23* CA > NC
Restrictiveness	1.54	1.46	1.62	1.93
Detachment	1.65	1.47	1.71	2.49
Observations				
Low involvement	.09	.33	.32	23.44* NC, TX > CA
Responsive involvement	.74	.52	.38	28.25* CA > NC > TX
Limit-setting	.56	3.61	1.87	14.13* NC > CA, TX
Self-report				
Restrictiveness	3.10	3.82	4.46	9.84* NC, TX > CA
Nurturant	6.24	6.35	6.42	1.06

*p < .001

The effects for state on restrictive child-rearing attitudes were no longer present when demographic variables were controlled. The other effects were still present when demographic variables were controlled.

Structural Quality

A multivariate analysis was not conducted for structural quality variables because the amount of missing data on several variables rendered the sample size too small (see Table 10.3). Ratio, provider experience, as well as family child care training did not differ across states. On the other hand, group size, number of toddlers, and provider formal education were different by state. On average, providers in California had larger group sizes than did providers in North Carolina, and were caring for more toddlers than were providers in either North Carolina or Texas. Although there was an overall state effect for provider formal education, the Scheffe test indicated that no two pairs of states were significantly different from one another. Texas providers had less education than did providers in the other two states. The effect for state on formal education was no longer present when demographic variables were controlled. However, the effects for group size and for number of toddlers remained when demographic variables were controlled. It is important to point out that, *on average,* providers in all three states were in compliance with their states' ratio and group size regulations.

TABLE 10.3. STRUCTURAL QUALITY BY STATE

Structural Quality	California (n = 76)	North Carolina (n = 75)	Texas (n = 76)	F-test/ Scheffe
Ratio	3.3	3.05	3.55	1.15
Experience	6.49	5.39	5.25	.72
Group size: all ages	4.55	3.43	3.96	3.41 *CA > NC
Number of infants (0–12 m.)	.54	.43	.55	.54
Number of toddlers (12–29 m.)	2.19	1.34	1.24	10.13 **CA > NC, TX
Formal education	3.69	3.61	3.16	3.17* Scheffe NS
Family child care training	-1.41	-3.18	-.91	1.32

*p < .05; **p < .001

Additional Quality Components

There was no multivariate main effect for state on adult work environment (see Table 10.4); global quality (see Table 10.5); or provider definitions of quality (see Table 10.6).

TABLE 10.4. ADULT WORK ENVIRONMENT BY STATE

Adult Working Conditions	California (n = 75)	North Carolina (n = 75)	Texas (n = 73)	F-test/ Scheffe
Adult work environment				.27
Hassles	1.75	1.70	1.78	.52
Job satisfaction	5.60	5.56	5.58	.02
Job commitment	4.31	4.32	4.34	.03

TABLE 10.5. GLOBAL QUALITY BY STATE

Global Quality	California	North Carolina	Texas	F-test/ Scheffe
FDCRS	3.54	3.37	3.25	1.36

TABLE 10.6. PROVIDER DEFINITIONS OF QUALITY, BY STATE

	California (n = 75)	North Carolina (n = 74)	Texas (n = 71)	F-test/ Scheffe
Provider definitions of quality				1.56
Parents as partners	1.67	1.54	1.60	.61
Cost and convenience	2.16	1.96	2.12	1.20
Clean and safe	1.52	1.47	1.53	.30
School-like	2.37	2.13	2.07	2.42
Home-like	3.03	2.63	2.66	2.88
Warmth	1.36	1.38	1.43	.37
Structure	1.88	2.05	2.06	2.00
Ratio/group size	1.95	1.87	2.20	1.85

Summary

The differences by state were clustered in the areas of process and structural quality. Essentially, the differences indicated that California providers engage in more sensitive, responsive caregiving than do those in the other two states, even though they are caring for more toddlers and have larger group sizes than do North Carolina providers. North Carolina providers, on the other hand, engage in the most frequent limit setting, in spite of the fact that they have smaller groups. An important finding is that, on average, providers in all three states were well within the state regulations regarding ratio and/or group size. Another important finding is the absence of state differences in global quality. Overall, the differences in quality among states were nearly as undramatic as were the differences in regulatory climates.

PROVIDERS' COMPLIANCE WITH STATE REGULATIONS AND OPTIMAL STANDARDS

Our investigation of compliance to regulation by family child care and relative care providers focused primarily on ratio and group size. The rationale was two fold. First, ratio and group size comprise two of three sides of the "iron-triangle" depicted by Phillips (1988, as cited in Hayes, et al., 1990) as a sum of the critical components of child care quality. The third side, provider training, is not regulated for family child care in many states, including two of the three states participating in this study. Second, among the myriad aspects of family child care that are regulated, ratio and group size are not only regarded as critical to quality but are reliably and unobtrusively measured through observation. Safety, another critical aspect of state family child care regulations, was not assessed because it could not be reliably and unobtrusively measured during our visits.

Even though the state comparisons, reported in the previous section, revealed that providers are, on average, in compliance with ratio and group size regulations, a measure of central tendency does not tell us to what extent providers vary outside the compliance level. The range for adult–child ratio in our sample was .4–10.7 children per adult. The range for group size was 1–13 but, consistent with the regulatory climate in each state, the vast majority of providers (83%) cared for six or fewer children. One third of the providers cared for only one or two children. Sixteen providers (7%) cared for more than six children per adult, and 37 (16.3%) had more than six children in their home . Clearly, a relatively small number of providers in each state was out of compliance with the ratio and group size regulations. No provider was out of compliance with the applicable state regulation regarding number of infants.

Although we are using the term *compliance*, we recognize that some of the providers are exempt from regulation and are under no obligation to comply. Compliance as applied to this group refers to whether they conform to the regulations in spite of their exemption from them. It is also important to point out that knowing how many providers are in compliance with the ratio and group size regulations does not tell us how many are legally—versus illegally—unregulated. States stipulate the number of children beyond which providers cannot go without becoming regulated (refer to Table 2.8 for the requirements of the three states in the sample). In our sample of providers, 81% of the nonregulated providers were illegally nonregulated.

Compliance with State Ratio and Group Size Regulations

Determining compliance with ratio and group size regulations is not completely straightforward because frequently one regulation (e.g., number of infants allowed) is tied to another regulation (e.g., total number of children allowed). Consequently, to determine compliance rates for the providers in the sample, a calculation was made for providers in each state according to the complex web of ratios, group sizes, and ages of children allowed. This number, because of the interrelated criteria of the regulations, is a single indicator of compliance with ratio, group size, and age ranges of children. The number of providers exceeding the regulated criteria were calculated. The results of this calculation revealed significant differences in compliance with ratio/group size/age range regulations by state. California providers were more likely to be out of compliance (34%) than were North Carolina (11%) or Texas (7%) providers [χ^2 (2) = 23.73, $p < .001$]. Across states, 17% of providers were out of compliance with these regulations.

Because it is likely that compliance with regulations is related to type of provider (regulated, nonregulated nonrelative, nonregulated relative), the association between these two variables was examined. Results of these analyses show that regulated providers are the least likely (78%) and relatives are the most likely (91%) to be in compliance; nonregulated providers were in the middle (91%) [χ^2 (2) = 5.15, n.s.]. The association between type of care and compliance was not statistically significant, however.

Optimal Standards

Quality criteria for family child care are in the process of being developed by the Family Child Care Quality Criteria Advisory Board (Harms & Cryer, 1994). Included in those criteria are optimal standards for ratio, group size, and age mix. The development of optimal standards by a nonregulatory group acknowledges that state regulatory standards may be set for reasons other than what is best for children. The recommended standards are that one provider care for no more than five children, ages birth to five (including her own children under the age of ten), and that no more than two of these children be under 30 months of age. Also, no more than two additional school-age children will be served. In our sample of providers, 58% were in compliance with the optimal standards. Rates of compliance varied by state [χ^2 (2) = 7.55, $p < .05$] and by type of provider [χ^2 (2) = 38.27, $p < .001$], however. California providers were the least likely to comply with optimal standards (46%) whereas North Carolina providers were the most likely to comply (68%); Texas fell in the middle (59%). Regulated providers were significantly less likely to be in compliance with optimal regulations (37.5%) than were relatives (80%) or nonregulated providers (77%).

Summary

The majority of providers (83%) is in compliance with state regulations, although the proportion varies by state and, to a lesser extent, by type of care.

A majority of providers, if just barely, comply with optimal standards for ratio, group size, and age mix. Unfortunately, there was not a majority of providers who were regulated or in California who were in compliance with optimal standards.

Providers who object to the limits states place on group size regulations frequently indicate that they "know their own limits" regarding the number of children for whom they are capable of providing quality child care (Leavitt, 1991). Thus, the question we address next is whether providers who are out of compliance with state regulations or optimal structural quality vary in their ability to maintain process quality.

RELATIONSHIP BETWEEN PROVIDER COMPLIANCE AND QUALITY OF CARE

Recall from Chapter 4 that larger ratios and group sizes were positively correlated with global quality, although research conducted in center-based child care suggests that a negative relationship would be expected (Hayes et al., 1990; Howes & Hamilton, 1993). Policymakers and practitioners could be tempted to infer that ratio and group size regulations are unnecessary or, at the very least, are not having their intended effect of maximizing quality by maintaining smaller groups. Interpreting this positive association requires taking cognizance of the fact that the three states included in this study had group size regulations similar or equal to the optimal number recommended by the Harms and Cryer (1994) Advisory Board. Thus, even though the group size range in our study goes beyond this number, it is nonetheless restricted in the appropriate direction. If states with more lax group size regulations had been included, the results might have been quite different.

The positive association of larger ratios and group sizes with global quality (and, to a much lesser extent, process quality) may be masking a nonlinear relationship such that providers who exceed the legal or optimal limits may be less responsive in their interactions with children than are providers who are at the upper end of the legal or optimal limits. To test this possibility, a multiple regression analysis was conducted, with proportion of high-level interactions with children as the outcome measure and group size and group size-squared (the curvilinear predictor term) as predictors, controlling for amount of family child care training, regulatory status, and professionalism or intentionality (job commitment and whether family child care or relative care was the provider's chosen profession). The model was statistically significant [F (6, 114) = 2.33, $p < .04$], and accounted for 11% of the variance in proportion of providers' high-level interactions with children. The only significant predictor, however, was regulatory status [Beta = $-.023$, $p < .006$]. Regulated providers were more likely to have responsive interactions with children than were nonregulated providers when all other variables were held constant. Group size had neither a linear nor curvilinear relationship with this aspect of process quality.

We compared providers who were in and out of compliance with both state regulations and optimal standard for ratio and group size. There was a multivariate main effect for compliance with optimal standards on process quality [F (8, 181) = 2.4, $p < .02$] but not for compliance with state regulations. Providers who were out of compliance with optimal standards of structural quality had more responsive interactions with children, and reported less restrictive child-rearing attitudes, than did providers who were in compliance. When regulatory status was controlled, however, there were no differences in process quality between providers who vary in their compliance with optimal standards for structural quality. Once again, regulatory status was the key variable.

There was a significant association between compliance with state regulations and optimal standards and level of global quality (see Table 10.7). Providers offering high quality care (FDCRS scores of 5 or higher) were less likely than were those providing adequate/custodial quality (FDCRS scores of 3 to 4.99) to be in compliance with state regulations or optimal standards who, in turn, were less likely than those provid-

TABLE 10.7. COMPLIANCE BY LEVEL OF GLOBAL QUALITY

Regulatory Comparisons	Level of Global Quality			
	Low (n = 80)	Adequate (n = 126)	High (n = 17)	χ^2
Compliance with state regulations	91%	82%	71%	6.11*
Compliance with optimal standards	71	52	38	10.79*
More than 6 children per adult	4	8	17	24.43**
More than 6 children total	9	19	30	17.04**

*$p < .05$; **$p < .01$

ing inadequate quality care (FDCRS scores of less than 3). Table 10.7 also indicates the proportion of providers caring for more than six children (total and per adult) by level of global quality. As we might expect, these data reflect the results for compliance.

It was conceivable that, exclusively among regulated providers, those who were in compliance with state regulations or with optimal standards were providing higher quality care. To test this hypothesis, global quality and responsive interactions for regulated providers were compared by whether they were in or out of compliance with state regulations and with optimal standards. These comparisons revealed that there were no differences between those who were or were not in compliance with state regulations and optimal standards for global quality or responsive caregiving. Thus, it does not appear that regulated providers who are in compliance are necessarily doing a better job than are regulated providers who are not in compliance.

Summary

The results clearly indicate that, within the regulatory climates of the participating states and the ranges of ratio and group size present in the sample, compliance with state regulations and optimal standards regarding ratio and group size is not a key factor associated with process or global quality. On the other hand, being regulated—and all the characteristics associated with being regulated, such as greater training, support, and intentionality—appear to be the most critical factors. These results are consistent with a recent review suggesting that, since they co-occur in a single setting, clusters of quality indicators are probably more important to children's development than is any single indicator (Dunn, 1993).

CONCLUSIONS

The positive aspect of these data is that the majority of providers, regardless of state or regulatory status, are in compliance with the ratio, group size, and age mix regulations in their respective states. On the other hand, it is disconcerting to learn that, although relatives and non-regulated providers have been shown to be providing care that is lower in process and global quality, they are nonetheless more likely to be in compliance with ratio/group size regulations. These data do not support the assumption that nonregulated providers (relatives or nonrelatives) are outside the regulatory system because of their desire to exceed the legal limit for group size. The data do reinforce the notion, however, that there is much more to process and global quality than number of children being served.

The explanation for the pattern of compliance among types of providers is likely to lie with the general tendency for regulated providers to care for larger numbers of children. Demands for their services and the need for a higher income may stretch their ability to keep their numbers within legal limits. The fact that regulated providers offering higher quality child care are serving more children may represent a "demand characteristic" of the child care marketplace. In other words, these numbers suggest that more families are choosing higher quality care for their children. Regulated providers are also more likely to be linked with the family child care community, and probably have more sources for referrals of families as a result.

The differences by state are also hard to explain, other than to once again point out that the California sample had a higher percentage of regulated providers who were caring for more toddlers, and who typically care for more children overall. In other words, state and type of provider are confounded. Another factor that probably differs by state is the level of enforcement of regulations. Enforcement can take two forms. One form involves making sure all providers who should be regulated *are* regulated. The other form involves monitoring compliance to regulations after becoming regulated. California child care resource and referral agencies have been recruiting family child care providers into the regulatory fold for 20 years, and then supporting them through training and other activities. Thus, California may do a better job of enforcing regulations regarding who should be regulated. But California regulatory agencies may not stress monitoring, once providers become regulated, as much as CCR&Rs stress recruiting.

The results for optimal ratio, group size, and age mix standards are predictable in light of the pattern of compliance with less stringent state regulations revealed above. These data further reinforce our earlier point regarding the results for compliance with state regulations. To achieve process and global quality involves more than just adequate or even optimal ratios and group sizes. Professionalism or "intentionality," as reflected in training, commitment to caring for children, and planned activities, is associated with sensitive, responsive caregiving and more prevalent among regulated providers. These aspects of providing care for children probably need stronger emphasis as crucial components of quality. As a prime example, states may need to pay more attention to training in the context of their family child care standards than they do now.

It is important to remember that these results do not tell us that ratio and group size are unimportant to quality of care under all circumstances. We can only interpret the results in light of the regulatory climates of the three states and the range for ratio and group size represented in this sample. We suspect that the results would have been quite different if the study had been conducted in a state that allows providers to care for larger groups of children, or to care for more than three infants.

11

Cost of Care

D ata on the cost of family child care and relative care are not abundant and can be hard to interpret due to inflation and geographic differences in cost of living. Our most recent data indicate that families with employed mothers and preschool children pay 10% of their family income on child care. For families earning under $15,000, however, 23% of their income goes toward child care, whereas for families earning $50,000 and over, only 6% goes toward child care (Willer et al., 1991). Parental expenditures for family child care (nonrelative in the nonrelative's home) for the youngest preschool child were $1.35 an hour in 1990; parental expenditures for relative care (in the relative's or parent's home) were $1.11 per hour (Hofferth et al., 1991). By comparison, parents report spending $1.67 per hour for center care in 1990 (Hofferth et al., 1991).

In this chapter, we present data on how much parents pay for care and compare that to what parents are willing to pay (based on the full sample of mothers participating in the study; $n = 820$). We also show that parents who earn less also pay less for family child care or relative care although they pay a larger proportion of their income. For the smaller sample of families whose provider participated in the study ($n = 226$), we examine the relationship between cost and quality of care.

It is important to remember that fees charged are an unreliable indicator of financial gain for providers. In a case study of the economics of family child care, Culkin et al. (1991) showed how the cost to providers of offering care can be more than the fees they are accepting from parents. Refer to Chapter 3 for a discussion of rates charged by providers and provider net income based on the companion study of the economics of family child care.

PAYMENTS FOR CARE

We found that 9 out of 10 families reported that they paid the provider to take care of their child. As might be expected, families were more likely to pay for care if their provider was regulated (98%) or nonregulated (97%) than if she was a relative (73%) [χ^2 (2) = 114.25, $p < .001$]. We asked if families compensated providers in ways other than cash, for example, buying groceries for the provider or looking after her children. Twenty-seven percent indicated that they did. Not surprisingly, in-kind payments were more likely among families who used a relative provider (49%) than among those who used a regulated or nonregulated provider (14% and 20%, respectively) [χ^2 (2) = 93.09, $p < .001$] and also more likely among families who did not pay (70%) than among those who did (22%) [χ^2 (1) = 85.5, $p < .001$].

Of the 736 families who paid the provider, over three quarters (76%) paid only for the care of the target child; the other 24% of the sample paid for additional children as well (one to seven additional children).The weekly cost for the target child alone, across all families who paid, ranged from $3.70–$225, with a median of $50. This is somewhat less than the average fee of $63 per week reported by the NCCS (Hofferth et al., 1991). The median weekly cost exclusively for regulated and nonregulated providers of $60 corresponds more closely to the NCCS figure. The 25% of families paying the least for care paid less than $37.50, and the 25% paying the most for care paid over $75. To verify the accuracy of the mothers' reports of costs, we examined the correspondence of mothers' reports of payments to providers' reports of fees in the smaller sample of families whose providers participated in the study. Mothers' reports corresponded closely to what the provider said she charged for a child the age of the target child, [r (169) = .75, $p < .001$]. Thus, we presume that our cost data are accurate.

Needless to say, families with more that one child in care with a provider paid more than did families with just one child in care. For this group of families, the total weekly cost for all children, as reported by mothers, ranged from $15 per week to $300 per week, with a median of $80.

According to mothers, the hourly rate for the target child, adjusted for the fact that families used care for different numbers of hours per week, ranged from $.04–$6.25, with a median of $1.40, among families who paid. The 25% of families paying the least paid $1.00 per hour or less, whereas the 25% paying the most paid $1.88 or more. These data are quite comparable to the amounts reported by the NCCS (Hofferth et al., 1991).

WILLINGNESS TO INCREASE PAYMENTS

Interestingly, the vast majority of mothers (92%) said that they would pay $5 to $50 more per week, if the provider asked, rather than seeking alternative arrangements for care. The median family would pay $10 more. One family in eight (12%) would pay $50 more per week before looking elsewhere; an additional 16% would pay $25 more. These figures are impressive, given that the median actual payment for care of the target child was $50 per week. Many families would pay substantially more before they would look elsewhere for care. Indeed, the median family would pay 22% more than they currently pay, 25% of families would pay 42% more, and 7% would pay double what they were paying at the time of the interview.

Families who currently paid in-kind were willing to increase their cash payments more (mean = $20.30) than were families who did not pay in kind (mean = $15.28) [$t\,(226) = -3.49$, $p < .001$]; the former group was also significantly more variable in what they were willing to pay [F (Levene's test) = 27.95, $p < .001$].

Among the 83 families in our full sample of mothers who did not pay for care, 90% (75) said they would be willing to pay, but only 59% said they were able to do so. We asked the 82 who were either able or willing whether they would pay the provider various amounts if she asked, or whether they would look for someone else to take care of their child. The majority of these families (57%) would pay $50 per week, another 21% would pay $25 per week, 15% would pay some lessor amount, and only 7% (six families) would pay nothing at all. Most families who paid nothing for care at the time of the interview were willing to pay something rather than look for another provider in the future.

VARIATION OF PAYMENTS WITH FAMILY INCOME

In contrast to the NCCS (Hofferth, et al., 1991), low-income families in our study were no less likely to pay than were families earning more [t (797) = -1.02, $n.s$]. Among families who did pay, however, the amount they paid for care of the target child was highly correlated with family income [$r\,(705) = .51$, $p < .001$] and with the mother's income [$r\,(708) = .56$, $p < .001$]. The cost for weekly care and annual care, assuming that families paid for care 52 weeks a year, by income, are shown in Table 11.1. Although poor families paid less for child care, they paid a larger portion of their income. This was also the case in the NCCS. The correlation between family income and the portion of income spent on care for the target child was $r\,(705) = -.63$, $p < .001$.

TABLE 11.1. MEAN COST OF CARE FOR TARGET CHILD, AMONG FAMILIES WHO PAID FOR CARE, BY FAMILY INCOME

Cost of Care	Family Income		
	< $20,000 (n = 147)	$20,000– < $40,000 (n = 247)	> $40,000 (n = 315)
Cost per week	$40.00	$48.51	$69.32
Cost per year	$2,080	$2,522	$3,605

There were small but statistically significant associations between the additional amount families were willing to pay and family income [r (715) = .19, $p < .001$] as well as mother's income [r (715) = .14, $p < .001$]. Income was more strongly related to actual amount paid than to the amount willing to pay.

In our sample, very few families received help in paying for child care: 3% ($n = 23$) got help from an employer; 2% ($n = 12$) got help from the government, and 2% ($n = 20$) got help from a relative. For the entire sample of 820 families, only 53 families (6%) received help from any source. The use of tax credits for child care was more prevalent. Just under two fifths of families (39%, $n = 317$) reported taking the Child and Dependent Care Federal Income Tax Credit on their previous year's taxes; 57% ($n = 469$) did not take it, and 4% ($n = 33$) were unsure. Among families with household incomes below $20,000, 51% ($n = 87$) reported that they would take an Earned Income Tax Credit on the following year's taxes, 33% ($n = 55$) said they would not, and 16% ($n = 27$) said they did not know. The proportion of families who reported using tax credits was greater than reported in the NCCS (Hofferth et al., 1991).

RELATIONSHIP OF COST TO QUALITY

Parents reported paying significantly more for regulated care (mean = $69.48 per week; $SD = 23.86) than for care they believed to be nonregulated (mean = $53.13, $SD = 21.78) which, in turn, was more than parents reported paying relative providers (mean = $40.22; $SD = 24.33) [F (2, 720) = 92.32, $p < .001$; Scheffe = .01]. Our data show that regulated care is higher quality than nonregulated care. Thus, parents who pay more are more likely to receive regulated, better quality care. Payments were barely related to overall satisfaction with care [r (721) = .10, $p < .01$].

Among the subset of families with providers in the study, costs per week, as reported by both mothers and providers, were strongly related to observed and rated quality, especially the total FDCRS Global Quality score and the Arnett sensitivity measure, as shown in Table 11.2.

TABLE 11.2. CORRELATIONS BETWEEN COST AND QUALITY

	Quality Rating			
Cost of Care	Global Quality (FDCRS)	Detached	Sensitivity	Restrictiveness
Reported by mother				
Overall	.51***	-.24**	.44***	-.09
Relative	.49**	-.33*	.53***	-.25
Nonrelative	.43***	-.18*	.36***	-.10
Reported by provider				
Overall	.42***	-.17*	.34***	.01
Relative	.16	-.23	.23	-.21
Nonrelative	.40***	-.14	.29***	.01

Note: ns = 175–197 overall, 137–156 for nonrelatives, and 38–59 for relatives
*p < .05; **p < .01; ***p < .001

Costs were more weakly related to levels of detachment on the Arnett measure. Correlations in the subsamples of regulated, nonregulated, and relative providers were generally consistent with those for the entire sample (although often smaller because of lesser variability within groups).

SUMMARY AND CONCLUSIONS

Costs for child care per hour and per week are quite low, with a median cost of only $50 per week, among the 90% of families who pay for care. One fourth of families supplemented their payments with in-kind contributions. Although these rates are low from the perspective of providers, they represent a substantial portion of income for low-income families. Very few families receive direct help with child care payments, and a minority took advantage of federal tax credits for child care. Instead, it appears to be providers who are subsidizing family child care and relative care by charging very low rates.

Whenever the issue of increasing compensation for providers is raised, it is usually countered with arguments that many parents are unable or unwilling to pay higher rates. An important finding of this study was that the vast majority of families would be willing to pay more for care, if asked, rather than look for an alternative form of care.

In family child care and relative care, what you pay is closely related to what you get. Providers with higher rates, by their own and by mothers' reports, provided care that was of higher global quality, responded more sensitively to children, and were somewhat less detached. Payments appear to be strongly related to the provider's investment in providing high-quality care.

12

Turnover and Its Relationship to Quality

Turnover among child care workers is a concern among parents and child care advocates (Bollin, 1993; Whitebook & Granger, 1989). Although we now have fairly solid data regarding the turnover of staff in child care centers (Whitebook, et al., 1989), similar longitudinal data for a large, multisite sample of family child care providers has not been forthcoming. Existing estimates of family child care turnover come from a variety of sources: Atkinson (1993)—35% for small sample of Iowa providers; Nelson (1990)—37% for small sample of Vermont providers; National Association for the Education of Young Children (1985)—59%; Stentzel (1985)—41%; and Majeed (1983)—10% for regulated and 61% for nonregulated, over seven months. These data suggest that turnover for family child care providers is similar to or worse than turnover rates for staff in child care centers (41%) (Whitebook et al., 1989). Several of these studies were conducted a decade ago ago or more, however, and thus cannot be assumed to be accurate any longer. Although the two most recent studies suggest that turnover may be slightly less for family child care providers than for centers, their results are based on the smallest samples of all the studies reporting data on turnover. The need for current turnover data from more representative samples of providers is readily apparent. Our study was designed with that need in mind.

Twelve months after our initial visits to the providers we contacted them by telephone to determine which providers continued to provide care. We were able to contact 176 providers, 78% of our original sample. The remaining 51 providers were unreachable. In most cases (76%) they had moved, leaving no forwarding number, or the number was inexplicably disconnected. The other unreachable providers (24%) did not answer the phone or failed to return our messages.

COMPARISONS OF THOSE WHO CONTINUED VERSUS STOPPED PROVIDING CARE

We compared providers who were still providing care, were no longer providing care, and were unreachable to examine characteristics of providers and of their caregiving that distinguish between those providers who did and did not continue to provide care. We also asked the providers who were still providing care why they continued and the providers who were no longer providing care why they quit and what might change their minds.

Provider Groups. First we determined whether there were differences between regulated, nonregulated, and relative providers in whether they were still providing care. These results are shown in Table 12.1. Regulated providers were more likely than were either nonregulated or relative providers to continue to provide care. More nonregulated providers were unreachable than were regulated or relative providers.

Demographic Characteristics. Providers who continued differed from those who did not in age, ethnicity, and employment history but not in marital status. Demographic characteristics comparisons are found in Table 12.2. Providers who continued to provide care were older than providers who stopped or were unreachable. White providers were most likely to continue to provide care. Latino providers were most likely to be unreachable. Providers who were unreachable were more likely than were providers who had either continued or stopped to have had outside employment prior to becoming providers [$\chi^2 (2) = 7.42$, $p = .03$]. There were no differences in the type of prior employment.

Families Served. The families served by providers who did and did not continue to provide care also differed. Family characteristics are

TABLE 12.1. COMPARISON OF PERCENT OF PROVIDERS WHO CONTINUED TO PROVIDE CARE

	All	Regulated	Non-regulated	Relative	χ^2
Still providing care					38.73*
No	18	8	25	30	
Yes	60	79	37	44	
Unreachable	22	13	38	26	

*$p < .01$

shown in Table 12.3. White and African-American children were most likely to be served by a provider who continued while Latino children were most likely to be served by a provider who was unreachable. There were no differences for family income.

TABLE 12.2. COMPARISONS OF DEMOGRAPHIC CHARACTERISTICS OF PROVIDERS WHO DID AND DID NOT CONTINUE TO PROVIDE CARE

Family Characteristics	Continued	Stopped	Unreachable	χ^2/ F-test
Age in years (when observed)	44.3	39.2	39.5	3.56*
Ethnicity				20.77**
White	62%	51%	48%	
African American	24	23	17	
Latino	7	23	33	
Other	7	3	2	
Marital status (when observed)				11.62
Never married	6%	10%	8%	
Married/living with a partner	74	83	65	
Divorced	16	7	21	
Widowed		4	6	

*$p < .05$; **$p < .01$

TABLE 12.3. COMPARISONS OF FAMILIES SERVED BY PROVIDERS WHO DID AND DID NOT CONTINUE TO PROVIDE CARE

Family Characteristics	Stopped	Continued	Unreachable	χ^2/ F-test
Ethnicity				20.49*
White	17%	65%	18%	
African American	16	71	13	
Latino	24	27	49	
Family income (when observed)				9.09
Less than $20,000	21%	44%	35%	
$20,000–$40,000	20	54	26	
Over $40,000	15	69	16	
Widowed		4	6	

*$p < .01$

Motivation for Becoming a Provider. We examined differences in motivations for becoming a provider in those who did and did not continue. We compared providers' earlier responses on the four most highly ranked reasons. There were no significant differences. We then compared providers' choices of four alternative descriptions of child care as their chosen profession. There were significant differences among the providers who did and did not continue. These comparisons are in Table 12.4. Providers who continued were most likely to describe child care as their chosen occupation, whereas those who stopped or were unreachable were most likely to describe child care as good while their children were young.

Social Support Networks. Not surprisingly, providers who continued to provide care were more integrated into family child care support networks than were providers who either stopped or were unreachable [$F(2, 214) = 4.63$, $p = .01$,Scheffe = .05]. There were no differences among providers who continued, stopped, or were unreachable in their integration into general social support networks.

Organization of Child Care Services. Providers' perceptions of their organization of services were similar whether or not they continued to provide care. Providers who continued, stopped, or were unreachable were no different in whether they had children living at home or in the number of children they had living at home. Providers who continued, stopped, or were unreachable also were no different in their use of formal/planned versus informal/not planned activities, and in whether or not they felt they were able to do housework while the children were present.

TABLE 12.4. COMPARISONS OF CHILD CARE DESCRIPTIONS BY PROVIDERS WHO DID AND DID NOT CONTINUE TO PROVIDE CARE

Description of Job	Stopped	Continued	Unreachable	χ^2
Description				25.89*
Chosen occupation	31%	63%	41%	
Stepping stone to related work	9	14	9	
Good while my children are young	43	20	46	
Temporary employment	17	3	4	

*$p < .01$

Business Practices. The weekly rates and business practices reported a year earlier differed among providers who continued or stopped providing care, or were unreachable. Considering only those providers who charged, the estimated income of providers who continued was higher than the estimated income of providers who stopped or were unreachable [$F(2, 152) = 7.66$, $p = .0007$, Scheffe = .05]. Providers who continued charged more for infants [$F(2, 131) = 4.41$, $p = .01$, Scheffe = .05], for toddlers [$F(2, 169) = 3.40$, $p = .04$, Scheffe = .05], and for preschoolers [$F(2, 146) = 3.00$, $p = .05$, Scheffe = .05] than did providers who stopped or were unreachable. Providers who continued had higher business practices scores [$F(2, 183) = 18.56$, $p = .0001$, Scheffe = .05] than did providers who stopped or were unreachable.

Quality of Care. Providers who continued, stopped, or were unreachable were not significantly different in process quality (observed sensitivity, responsiveness, or harshness), nor in their child-rearing attitudes.

Providers who continued, stopped, or were unreachable were different in structural quality. These comparisons are in Table 12.5. Providers who continued cared for more children, had larger ratios and had more informal training than did providers who stopped or were unreachable. There were no differences between groups in formal education or training or in number of years as a provider.

Providers who continued had, a year earlier, rated their job commitment higher than had providers who stopped or were unreachable [$F(2, 210) = 13.27$, $p = .0001$; Scheffe = .05]. There were no differences among providers who continued, stopped, or were unreachable in job satisfaction and hassles scores.

TABLE 12.5. COMPARISONS OF STRUCTURAL QUALITY BY PROVIDERS WHO DID AND DID NOT CONTINUE TO PROVIDE CARE

Structural Quality (When Observed)	Stopped	Continued	Unreachable	F-test
Group size	2.73	4.59	3.34	10.12*
Ratio of children to adults	2.66	3.67	2.80	6.19*
Years of experience	4.00	6.42	5.09	2.19
Formal school	3.33	3.61	3.33	1.09
Formal training	2.11	2.02	1.95	.17
Informal training	-4.01	-.26	-4.45	5.09*

*$p < .01$

Providers who continued to provide care had higher global quality scores (M = 3.61) than did providers who stopped(M > = 3.08) or providers who were unreachable (M = 3.04) [F (2, 220) = 7.51, p = .007, Scheffe = .05]. The differences in global quality are dramatic when the categories of quality are considered. These are displayed in Table 12.6. Seventy-six percent of the providers observed to provide good care continued to provide care, as opposed to 45% of the providers observed to provide inadequate care.

Reasons for Leaving, Staying, or Returning. We asked the providers who had stopped providing care "What were the main reasons you stopped taking care of children?" The most frequent responses to this question are presented in Table 12.7. Providers could give multiple responses. Providers most frequently left to go to school or to take another job.

We asked the providers who continued to provide care to tell us "What keeps you in the field?" The most frequent responses to this question are presented in Table 12.8. Providers could give multiple

TABLE 12.6. COMPARISON OF GLOBAL QUALITY RATINGS OF PROVIDERS WHO DID AND DID NOT CONTINUE TO PROVIDE CARE

Structural Quality (When Observed)	Continued	Stopped	Unreachable	χ^2
Global quality (when observed)				12.80*
Inadequate	45%	23%	33%	
Adequate/custodial	66	17	17	
Good	76	6	18	

*p < .01

TABLE 12.7. REASONS FOR STOPPING PROVIDING CARE

Reason	Percentage of Those Who Stopped Giving This Reply
Returned to or started school	25
Found another job	23
Illness or poor health	13
Pregnant or had another child	10
Hassles of the job	5
Her own child needed to be around other children	5
Child or children no longer needed care	3

responses. Providers were most likely to enjoy the children and like staying home with their own children.

We then asked the providers who had stopped what changes would make them change their minds about returning to the field. The most frequent responses to this question are presented in Table 12.9. Providers could give multiple responses. Better salary was the most frequent response.

Summary

Our one-year, follow-up data reveal that the providers most likely still to be offering care were white, regulated, and had chosen family child care as their occupation. Compared to providers who had stopped offering care or were unreachable, they were older, had higher job commitment, cared for more children, had more family child care training, charged more and were more business-like, were more likely to be

TABLE 12.8. Reasons for Continuing to Provide Care

Reason	Percentage of Those Who Stopped Giving This Reply
Enjoy children	32
Can stay home with own children	27
Need the income	15
Enjoy the diversity of the work	14
Provide care for grandchildren and help my grown children	11
Convenient/enjoy working at home	7
Like the job	7
Child care is needed by working parents	6
Able to have an irregular schedule	2
Am satisfied	2
Can't work anywhere else	2
Get to watch children grow	2
Job requires little skill	2

TABLE 12.9. Reasons to Change Mind and Stay in the Field

Reason	Percentage of Those Who Stopped Giving This Reply
Better salary	13
Cooperation from parents	7
Regaining health	7
If could do it on a drop-in basis	7

involved in family child care networks, and were offering care that was higher in global quality. They stayed in family child care because, most often, they enjoyed the children in their care and appreciated the opportunity to stay home with their own children.

Of the providers who stopped doing family child care, nearly half left for another job or to obtain more schooling. For them, family child care was not a chosen profession but something that was good while their children were young. The most frequently cited incentive to stay in family child care would have been a better income.

CONCLUSIONS

The follow-up data reinforce the importance of the "intentionality" factor in the retention of family child care providers. The components of intentionality addressed in Chapter 7 (e.g., regulation, job commitment, training, business practices) appear to be more prevalent among providers who stay in family child care. It is reassuring to know that those who stay are the "cream of the crop." Providers who leave family child care appear to have had more difficulty making it an economically viable occupation, but they were also more likely to have seen their work as temporary. Thus, a certain amount of the turnover in family child care may be a built-in "weeding out" process.

13

Final Conclusions

The purpose of this study was to provide up-to-date information on family child care and relative care from the perspective of families, children, and providers. We were concerned about the typical level of quality in family child care and relative care for all children, but were especially concerned about quality for low-income children and minority children. In addition, a primary focus was on relative care and how it differs from regulated and nonregulated family child care.

The sampling strategy involved over 26,000 telephone calls resulting in interviews of 820 employed mothers with a preschool child enrolled in family child care or relative care in Charlotte, North Carolina, Dallas/Forth Worth, Texas, and San Fernando/Los Angeles, California. Approximately half of the interviewed mothers referred their providers to the study, and approximately half of the providers were eligible and agreed to be observed. Ultimately, 226 family child care and relative care providers were observed and interviewed, and the target child in each provider's home was observed as well.

KEY FINDINGS

The results of this study are complex and have far-reaching implications. Summing up the data from our study as presented in the previous chapters, the key findings are as follows:

• Both parents and providers see a warm, caring, responsive relationship between the child and the provider, a safe environment, and good communications between the parent and provider as the crux of quality.

202

• When the care children receive is sensitive, responsive, and of better quality, children are more likely to be securely attached to their providers and to achieve higher levels of cognitive competence.

• Providers who offer more sensitive, more responsive, and overall better quality care are more "intentional" in their approach to caregiving. One feature of intentionality is being committed to taking care of children. Another indicator of intentionality is seeking out opportunities to learn about child care and children's development. Accordingly, providers who have professional preparation are more likely to be sensitive. Planning experiences for the children is another aspect of intentionality. Providers who think ahead about what the children are going to do and plan for their involvement are more likely to be rated as sensitive, and observed as more responsive. Still another aspect of intentionality is seeking out the company of others who are providing child care. Providers who are involved with other family child care providers are more likely to be sensitive and responsive.

• Providers who are regulated by their states are more likely to be sensitive and responsive. Being regulated is more predictive of quality than is conforming with the features of state laws that regulate ratios, group size, and the age mix of children.

• Providers with somewhat larger groups are more likely to be sensitive; providers with somewhat larger groups and somewhat higher number of children per adult are more likely to have higher global quality scores.

• Providers who report charging higher rates and following standard business and safety practices are more likely to offer higher quality child care.

• The majority of parents, regardless of income, report that they would be willing to pay more for child care.

• Providers who are still offering child care after one year are more likely to be white, regulated, have more training, be more business-like, and to have chosen family child care as a profession.

IMPLICATIONS OF THE STUDY

The results of our study contradict some assumptions about what makes family child care and relative care good, and raise concerns about families' child care choices and our nation's support of quality child care. They also have implications for policies concerning child care subsidies, the Child and Adult Care Food Program, and welfare reform.

• *Care in a home setting is naturally better for children than in centers.* Based on our definitions of quality for family child care and relative care, our data show that family child care is, on average, just adequate and almost identical to quality in centers (Whitebrook, et al., 1989). Children were no more likely to be securely attached to their family child care or relative providers than were children in centers (about 50% in either setting). Thus, there is no reason to believe that children are more or less better off in care simply on the basis of the form of care (home versus center). Rather, we now know that there is a wide range of quality in all types of care.

• *Experience is a better indicator of quality caregiving than training.* Our results show that the opposite is true. Providers with more experience were *not* offering more responsive, sensitive caregiving than were those with less experience. Providers with more training, on the other hand, were offering more responsive, sensitive care than were those with less or no training. The most common type of training received by providers was through the Child and Adult Care Food Program, and through other informal sources. This study documents the importance of family child care training to providers and also shows how important the food program has become to quality child care. Thus, dropping or reducing the food program as a cost-saving component of welfare reform would probably have broader ramifications than just an effect on child nutrition. We could expect the quality of child care for large numbers of children to be affected as well.

• *Children will receive the best care from a relative.* In this study, relative providers were less sensitive and responsive in their interactions with the target child (usually a grandchild) and were more likely to be providing care that was rated as inadequate. Children were no more likely to be securely attached to a relative than they were to a provider who was a nonrelative. Recall, however, that the relative providers were more likely to be low-income women who were more socially isolated than were the other providers, and who were more likely to be providing care in order to assist the mother, as opposed to providing care out of a desire to spend the day with children. Thus, even though they cared for the fewest children on average, the relative providers were not providing the highest quality care according to either parents' and providers' own definitions of quality, or to standards within the field. Our measures did not address the importance of a culturally familiar child care environment, nor examine the various unique ways that family members can express their affection for one another. Nonetheless, the results do indicate that when adults care for children under less than ideal circumstances (poverty, social isolation, not their chosen occupation), the children are less likely to get the warmth and attention that parents rate as important attributes of quality child care.

• *Children are likely to get more personal attention in very small groups.* Our results revealed that children are more likely to get sensitive, responsive caregiving when the group sizes are from three to six rather than just one or two. This is very different from the consistent finding in center-based child care, that smaller group sizes are associated with quality. We think the difference has two causes. First, providers in our study typically did not take care of large groups of children, such as those associated with poor quality in centers. Second, this appears to happen because the providers who have larger groups of children are more likely to be trained or to belong to a family child care network, are more likely to see family child care as their chosen occupation, and are doing child care for child- rather than adult-focused reasons. Some providers informally report that when they care for one or two children, they feel as though they are simply at home with children, but when they have three or more, they see themselves as "at work."

• *Regulation is unimportant for quality in family child care.* Our results show that the single best indicator of quality in family child care is the provider's regulatory status. Being regulated is strongly associated with the other important predictors of quality, such as training, membership in family child care networks, planning activities for children, using sound business practices, doing family child care for child-focused reasons, and choosing family child care as an occupation. All of these factors combined appear to promote sensitive, responsive caregiving on the part of providers (although our correlational data do not allow causal inferences to be made).

Parents, professionals, and advocates can rest assured that the key to quality child care in the home is *not necessarily* finding a relative to provide the care. Parents with relatives close-by should be cautioned against convincing reluctant grandmothers and aunts to do child care. If relatives are committed to caregiving, the results can be positive. As an alternative to using reluctant relatives, parents can be counseled regarding the potential choices among regulated providers. Likewise, policymakers should not push welfare or job training recipients to find child care with a relative under the assumption that such care will be *both* cheap and good. Because regulated care costs more than unregulated or relative care, and because higher quality costs more than lower quality, parents may need assistance in purchasing quality care.

CAUSES FOR CONCERN

• *Few homes are rated as "good quality."* Only 9% of the providers
were observed to be providing good quality care, whereas 35% were
rated as providing inadequate quality care. The remaining providers
(56%) were rated as providing adequate or custodial quality care. It is
disturbing to think that over one third of providers are offering care
that may be detrimental to the development of children (because our
sample is biased toward regulated providers, we may actually overestimate the average quality of care available to children in the three communities). It is important to point out, however, that only 13% of regulated providers offered inadequate care. The vast majority of providers
offering inadequate care are nonregulated (82%), and the relative
providers are the largest group (46%). More than two thirds of relatives
and half of nonregulated providers are offering care of inadequate quality. Thus, regulation appears to serve as a relatively reliable indicator
of care that is at least adequate in quality.

The small group of providers offering good care demonstrates the
potential for family child care as a developmentally enhancing setting for
young children, and points to the types of supports necessary to increase
the amount of care of this quality. Providers offering good quality care
were overwhelmingly regulated, trained, and involved in family child care
networks. Our study supports the notion of expanding training, support,
and technical assistance opportunities for family child care providers, as
well as increased efforts to bring providers into the regulatory system.
Being regulated does not itself improve quality, but it increases the access
of providers to the resources they need to do a good job.

• *Parents found few options for care.* Although mothers report being
satisfied with the quality of care they were using, 28% of them would
use other care were it available. Of the 62% of mothers who searched
for alternative child care arrangements, nearly two thirds (65%)
reported no other available options. Just over half of the mothers who
use nonrelatives as providers (54%) said finding care was difficult.
Thus, even though parental choice is a prevalent theme for child care
policies in this country, the reality for parents appears to be much different. Parents might find their search for child care to be less of a bur-
den if states and communities were able to provide better consumer
education and resource and referral services, and if the quality of child
care services available were improved.

• *Children of low-income families and minority families were receiving poorer quality care than were their higher income and nonminority
counterparts.* White and middle-income families were more likely to use

regulated family child care that was higher in quality. Low-income and minority families were more likely to use relatives. Not surprisingly, low-income and minority families paid less for child care, on average, and received poorer quality of care in return. These data run counter to those from child care centers, where low-income children receiving child care subsidies are in higher quality care than their middle-class counterparts, whose parents also cannot afford to pay for quality care but are ineligible for subsidies (Kontos, 1991; Whitebook & Granger, 1989). In our sample, few of the families using family child care or relative care received any type of subsidy. Thus, the "safety net" for the low-income and minority children in center-based care was not present for children in family child care and relative care. Public subsidies and employer investments in child care that can be accessed by all eligible families, regardless of type of care preferred, are necessary to affect any changes in this pattern.

CONCLUSIONS AND RECOMMENDATIONS

This study sheds some light on the characteristics associated with more sensitive, responsive, and better quality family child care and relative care. The results point toward the importance of providers who go about their work in an "intentional" or professional manner. The study also reveals how variations in family child care and relative care settings are related to children's development. These data provide new insights into parents' perceptions of child care—finding it, recognizing quality, and paying for it. Concerns are raised regarding the range of quality and lack of good quality care available, the lack of choices perceived by parents, and the poorer quality of care received by low-income and minority children. The following recommendations emerged from the findings of the study (see Galinsky, Howes, Kontos, & Shinn [1994], for implications of these recommendations):

- No public policies at the federal or state level should push or require people to care for children if they do not want to be providers.
  Rationale: Providers who are committed to caring for children are more sensitive and more responsive.

- There should be public and private investments in child care consumer education and advocacy.
  Rationale: The responsibility for evaluating and assuring child care quality falls mainly on parents as consumers.

- Government and business should fund high-quality family child care training initiatives.

Rationale: Providers who have participated in family child care training offer more sensitive and more responsive care.

- Family child care providers should have access to resources that help them anticipate and create learning experiences for the children.
  Rationale: Providers are more sensitive and more responsive when they plan ahead about what the children will do in care.

- National, state, and local associations should be developed and supported to involve providers in social support and technical assistance networks.
  Rationale: Providers who are involved with other providers are more sensitive and responsive.

- States and businesses should undertake efforts to bring family child care providers into the regulatory system and ensure that the regulatory system helps providers improve the quality of care they offer.
  Rationale: Providers who are regulated are more sensitive and more responsive.

- Government and business should undertake efforts to help families pay for child care.
  Rationale: Parents who pay more receive better quality care for their children.

- Studies of various public and private efforts to improve the quality of regulated, nonregulated, and relative care should be conducted.
  Rationale: Research helps to determine the effectiveness of strategies undertaken to improve access to quality family child care and relative care.

Our study shows that quality family child care and relative care does not happen by chance. It takes knowledge and resources on the part of the families to identify and pay for it, assuming it is available in their neighborhood or community. It takes sensitivity, planning, and commitment on the part of providers to balance family, home, and child care responsibilities in a way that is developmentally enhancing to the children. It also takes training and support for providers in the community—through resource and referral agencies, family child care associations, and the like. Although our results show that providers offering good quality care are in the minority, they also provide correlational evidence for how to bring more providers into that elite group. In so doing, we hope our study helps to chart the course for the bright future that belongs to family child care and relative care.

Appendices

APPENDIX A:
ADDITIONAL DATA ON SAMPLE VARIATION AND BIAS

This appendix provides additional detail on three topics. First it examines variation in the sample of families by state and sampling method. Second, it examines variation in characteristics of care, as described by mothers, by state and sampling method. Variation in both families and provider groups is consistent with the goals of obtaining substantial numbers of both minority and low-income families in the community samples. Because providers in the provider referral group were much more likely than were the others to be regulated, it is important to ask whether regulated providers from the community groups were similar to or different from regulated providers in the provider referral sample, and whether the families served by regulated providers obtained by these different methods also varied. This is the final issue addressed in the appendix.

Differences by State and Sampling Method in
Characteristics of Families

The sampling strategies were differentially successful in obtaining minority families, as shown in Table A.1: collapsing across states, the samples obtained from birth records and from random-digit dialing did not differ from each other in ethnicity [χ^2 (2) = 2.53, n.s.] but respondents from the commercial list were more likely than were those from the other two community samples to be white [χ^2 (4) = 58.87; $p < .001$]. Respondents from the provider referral sample, who were not targeted by ethnicity, were more likely than respondents from the list frame to be white, [χ^2 (2) = 26.53, $p < .001$]. Even in the provider referral sample, only 76% of respondents were white. (Note: in analyses involving ethnicity, the three percent of families in the "other" category are included with Latinos.)

The four sampling methods in three states yielded 11 sample-by-state groups (birth records were not sampled in Texas). We compared these 11 groups using analysis of variance, with a priori contrasts or chi square analyses, to examine the following differences by state and by sampling method:

TABLE A.1. ETHNICITY BY SAMPLING METHOD

Ethnicity	Random Digit Dial	Birth Records	List Frame	Reverse	Total
White					
n =	14	25	246	62	347
% =	24%	17%	46%	76%	42%
African American					
n =	18	62	100	10	190
% =	30%	41%	19%	12%	23%
Latino/Other					
n =	27	64	183	9	283
% =	46%	42%	35%	11%	34%
Total					
n =	59	151	529	81	820
% =	100%	100%	100%	100%	100%

- *Income* [F (10, 788) = 9.23, $p < .001$]. Respondents in California were wealthier than were those in Texas [t (788) = 2.42, $p < .05$], respondents from the commercial list were wealthier than were respondents from the other community sampling methods combined [t (788) = 4.80, $p < .001$], and respondents from the reverse sample were in turn wealthier than those from the commercial list [t (788) = 2.43, $p < .05$].
- *Education* [F (10, 809) = 4.07, $p < .001$]. Differences between states did not reach significance, but differences between samples paralleled those for income: Respondents from the commercial list were better educated than were those from the other community samples [t (809) = 2.67, $p < .01$] and respondents from the reverse sample were better educated than were those from the list sample [t (809) = 2.20, $p < .05$].
- *Age* [F (10, 808) = 2.58, $p < .01$]. Respondents from the commercial lists were slightly older than those from the other community sample groups [(808) = 3.04, $p < .01$], but did not differ from respondents from the reverse sample [t (808) = 0.97, n.s.]. Respondents from different states did not differ in this respect.
- *Marital status* [χ^2 (10) = 49.71, $p < .001$]. Respondents in the North Carolina birth records sample were least likely to be married (46%). In contrast, the California and Texas commercial list samples and the California provider referral samples each had between 87% and 89% married. Whites were most likely, and

African Americans were least likely, to be married [χ^2 (2) = 67.52; $p < .001$].

- *Ethnicity.* Site and sample differences were reduced, although not eliminated, within ethnic groups.
- *First-born target children* [χ^2 (10) = 19.5; $p < .05$]. The groups differed slightly but there was no pattern to the differences. The California provider referral sample (61%) and both the California and North Carolina commercial list samples (57% each) had the largest proportion of first-borns; the California random-digit dial sample (38%) and the Texas commercial list sample (41%) had the smallest.

Differences by State and Sampling Method in Characteristics of Care

There were large variations in characteristics of care by sample, due primarily, but not entirely, to differences between the provider referral sample and the three community samples. Membership in the eleven groups formed by state and sampling method was strongly related to whether or not the provider was a relative [χ^2 (10) = 73.89 $p < .001$], with a phi coefficient of. 27. Overall, 35% of the providers were relatives, but in the three provider referral sample groups, only 4% were related to the child. The χ^2 (7) was reduced to 19.66, $p < .01$, and the phi to .16 by removing the three provider referral groups from the analysis. The California samples had fewer relative providers across the board (32% on average).

The family child care homes in the 11 state and sample groups varied greatly in composition, again because of differences between the provider referral and community samples [χ^2 (30) = 103.21 $p < .001$], phi = .33. Overall, 23% of providers cared only for the respondents' children, but no provider in the provider referral sample served only the family she referred to the study. Another eight percent of the full sample cared only for the respondent's children and her own, but this proportion was two percent in the provider referral sample. Mothers in the provider referral sample were correspondingly more likely to have other children who were neither the respondent's nor the provider's in the child care home. The χ^2 (21) was reduced to 28.00, n.s., and the phi to .19, when the provider referral samples were removed from the analysis.

Similarly, the proportion of providers who were regulated, according to mothers' reports, was 38%, but was 89% in the provider referral sample. Thus, the 11 groups created by crossing state with sample (including the provider referral samples) differed strongly [χ^2 (10) = 124.06, $p < .001$], but the 8 community groups differed less [χ^2 (7) = 16.24 $p < .05$] and the phi coefficient was reduced from .40 to .15. Respondents sampled from the commercial list were somewhat more likely than were those from the random-digit dial and birth-record samples to report using regulated care (35% vs. 32% overall in the three community samples).

The number of children in care reported by the mothers varied by the eleven sample and state groups [$F(10, 807) = 6.52$, $p < .001$]. This was entirely due to the larger size of the family child care and relative care homes in the provider referral sample (mean across states = 5.6 children, $SD = 2.3$), which differed significantly from the homes in the commercial list sample (the next largest group, mean = 3.5, $SD = 2.8$) [$t(807)$ for the contrast = -6.30, $p < .001$]. When the provider referral samples were eliminated, no differences among groups remained [$F(7, 729) = 1.31$, n.s.].

Finally, although mothers' overall satisfaction with care did not differ by group [$F(10, 809) = 1.29$, n.s.], an a priori contrast between the provider referral sample and the commercial list sample was significant [$t(809) = -2.46$, $p < .05$], with mothers in the provider referral sample more satisfied.

Differences Between Regulated Providers and the Families They Serve by Source of Sample (Community Versus Provider Referral)

Given the substantial differences between the provider referral sample, which was made up primarily of regulated providers, and the three community samples, which included a majority of unregulated providers, it is important to determine whether the provider referral sample differed from the community samples when we consider only providers whom the mother believes to be regulated by the state. Altogether, there were 215 such providers in the community samples and 73 in the provider referral samples. We consider both characteristics of the families using care and characteristics of the child care arrangements.

Among families who used regulated care (according to the mother), there were no differences between the provider referral sample and the community samples on family income [$t(277) = 0.16$, n.s.], mothers' education [$t(286) = 0.25$, n.s.], marital status [$\chi^2(1) = 0.07$, n.s.], or whether the target child was a first-born [$\chi^2(1) = 0.76$, n.s.]. The samples did differ by ethnicity [$\chi^2(2) = 8.69$, $p < .05$]. Consistent with the overall sample design, a larger proportion of families in the community sample were African American (27% vs. 12% in the provider referral sample) or Latino (14% vs. 11%), and a smaller proportion were white (59% vs. 77%).

Only eight of regulated providers were relatives of the child, and this did not differ by sample [$\chi^2(2) = 2.27$, n.s]. Regulated providers in the provider referral sample and in the community sample differed in whom they cared for [χ^2 (3) = 26.42, p < .001], according to mothers' reports: Regulated providers in the community samples were most likely to care for the respondent's children and others, but not for their own (65%), whereas regulated providers in the provider referral sample were most likely to care for their own children in addition to the respondent's and children from another family (55%). Some regulated providers from the community sample cared for only the respondent's children (6%) or for only the respondent's children and her own (3%), but neither arrangement was found in the provider referral sample. Nevertheless, the mean number of children cared for did not differ by sample [t (184) = –0.56, n.s.], although there was more variability in this number in the community sample (mean = 5.6, SD = 3.4) than in the provider referral sample (mean = 5.8, SD = 2.3) [F for equality of variance by Levene's Test = 6.37, p < .05] . That is, there were somewhat more quite small and quite large regulated family child care and relative care homes in the community sample than there were in the provider referral sample. According to mothers, regulated providers in the community sample were marginally more likely to have an assistant (44%) than were those in the provider referral sample (32%) [χ^2 (1) = 3.81, p < .06].

Mothers in the provider referral sample were significantly more satisfied with family child care and relative care homes than were those in the community sample [t (251) = –3.32, p < .001 (test for unequal variances, because the less satisfied group was also more variable, probably due to ceiling effects in the more satisfied group)].

APPENDIX B: PREDICTORS OF MATERNAL OUTCOMES

Factor Structure of Characteristics of Care

Principal components analysis of the characteristics of care yielded 3 eigen values greater than 1, and explaining 52% if the variance. The scree criterion suggested 3 or 4 factors. The 3-factor solution was chosen because of interpretability and lack of double loadings. The 4-factor solution included double loadings and two one-item factors. The rotated factor matrix is shown in Table B.1. Items were z-scored because of different response formats and unit-weighted to form indices for analysis.

Factor Structure of Facet Satisfactions

The factor analysis of the measure of facet satisfaction with child care produced a 5-factor solution:

TABLE B.1. FACTOR STRUCTURE OF CHARACTERISTICS OF CARE

Variable (loadings below .35 omitted)	Professional Provider	Friendly Communication	Availability
Regulated provider	.78		
Relative	-.76		
Cost	.69		
Ratio	.68		
Provider a personal friend		.65	
Talk with provider about child		.64	
Provider encourages mother to drop in		.63	
Hours per week			.76
Frequency of special child care arrangements because provider is unavailable			-.65

1. Satisfaction with size included satisfaction with the number of children in the home and the ratio of children to adults (alpha = .79).
2. Satisfaction with parental needs was a 4-item index (alpha = .72), including hours in care, and the provider's flexibility about schedules, costs, and continued availability ("care that is available day-in and day-out").
3. Satisfaction with the provider was a 5-item index (alpha = .65) that included satisfaction with the provider's licensure and training, the home-like atmosphere, the way the provider taught children to get along, and teaching of cultural or religious values.
4. Satisfaction with warmth was a 4-item index (alpha = .74) including satisfaction with the provider's attention to children, her warmth, her experience, and her openness to the mother's dropping in to see the child.
5. Satisfaction with shared values was a 7-item index (alpha = .78) including cleanliness, safety, attention to nutrition, the degree to which the provider shares the mother's values, her style of discipline, her communication with parents, and her relationship to the child's family.

One item, satisfaction with the location, failed to load on any factor. The five satisfaction indices were even more highly related to one another than were the characteristics of care. Thus, we subjected them to a secondary principal components analysis, which yielded one factor with eigenvalue greater than one. A scree plot also strongly suggested a single factor. The first principal component esplained 57.8%

TABLE B.2. SIGNIFICANT BETA WEIGHTS PREDICTING MATERNAL OUTCOMES FROM MOTHERS' DEMOGRAPHIC CHARACTERISTICS, CHARACTERISITICS OF CHILD CARE, SATISFACTION WITH CHILD CARE, AND JOB CHARACTERISTICS

Step Variable	Global Satisfaction $F_{(11, 757)} = 59.19$****		Benefits to Child $F_{(11, 757)} = 2.87$***		Separation Anxiety $F_{(11, 757)} = 26.24$****		Stress $F_{(11, 757)} = 13.93$****	
	At Entry	Final Step	At Entry	Final Step	At Entry	Final Step	At Entry	Final Step
1. Demographics								
Family income	.11**				-.24***	-.21****		
Mother's education					-.11**	-.12***		.07*
Child's age								
African American								
Latino/other ethnicity			-.09**		.27****	.25****		
2. Characteristics of care								
Professional care	.34****	.11****	.17****	.16****		-.07+	.13***	.07*
Friendly communication	.09**	.06*		.07+	-.06*		-.13****	
Available care					-.06+		-.07*	
3. Facet satisfaction								
Facet satisfaction	.65****	.65****			-.16***	-.15****	-.21****	-.17****
4. Job characteristics								
Autonomy							-.13****	-.13****
Job demands					.14***	.14****	.27****	.27****

*$p < .10$; **$p < .05$; ***$p < .01$; ****$p < .001$

of the total variance. Indices were unit-weighted to form a single super-ordinate index of facet satisfaction. This differed from global satisfaction in that global satisfaction was facet free. It is composed of three items, including overall satisfaction, whether or not the mother would send the child again if she had the decision to do over, and whether or not she would recommend the provider to a friend.

Table B.2 shows beta weights predicting maternal well-being from maternal demographic characteristics, characteristics of child care, satisfaction with child care, and job characteristics.

References

Adams, G.C. (1990). *Who knows how safe?: The status of state efforts to ensure quality child care.* Washington, DC: Children's Defense Fund.

Ainsworth, M., Behar, M., Waters, E., & Wall, S. (1978). *Patterns of attachment: A psychological study of the Strange Situation.* Hillsdale, NJ: Lawrence Erlbaum.

Arnett, J. (1989). Caregivers in child care centers: Does training matter? *Journal of Applied Developmental Psychology, 10,* 541–552.

Atkinson, A. (1993). Evaluation of career and family roles by family day care providers, mothers at home, and employed mothers.*Early Childhood Research Quarterly, 8,* 445–456.

Behar, L. (1977). The Preschool Behavior Questionnaire. *Journal of Abnormal Child Psychology, 5,* 265–275.

Behar, L., & Stringfield, S. (1975). A behavior rating scale for the preschool child. *Developmental Psychology, 10(5),* 601–610.

Blank, H. (1994). *Protecting our children: State and federal policies for exempt child care settings.* Washington D.C.: Children's Defense Fund.

Bollin, G.G. (1993). An investigation of job stability and job satisfaction among family day care providers. *Early Childhood Research Quarterly, 8(2),* 207–220.

Bronfenbrenner, U. (1979). *The ecology of human development: Experiments by nature and design.* Cambridge, MA: Harvard University Press.

Buchanan, T. (1993). *The relationship of child care and employer support to maternal well-being.* Unpublished doctoral dissertation, Purdue University, IN.

Butts, M. (1993). Daycare laws: An essental guide. *Parenting,* November, 129–132.

Children's Foundation. (1993). *Issues in the regulation of family day care.* Washington, DC: Author.

Clarke-Stewart, A., & Gruber, C.P. (1984). Day care forms and features. In R. Ainslie (Ed.), *The child and the day care setting: Qualitative variations and development* (pp. 35–62). New York: Praeger.

Class, N.E. (1980). Some reflections on the development of child day care faculty licensing. In S. Kilmer (Ed.), *Advances in early education and day care* (Vol.1, pp. 3–18). Greenwich, CT: JAI Press.

Clifford, R.M., Harms, T., & Cryer, D. (1991, November). *Assessing the early childhood environment for infants and toddlers, family day care, and preschoolers: Three rating scales.* Paper presented at the Annual Conference of the National Association for the Education of Young Children, Denver.

Clifford, R.M., Harms, T., Pepper, S., & Stuart, B. (1992). Assessing quality in family child care. In D. Peters & A.R. Pence (Eds.), *Family child care: Current research for informed public policy* (pp. 243–265). New York: Teachers College Press.

Cochran, M.M. (1977). A comparison of group day and family child-rearing patterns in Sweden. *Child Development, 48,* 702–707.

Cohen, S., Karmach, T., Mermelstein, R. (1983). A global measure of perceived stress. *Journal of Health and Social Behavior, 24*, 385-396.

Crnic, K., Greenberg, M., Ragozin, A., Robinson, N., & Basham, N. (1983). Effects of stress and social supports in mothers in premature and full term infants. *Child Development, 54*, 209-217.

Culkin, M., Morris, & Helburn, S. (1991). Quality and the true cost of child care. *Journal of Social Issues, 47*, 71-86.

Divine-Hawkins, P. (1981). *Family day care in the United States: Executive summary.* (Final report of the National Day Care Home Study) (Report No. DHHS-OHDS-80-30287). Washington, DC: Administration of Children, Youth, and Families. (ERIC Document Reproduction Service No. ED 211 224)

Dunn, L. (1990). *Structural, global, and specific features of day care quality and children's development.* Unpublished doctoral dissertation. West Lafayette, IN: Purdue University, Department of Child Development and Family Studies.

Dunn, L. (1993). Ratio and group size in day care programs. *Child and Youth Care Forum, 22*, 193-226.

Eheart, B.K., & Leavitt, R.L. (1989). Family day care: Discrepancies between intended and observed caregiving practices. *Early Childhood Research Quarterly, 4*, 145-162.

Feagans, L.V., & Farran, D. (1979). Adaptive language inventory. Unpublished manuscript. Chapel Hill, NC: University of North Carolina at Chapel Hill.

Feagans, L.V., Fendt, K., & Farran, D. (1991, April). *The effect of day care intervention on teacher ratings of the elementary school discourse skills in disadvantaged children.* Paper presented at the biennial meeting of the Society for Research in Child Development, Seattle, WA.

Fischer, J.L. (1989). *Family day care: Factors influencing the quality of caregiving practices.* Unpublished doctoral dissertation, University of Illinois, Urbana-Champaign, IL.

Fosburg, S. (1982). Family day care: The role of the surrogate mother. In L. Laosa & I. Sigel (Eds.), *Families as learning environments for children* (pp. 223-260). New York: Plenum.

Galinsky, E., Bond, J.T., & Friedman, D. (1993). *National study of the changing workforce.* New York: Families and Work Institute.

Galinsky, E., Howes, C., Kontos, S., & Shinn, M. (1994). *The study of children in family child care and relative care: Highlights of findings.* New York: Families and Work Institute.

Galinsky, E., & Hughes, D. (1985). *Final report of the Merck work and family life study.* New York, NY: Bank Street College of Education.

Galinsky, E., & Shinn, M. (1994). Unpublished measures.

Goelman, H., & Pence, A. (1987). Some aspects of the relationship between family structure and child language in three types of day care. In D. Peters & S. Kontos (Eds.), *Annual Advances in Applied Developmental Psychology*, Vol. II, (129-146). Norwood, NJ: Ablex.

Goelman, H., Shapiro, E., & Pence, A.R. (1990). Family environments and family day care. *Family Relations, 39*, 14-19.

Harms, T., & Clifford, R. (1989). *Family Day Care Rating Scale.* New York: Teachers College Press.

Harms, T., & Cryer, D. (1994). *Quality criteria for family child care.* Chapel Hill, NC: University of North Carolina at Chapel Hill.

Hayes, C., Palmer, J., & Zaslow, M. (1990). *Who cares for America's children? Child care policy for the 1990's.* Washington, D.C.: National Academy Press.

Hill-Scott, K. (1989). No room at the inn: The crisis in child care supply. In J. Lande,

S. Scarr, & N. Gunzenhauser (Eds.), *Caring for children: Challenge to America.* Hillsdale, NJ: Erlbaum.

Hock, E., Gnezda, M.T., & McBride, S. (1983). *The measurement of maternal separation anxiety.* Paper presented at the biennial meeting of the Society for Research in Child Development, Detroit, MI.

Hofferth, S.L., Brayfield, A., Deitch, S., & Holcomb, P. (1991). *National child care survey, 1990.* Washington, DC: The Urban Institute.

Hofferth, S.L., & Kisker, E.E. (1992). The changing demographics of family day care in the United States. In D. Peters & A.R. Pence (Eds.), *Family Day Care: Current research for informed public policy.* New York: Teachers College Press.

Howes, C. (1980). The peer play scale as an index of complexity of peer interaction. *Developmental Psychology, 16,* 371-372.

Howes, C. (1983). Caregiver behavior in center and family day care. *Journal of Applied Developmental Psychology, 4,* 99–107.

Howes, C. (1988). Peer interaction of young children. *Monographs of the Society for Research in Child Development. 53*(1): Serial No. 217.

Howes, C., & Hamilton, C.E. (1992a). Children's relationships with caregivers: Mothers and child care teachers. *Child Development, 63,* 859–866.

Howes, C., & Hamilton, C.E. (1992b). Children's relationships with child care teachers: Stability and concordance with parental attachments. *Child Development, 63,* 867–878.

Howes, C., & Hamilton, C.E. (1993). Child care for young children. In B. Spodek & O.N. Saracho (Eds.), *Yearbook in early childhood education, Vol.3: Issues in child care* (pp. 31–46). New York: Teachers College Press.

Howes, C., Keeling, K., & Sale, J. (1988). *The home visitor: Improving quality in family day care homes.* Unpublished manuscript, University of California–Los Angeles.

Howes, C., & Matheson, C. (1992). Sequences in the development of competent play with peers: Social and social preferential play. *Developmental Psychology, 28,* 961–974.

Howes, C., Matheson, C., & Hamilton, C. (1994). Maternal, teacher, and child care history: Correlates of children's relationships with peers. *Child Development, 65,* 264–272.

Howes, C., Phillips, D., & Whitebook, M. (1992). Threshholds of quality: Implications for the social development of children in center-based care. *Child Development, 63,* 449–460.

Howes, C., & Rubenstein, J.L. (1985). Determinants of toddler's experience in day care. *Child Care Quarterly, 14,* 140–151.

Howes, C., Sakai, L.M., Shinn, M., Phillips, D., Galinsky, E., & Whitebook, M. (in press). Race, social class, and maternal working conditions as influences on children's development . *Journal of Applied Developmental Psychology.*

Howes, C., & Smith, E.W. (1994). *Relations among child care quality, teacher behavior, and children's play activities, emotional security, and cognitive activity in child care.* Manuscript submitted for publication.

Howes, C., & Smith, E.W. (in press). Children and their child care caregivers: Profiles of relationships. *Social Development.*

Howes, C., & Stewart, P. (1987). Child's play with adults, toys and peers: An examination of family and child care influences. *Developmental Psychology, 23,* 423-430.

Hughes, D. (1988). *Relations between characteristics of the job, work-family interference, and marital outcomes, Dissertation Abstracts International.*

Jendrek, M.P. (1993). Grandparents who parent their grandchildren: Effects on lifestyle. *Journal of Marriage and the Family, 55,* 609–621.

Karasek, R.A. (1979). Job demands, job decision latitude, and mental strain: Implications for job redesign. *Administrative Science Quarterly, 24,* 285–314.

Kisker, E.E., Maynard, R., Gordon, A., & Strain, M. (1989). *The child care challenge: What parents need and what is available in three metropolitan areas.* Princeton, NJ: Mathematica Policy Research, Inc.

Kisker, E.E., Piper, V., Maynard, R., Ensor, T., Hall, E., Hofferth, S.L., Brayfield, A., Phillips, D., & Farquhar, E. (1991). *A profile of child care settings: Early education and care in 1990.* Washington DC: U.S. Department of Education, Office of the Under Secretary.

Kontos, S. (1991). Child care quality, family background, and children's development. *Early Childhood Research Quarterly, 6,* 249–262.

Kontos, S. (1992). *Family day care: Out of the shadows and into the limelight.* Washington, DC: National Association for the Education of Young Children.

Kontos, S. (1994). The ecology of family day care. *Early Childhood Research Quarterly, 9,* 81–110.

Kontos, S., & Dunn, L. (1993). Caregiver practices and beliefs in child care varying in developmental appropriateness and quality. In S. Reifel (Ed.), *Perspectives in developmentally appropriate practice: Vol. 5. Advances in early education and day care,* pp. 133–185. Greenwich, CT: JAI Press.

Kontos, S., Hsu, H-C., & Dunn, L. (1994). Children's cognitive and social competence in child care centers and family day care homes. *Journal of Applied Developmental Psychology, 15,* 87–111.

Kontos, S., & Riessen, J. (1993). Predictors of job satisfaction, job stress, and job commitment in family day care. *Journal of Applied Developmental Psychology, 14,* 427–441.

Leavitt, R.L. (1991). Family day care licensing: Issues and recommendations. *Child and Youth Care Forum, 20,* 243–254.

Majeed, A. (1983). *Casper family day care study.* Casper, WY: Nutrition and Child Development, Inc. (ERIC Document Reproduction Service No. ED 315 180).

Mason, K., & Kuhlthau, K. (1989). Determinants of child care ideals among mothers of preschool-aged children. *Journal of Marriage and the Family, 51,* 593–603.

McBride, B.A., & Rubenstein, J.L. (1990). *Influence of family and child care systems on child functioning.* Paper presented at the annual meeting of the American Educational Research Association, Boston, MA.

McCartney, K. (1984). The effect of quality day care environment upon young children's language development. *Developmental Psychology, 20,* 249–260.

McCartney, K., & Phillips, D. (1988). Motherhood and child care. In B. Birns & D. Hay (Eds.), *Different faces of motherhood.* New York: Plenum.

McLloyd, V.C. (1990). The impact of economic hardship on black families and children: Psychological distress, parenting, and socioemotional development. *Child Development, 61,* 311–346.

Minton, C., Kagan, J., & Levine, J. (1971). Maternal control and obedience in the two-year-old child. *Child Development, 42,* 1873–1894.

Modigliani, K. (1991). *Assessing the quality of family child care: A comparison of five instruments.* Hayward, CA: Mervyn's Public Affairs Office.

Morgan, G. (1980). Can quality family day care be achieved through regulation? In S. Kilmer (Ed.), *Advances in early education and day care* (Vol. 1, pp. 91–102). Greenwich, CT: JAI Press.

National Association for the Education of Young Children (1985). *In whose hands? A demographic fact sheet on child care providers.* Washington, D.C.: Author.

Nelson, M.K. (1991a). Mothering others' children: The experiences of family day care providers. In E. Abel & M. Nelson (Eds.), *Circles of care: Work and identity in women's lives* (pp. 210–232). Albany, NY: State University of New York Press.

Nelson, M.K. (1991b). A study of family day care providers: Attitudes towards regulation. *Child and Youth Care Forum, 20,* 225–242.

Pence, A.R., & Goelman, H. (1991). The relationship of regulation, training, and motivation to quality of care in family day care. *Child and Youth Care Forum, 20,* 83–101.

Perrault, J. (1992). Models of family child care and support services in the United States. In D. Peters & A. Pence (Eds.), *Family child care: Current research for informed public policy* (pp. 229–243). New York: Teachers College Press.

Phillips, D. (1988, June). *Quality in child care: Definitions at the A.L. Mailman Family Foundation, Inc.* Paper presented at Symposium on Dimensions of Quality in Programs for Children, White Plains, NY.

Phillips, D., & Howes, C. (1987). Indicators of quality in child care: Review of the research. In D. Phillips (Ed.), *Quality in child care: What does research tell us?* Research monograph of the National Association for the Education of Young Children, Vol.1., pp. 1–19. Washington, DC: NAEYC.

Phillips, D., Lande, J., & Goldberg, M. (1990). The state of child care regulation: A comparative analysis. *Early Childhood Research Quarterly, 5,* 151–179.

Phillips, D., Scarr, S., & McCartney, K. (1987). Child care quality and children's social development. *Developmental Psychology, 23*(4), 537–543.

Piotrkowski, C.S., & Katz, M.H. (1983). *Work experience and family relations among working class and lower middle-class families.* In H.Z. Lopata and J.H. Pleck (Eds.), Research in the interweave of social roles: Families and jobs (Vol. 3). Greenwich, CT: JAI Press, Inc.

Pollard, J., & Fischer, J. (1992). Research perspectives on family day care. In D. Peters & A. Pence (Eds.), *Family day care: Current research for informed public policy* (pp. 92–112). New York: Teachers College Press.

Presser, H.B. (1989). Some economic complexities of child care provided by grandmothers. *Journal of Marriage and the Family, 51,* 581–591.

Quinn, R.P., & Staines, G.L. (1979). *The 1977 Quality of Employment Survey: Descriptive Statistics with Comparison Data from the 1969–70 and the 1973–74 Surveys.* Ann Arbor, MI: Institute for Social Research.

Rickel, A., & Biasatti, L. (1982). Modification of the Block childrearing practices report. *Journal of Clinical Psychology, 38,* 129–134.

Rosenthal, M.K. (1988). *Attitudes and behaviors of caregivers in family day care: The effects of personal background, professional support systems, and the immediate caregiving environment.* Jerusalem: The Hebrew University of Jerusalem. (ERIC Document Reproduction Service No. ED 306 040).

Rosenthal, M.K. (1990). Social policy and its effects on the daily experiences of infants and toddlers in family day care in Israel. *Journal of Applied Developmental Psychology, 11,* 85–104.

Rosenthal, M.K. (1991). Behaviors and beliefs of caregivers in family day care: The effects of background and work environment. *Early Childhood Research Quarterly, 6,* 263–283.

Sale, J., & Torres, Y. (1973). *Final report: Community family day care project.* Pasadena, CA: Pacific Oaks College.

Schaefer, E., & Edgerton, M. (1978). *A method and a model for describing competence and adjustment: A preschool version of the Classroom Behavior Inventory.* Paper presented at the American Psychological Association annual meeting, Toronto, Canada. (ERIC Document Reproduction Service No. ED 183 262).

Shinn, M., Phillips, D., Howes, C., Whitebook, M., & Galinsky, E. (1990). *Correspondence between mothers' perceptions and observer ratings of quality in child care centers.* New York: Families and Work Institute.

Simon, H. (1956). Rational choice and the structure of the environment. *Psychological Review, 63,* 129–138.

Smilansky, S. (1968). *The effects of sociodramatic play on disadvantaged preschool children.* New York: Wiley.

Sonenstein, F.L., & Wolf, D.A. (1988). *Caring for the children of welfare mothers.* Paper presented at the annual meeting of the Population Association of America, New Orleans, LA.

Stentzel, C. (1985). *Child care fact sheet: Working mothers and children.* Washington, DC: National Commission on Working Women.

Stoakley, D.V. (1994). *Ethnic differences in what parents want their children to learn.* Unpublished master's thesis, New York University.

U.S. House of Representatives Committee on Ways and Means. (1992). *Overview of entitlement programs: 1992 Green Book.* Washington, DC: U.S. Government Printing Office.

Waters, E., & Deane, K.E. (1985). Defining and assessing individual differences in attachment relationships: Q-methodology and the organization of behavior in infancy and early childhood. In I. Bretherton & E. Waters (Eds.), Growing points of attachment theory and research, *Monographs of the Society for Research in Child Development, 50,* (1-2, Serial No. 209), pp. 41–65.

Whitebook, M., & Granger, R. (1989). Assessing teacher turnover. *Young Children, 44,* 11–14.

Whitebook, M., Howes, C., & Phillips, D. (1989). *Who Cares?: Child care teachers and the quality of care in America.* Executive Summary, National Child Care Staffing Study. Oakland, CA: Child Care Employee Project.

Whitebook, M., Howes, C., & Phillips, D. (1990). *Who Cares?: Child care teachers and the quality of care in America.* Final report of the National Child Care Staffing Study. Oakland, CA: Child Care Employee Project.

Willer, B., Hofferth, S., Kisker, E., Divine-Hawkins, P., Farquhar, E., & Glantz, F. (1991). *The demand and supply of child care in 1990: Joint findings from The National Child Care Survey 1990 and A Profile of Child Care Settings.* Washington, D.C.: National Association for the Education of Young Children.

Zinsser, C. (1991). *Raised in East Urban: Child care changes in a working class community.* New York: Teachers College Press, Columbia University.

Index

About the Authors

Susan Kontos is a Professor in the Department of Child Development and Family Studies at Purdue University, where she is also Director of the Center for Families. Dr. Kontos received her MA in psychology from Southern Illinois University, Edwardsville, and her PhD in child development from Iowa State University. She is the author of numerous articles and book chapters on child care and early intervention and wrote a research monograph for the National Association for the Education of Young Children summarizing the existing research on family child care *(Family Day Care: Out of the Shadows and into the Limelight)*. Dr. Kontos currently serves as Associate Editor for *Early Childhood Research Quarterly*.

Carollee Howes is a Professor of Developmental Studies in the Graduate School of Education, University of California, Los Angeles. The Developmental Studies Program is an NIMH-funded program of graduate training in applying the principles and research methods of developmental psychology to the problems of education. Dr. Howes received her MA from the Child Study Department of Tufts University and her PhD in developmental psychology from Boston University. Dr. Howes is the author of numerous published studies examining the social and emotional development of children who are enrolled in child care at young ages. She was a principal investigator of the National Child Care Staffing Study (NCCSS) and served on the advisory panel for the recent Profile of Child Care Settings survey study of child care.

Marybeth Shinn is Professor of Psychology and Coordinator of the Community Psychology Program at New York University. Dr. Shinn received her PhD in social psychology and community psychology from the University of Michigan. She is Associate Editor of the *American Journal of Community Psychology* and a past president of the Society for Community Research and Action, the Community Psychology Division, 27, of the American Psychological Association. In addition to research on work and family issues, Dr. Shinn is conducting a longitudinal study of homeless and housed poor families in New York City.

Ellen Galinsky is the Co-President of the Families and Work Institute. This nonprofit institute is a national center for policy research on issues of the changing workforce and changing family life. She received her BA from Vassar College and her MS from Bank Street College.

At the Families and Work Institute, Ellen Galinsky directs a nationally representative longitudinal study of the U.S. workforce, a cost/benefit analysis of Johnson & Johnson's work-family program, a Department of Labor study of work-family and productivity, and a series of studies on how quality improvements affect the early childhood marketplace.

Ellen Galinsky is a past President of the National Association for the Education of Young Children. She also serves on the Advisory Committee to the New York State Permanent Interagency Committee on Early Childhood Programs and on the boards of Child Care Action Campaign and Parent Action. She is the author of 13 books and has published over 70 articles in academic journals and magazines.